Newspaper Layout & Design

Newspaper Layout & Design

A Team Approach

Fourth Edition

Daryl R. Moen

Iowa State University Press / Ames

Daryl R. Moen is a professor in the School of Journalism, University of Missouri, Columbia.

© 1984, 1989, 1995, 2000 Iowa State University Press, Ames, Iowa 50014

♾ Printed on acid-free paper in the United States of America

Orders: 1-800-862-6657
Office: 1-515-292-0140
Fax: 1-515-292-3348
Web site: www.isupress.edu

Fourth edition, 2000

International Standard Book Number: 0-8138-0729-8/2000

Library of Congress Cataloging-in-Publication Data
Moen, Daryl R.
      Newspaper layout and design : a team approach / Daryl R. Moen—4th ed.
          p. cm.
      Includes bibliographical references and index.
      ISBN 0-8138-0729-8
      1. Newspaper layout and typography. I. Title: Newspaper layout and design.   II. Title.

   Z253.5. M63 2000
   686.2'252—dc21   00-035112

Last digit is the print number: 9 8 7 6 5 4

Contents

Preface

Brilliant reporting and writing, exceptional photographs and startling designs aren't enough these days. To entice the scanner to read and make sense of the content, newspapers must offer coherent packages. The brilliant writing and exceptional photographs must complement each other in order to illuminate. Headlines, pullouts and cutlines that are written to supplement each of the other elements in the package help turn mere data into information.

That's why this book is based on the premise that the new generation of journalists must be cross-trained. Reporters must know the value and role of photography and graphics. Designers must know the value of good stories told well. Photographers must recognize that the pictures and words must work in tandem. Designers are the only cross-trained specialists now in the newsroom, and that's not the way it should be.

All of us in the newspaper business have a challenge ahead. The philosophers Fritz Machlup and Theodore Rusik have eloquently made the case that the quantity of information does not correlate with understanding. Richard Saul Wurman popularized the theory in *Information Anxiety,* in which he talks about the need to help readers sort through the avalanche of data to find meaning. Journalists working in teams asking the right questions and presenting the information intelligently can offer understanding. This book shows you how.

But, first, it starts with the points and picas. It shows you how to fit elements onto a page, how to show the relationship among them, how to determine headline sizes, how to change the width of copy and photographs and still make them all fit. These chapters illustrate the nuts-and-bolts approach taken throughout the book. This book doesn't just talk about layout and design; it gives you the information you need to do it. In a sense, you have two books here. The first is for the beginner; the second is for the advanced designer.

Those still in college who master these basic skills will enter a workplace that will value them highly. Designers find more jobs available than most other specialties and are paid more on average.

Nearly 90 percent of the illustrations in this text are new. Unlike other newspaper design texts, this book gives you the historical background, the research support for applying techniques and the ethical questions you will encounter as you do your daily work. Also unique to this book is an emphasis on the accuracy of what we do. For instance, other books advise you how to create information graphics; this book tells you how to create and edit *accurate* information graphics. The need to have minorities represented in our photography and graphics is also emphasized. The section on ethics in photo manipulation and selection has been expanded again.

I've also added some format changes. Each chapter opens with a full-page illustration of the material to come. Also, several of the illustrations are larger in this edition to make sure you can read the material more easily. To make future editions even more useful, I'd like to hear from you. Write me at the Missouri School of Journalism; 203 Neff Hall, Columbia, MO 65211, or E-mail me at: *moend@missouri.edu.*

This book is the work of many people. Through my teaching at the University of Missouri and in seminars from British Columbia, Canada, to Madras, India, I have learned a great deal from students and professionals, much of which I have shared with you. Thanks for the special contributions from James Bennett of the Missouri School of Journalism, who created several graphics, Tony Sutton, designer and editor of the *DESIGN* journal, who helped on the chapter on tabloids, and the scores of newspapers who allowed me to use examples from their newspapers.

Most of all, thanks to my wife, Nancy, and Chad, Mia and Marisa, whose support is the most valuable thing I have.

Newspaper Layout & Design

Part I

Getting Ready: Training for a New World

1.1   What does a newspaper look like? The *New York Times*? *Wall Street Journal*? Or the *Virginian-Pilot* in Norfolk, Va.? The *Virginian-Pilot*'s front page varies significantly from day to day as its editors try to reflect the changing news flow. If the newspaper industry is to survive, more editors and designers will have to learn more effective ways to tell stories.

You must always ask the question "What is?"
before you ask the question "How to?"

Richard Saul Wurman
Author, *Information Anxiety*

1.2   In 1987 there were 1,645 daily newspapers in the United States. In 1997 there were 1,509. The *Phoenix Gazette* was one of the victims. During that same period, total morning and evening circulation fell from 62.8 million to 56.7 million.

1.3   Newspapers have found fertile ground on Sundays. From 1987 to 1997, Sunday circulation grew from 60.1 million to 60.4 million readers and the number of Sunday papers increased from 820 to 903. For marketing reasons, many newspapers have added the word *Sunday* to their flags.

We are awash in a sea of unconnected bits of information that used to float ashore daily but that now pound the shore minute by minute. Wars are televised live. Television news snippets beget Headline News sniplets. The amount of information doubles every six years, then five years. Like cholesterol shutting down the blood flow, information clogs the neural system. The question T. S. Eliot asked years ago remains unanswered: "Where is the knowledge we have lost in information?"

The expanding media mix is producing information in incomprehensible amounts at instantaneous speeds. The age is gone when Will Rogers could say, "Well, all I know is what I read in the newspaper." Newspapers, radio, television and electronic information systems jockey for position. Newspapers are too slow for sports enthusiasts, who call 900 numbers. Television is too slow for traders, who monitor business news on computers. Newspaper companies buy cable companies. Cable companies buy entertainment companies. A bigger company always appears to gobble a smaller company in an effort to roar into the next Information Age. But the Information Age becomes the Information Anxiety Age—the black hole, according to Richard Saul Wurman, between data and knowledge.

REEXAMINING JOURNALISTS' ROLES

So where does that leave newspapers? Newspaper penetration peaked in the mid-1940s, but the companies are still enjoying record profits. In 1987 there were 1,645 daily newspapers, and by 1997, 1,509 (Fig. 1.2). However, by 1997, there were also a record high number of Sunday newspapers: 903 (Fig. 1.3). Whether publishers, advertising managers and editors like it or not, the role of the newspaper is changing. Extinction is not inevitable. Newspapers do not have to disappear like dinosaurs; they can adapt and survive like shrews. Radio didn't make newspapers disappear. Television didn't make radio disappear. Newspapers can evolve if they can find their way out of the morass of information and start sharing knowledge. New sections, more precise zoning, better reproduction, content that speaks clearly and touches readers' lives, all will ensure newspaper survival. One of many people trying to engineer the new newspaper is Reid Ashe, formerly of the Wichita (Kan.) Eagle. "We have to recognize," he says, "that raw information is cheap, understanding is valuable and something you can act on is precious."

The best newspapers are fighting back by using some of the same technology that is assaulting them. Managers are ordering new presses to print papers with more and more color for smaller and smaller zones. They are developing databases to help the sales staff help advertisers. Desktop publishing systems are putting power into the hands of journalists and saving newspapers money at the same time.

Newspapers are still operating from strength. Almost six out of 10 adults, 112 million people, read a newspaper every day. Almost seven out of 10 adults read a paper every Sunday. Newspapers command 22 percent of all advertising dollars. Broadcast television, at 20 percent, ranks second.

The best newspapers are reexamining content, redefining news values and inviting readers into the process. Now some American newspapers have reporters covering malls, commuting, day care, and fitness programs. Food coverage has moved from the magnificent meal to microwaves. We are counting calories and nutritional benefits with health-conscious readers. We are following readers into video rental stores and health clubs. We are writing about relationships. We are offering readers time-saving tips. We are telling readers how to take action with instructions and addresses, phone and fax numbers. We are offering readers an opportunity to take command of the campaign agenda by asking them what they want the candidates to address rather than simply reporting what the candidates want to say. We are opening our phone lines to readers for story suggestions and opinions. We are reaching out to ethnic communities. We are correcting our errors and shoring up our credibility.

The best of us are also reexamining how we gather, process and present the news. From Norfolk, Va., to Santa Ana, Calif., newspapers are experimenting with innovative ways to gather information, new subjects to cover and better ways to present the information.

WELCOME TO JOURNALISM BY DESIGN

The assembly-line process that has produced raw information is changing in some newspapers and must in the rest. We are moving from a system that segregates journalists by their specialties—reporters, copy editors, photographers and designers—to a holistic system. Newspapers are a visual medium. The words, pictures and numbers all are visual. They work together synergistically, and the people who produce them separate themselves at the risk of fragmenting the message. If reporters intend to convey meaning rather than raw information, they must know the value of charts and pictures, photographers must know the value of words and charts, and graphic journalists must know the value of words and pictures. All must know that the presentation is part of the message. Individuals produce fragments of information; teams produce packages of knowledge. Together they can ask, "What is the best way to tell the story?" When they know what the whole is going to be, they can ask the specialists to produce the parts. On the best papers today, reporters are suggesting layouts, photographers are suggesting headlines, designers are suggesting photographs, copy editors are suggesting stories. You have reporters who understand that a zoning story needs a map, photographers who understand that a nutrition story needs a table, designers who understand that a good story told well needs space. The artificial and self-defeating distinction between word people and visual people must disappear.

Designers are the engineers who are making it happen. Designers are the only newsroom specialists who have a holistic view of the product. The best of the designers understand that the product is more than the sum of its parts, that we can tell stories using words, numbers and pictures only when the words, numbers and pictures work together. When all journalists recognize that symbiotic relationship and contribute to it, the designers will be no more—and no less—important than the others.

CONTRAST THESE SCENARIOS

In the traditional system, the city desk reacts to police scanner traffic about a drive-by shooting. The city editor dispatches two reporters to the scene. She sends another reporter to the police station, another to the files for background. Working in the lab, the photo editor has heard the same transmission. He sends a photographer to the scene. Working feverishly

1.4 One way of reaching out to readers is not only to report on society's problems but to offer solutions. The *Miami Herald* used its pages after a hurricane to help readers help readers.

against the deadline, the reporters report and the photographers shoot. In most cases they work independently, and their output arrives at the copydesk at the same time.

In the team system, the city desk alerts other members in the newsroom—photographers, graphic journalists and the news desk. A photographer and graphic journalist join the reporters at the scene. The reporters write a narrative account filled with suspense. The photographer gets action shots. The graphic journalist produces a diagram showing the sequence of events. The news desk monitors their progress and clears the space. The presentation takes advantage of the best ways to tell parts of the story to present a coherent whole. The team has asked "what is" before answering "how to."

Increasingly, the managers of these teams are themselves strong in words and visuals. Auman (1995) found that 73 percent of those in middle management and higher who responded to her survey said they were strong visual people. She also found that 64 percent said they were strong word people. In other words, the people moving into management positions in the new century will be those who have both visual and verbal skills.

LEARNING THE LESSONS

The big news event starts an adrenaline rush in journalists, who perform marvelously and creatively under deadline pressure. When a hurricane flattens South Florida, a flood engulfs the Midwest or a fire blackens Southern California, journalists find ways to tell stories with meaning. Fiefdoms disappear and teams appear. We can learn from these events and apply the lessons to our work daily.

In Miami, for instance, Hurricane Andrew tested the *Miami Herald* as well as the citizens of South Florida. Journalists were victims as well as observers. The newspaper had to find ways to print and then to re-create its distribution system. Through it all, the newspaper understood that to the thousands of people who had lost homes and jobs and who needed water and medical attention, something you can act on is precious. So in addition to the stories of heroes and villains, in addition to the photographs of devastation, in addition to the maps and charts, the newspaper told readers how and where to get help. The newspaper didn't just do it once, but every day. No longer just the town crier, the paper offered solution journalism (Fig. 1.4).

When a bomb destroyed the federal building in Oklahoma City, the entire nation felt the aftershocks. The *Virginian-Pilot* in Norfolk, Va., like hundreds of other newspapers, sent reporters and photographers. The paper was awash in stories and pictures. From the mass of information, it attempted to produce knowledge by summarizing the news and focusing on the key developments (Figs. 1.5-1.7).

APPLYING THE LESSONS

The teamwork and creativity shouldn't subside with the adrenaline. Big news sells newspapers to occasional readers. Making everyday news useful may convert occasional readers to frequent readers. The publisher Reid Ashe reminds us that traditional ways of delivering traditional news aren't

1.5 When newspapers cover big news events, such as the bombing of the federal building in Oklahoma City, the goal should be to bring order out of chaos. The *Virginian-Pilot,* with hundreds of photos and stories from which to choose, selected two photos and one story for its front page.

1.6 With dozens of angles to pursue, the newspaper tried to help readers through the thicket of information by providing labels that work like road signs.

1.7 As the story entered the mourning phase, the front page took on a distinctively different look and feel.

working. "The problem with newspapers is that we've grown too good at the wrong things, and neglected the things our readers and society value most," he says. "We've honed the art of compiling and delivering information and convinced ourselves that's our principal function at a time when information has grown cheap and abundant" (Ashe 1992).

Here are 10 ways to create knowledge, to communicate excitement daily and to give readers information on which they can act.

1. *Make everyone in the newsroom understand that he or she is a visual journalist.* Make specialists part of a team responsible for the package rather than the parts.

2. *Make sure stories clearly answer "what," "so-what" and "now what."* Answered properly, the question helps transform data into knowledge.

3. *Look for patterns.* Show connections. Explain. In 1979, long before most newspapers began thinking visually, the *Morning Call* in Allentown, Pa., offered readers coherence by pulling together the story of the Shah of Iran's journey around the world looking for cancer treatment. No country wanted to admit him because all were afraid of irritating Iran's new rulers. Besides, the rulers were holding Americans hostage. Readers had been bombarded for days with the odyssey. Each piece was part of the puzzle. The *Call* gave form to the puzzle by letting readers look at the big picture with a world map and copy blocks tracing the Shah's journey (Fig. 1.8). With the

1.8 This was one of the first efforts in a U.S. newspaper to tell a story with an information graphic. The techniques now are more sophisticated, but the methodology remains the same.

1.9   These days, with computer software, artists are able to show the news rather than merely *tell* the news.

1.10   The *Dayton Daily News'* page on the tobacco litigation demonstrates the range of story-telling devices available to journalists. Journalists used four different types of information graphics and segmented the copy so the length would not be intimidating.

help of computers, today's illustrations may look more polished, but the concepts are the same (Fig. 1.9).

Every day the wire is full of fragments. Fires. Shootings. Wars. Revolutions. Traditional categories of news don't always show the patterns. A plane crash in the United States runs on the national page. A plane crash in Germany runs on the world page. Gasoline prices in the United States run on the national page. OPEC decisions run on the world or business page. Scattering pieces of the puzzle throughout the paper is like offering a buffet. The diner has to select the right pieces to make a nutritious meal. The editor, like a chef, carefully plans what will be served and in what order. The useful newspaper adds value to the news.

One of the most useful additions to journalists' ability to find patterns is computer-assisted reporting. The computer allows us to find patterns in reams of data. Newspapers have used computers to show which banks discriminate against minority borrowers, to show that some judges deal more harshly with minority than with majority defendants, to show patterns in state bid-letting, and to identify campaign contributors who try to hide behind facades. The computer provides the data; it's up to the journalist to give it meaning through words, numbers and pictures.

4. *Use the newspaper's potential as a visual medium.* When the *Dayton Daily News* asked, "What's the best way to tell the story about the status of legal action against the tobacco industry?" the answer was to write stories, create lists and use a dateline, bar graphs and a map (Fig. 1.10). When the *Detroit News* told the story of a revival in downtown Detroit, it chose to tell part of the story visually (Fig. 1.11). The illustration was worth 1,000 words. These solutions to story telling combine the work of reporters, photographers and graphic journalists.

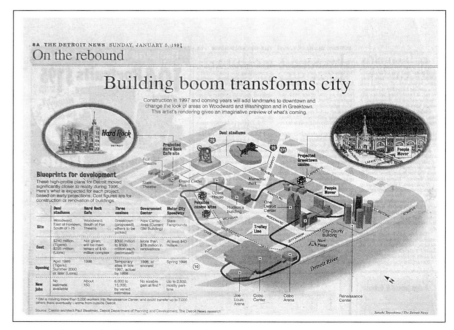

1.11   Artists are finding better ways all the time to show the news. Satoshi Toyoshima of the *Detroit News* used a different perspective so readers could look down on the map of Detroit. The perspective makes it easier for us to see the news.

5. *Anticipate.* Newspapers traditionally tell what happened. That continues to be important, but so is telling readers what will happen. Spurred by a reader's suggestion to tell her "what's next," the *St. Louis Post-Dispatch* tries to advance every major story. That's why you'll see a "what's next" item in most packages (Fig. 1.12). Most newspapers already offer lists of government meetings, entertainment and sports events. When they also preview important meetings, they are empowering readers to take action. Readers can write or call officials, they can protest, they can attend meetings and be heard.

6. *Practice service journalism.* Tell people what they need and want to know and how they can act. Include times, dates and places. Include phone and fax numbers and addresses. List the questions readers should ask to get help with their taxes. Newspapers traditionally write about the ups and downs of the stock market. *Money* magazine analyzes stocks and mutual funds, ranks them by various indicators and gives phone numbers and addresses. Newspapers publish unconnected bits of data; *Money* offers the information in a form that makes it useful and usable. Many newspapers run the annual two paragraphs warning readers to mail early at Christmas. One newspaper decided the best way to tell that story was with a photograph of a busy mailroom and a list of solutions (Fig. 1.13). Readers could act on that information.

7. *Offer solutions.* Don't just write about the problem of crime. Do a data-base search and find communities that have fought crime successfully. Don't just write about your city's lousy bus system; visit cities with successful systems and report why they work. Don't just chortle over catching your city's comptroller with a hand in the cookie jar; tell what the city should do to make sure it doesn't happen again.

Republicans craft four articles of impeachment

The Republicans
The House Judiciary Committee Republicans cited Clinton on two counts of perjury, one count of obstruction of justice and one count of abuse of power.

The Democrats
They drafted a proposal to censure Clinton, citing him for "reprehensible conduct with a subordinate," Lewinsky, and demanding his signature on the instrument of his censure.

What's Next?
The House Judiciary Committee will begin debate of the articles today. Committee approval would set the stage for a vote in the House next week, thus making Clinton only the second president to suffer an impeachment roll call.

1.12 Editors are listening. A reader in a *St. Louis Post-Dispatch* focus group told editors she simply wanted to know, "What, so what and what's next." Rather than burying the information in small text, the *Post-Dispatch* pulled out the "what" and "what's next" in large type as an introduction to the stories.

1.13 Many magazines, including *Ladies Home Journal* and *Money,* have built their publishing philosophy around service journalism. That requires editors not just to tell the news but also to tell readers how to act. Instead of doing the traditional "mail early" text story, the *Columbia Missourian* told readers what to do, how to do it and when to do it. That's service journalism.

1.14 The *Portland Oregonian* asked for readers' opinions on how to balance the budget. Rather than writing a traditional story, the *Oregonian* invented a grid to help readers through the responses.

1.15 In an attempt to increase circulation, newspapers have targeted single-copy buyers with some innovative approaches. One that has been tried in several cities, including Dallas, involves creating a billboard on the front page. All items on the page tease stories inside. Researchers at the Newspaper Association of America have found that 44 percent of single-copy buyers are between the ages of 18 and 34, an audience newspapers prize highly. The median income of this group in 1998 was $37,000.

8. *Invite readers to participate.* When Oregon's legislators were debating how to balance the budget, the *Oregonian* in Portland asked readers for suggestions. Not only did it get readers involved, the paper received several interesting solutions (Fig. 1.14). Other newspapers routinely seek readers' opinions and ideas on all kinds of issues.

9. *Reinvent the newspaper.* Richard Saul Wurman facetiously suggests in *Information Anxiety* (1990) that the newspaper could be divided into three categories: hope, absurdity and catastrophe. That may be too radical for some, but we should be willing to examine everything we do from the readers' viewpoint. As we enter the 21st century, what do readers want from our newspapers and how do they want it? Newspapers used to be the dominant information medium; now, for too many, they are a supplement. Readers say they don't have time, but they are spending more time watching television. Newspapers aren't important enough to them, especially to the younger generation. How can we change that?

Our front pages are static except for Big Events. Should they be? Should they offer an expanded table of contents? A diagram of the day's events? Should they be devoted to the topic of the day? In Pittsburgh and Dallas, the front page of some editions of the Sunday paper are turned into a billboard in an attempt to stimulate sales (Fig. 1.15).

Should the news continue to be divided into geographic categories—region, state, nation and world—or do other categories make sense in this "global village"? If not Wurman's "absurdity," how about hunger? If not "hope," how about solutions? If not "catastrophe," how about natural disasters? Does it make sense to treat the national debate about health care in the United States separately from the same debate in other countries? Does it make sense to treat U.S. trade problems separately from Germany's or Mexico's? Does it make sense to report on economic problems in the United States without linking them to Japan's or Canada's? Do traditional categories of news facilitate or impede understanding?

Reinventing the newspaper goes far beyond dealing with the great issues. It forces us to question everything we do. When we publish recipes, do we format them so readers can easily clip and save them, or do we wrap them from one column to the next or even jump them? Are school lunch menus formatted to be clipped? Obituaries? Weddings and engagements? Do readers want us to organize our entertainment listings by day or type of entertainment? Should sports agate be organized alphabetically?

The now-defunct *St. Louis Sun* published an innovative daily full-page television grid with color and advertisements built into it. Many other newspapers liked it so much they immediately adopted the idea. The *Sun* also published a weekly TV guide. One week when editors accidentally repeated the same grid two days running, they didn't receive a single call from their 100,000 subscribers. The readers obviously were ignoring the daily grid and using the weekly booklet, but no one at the newspaper knew.

Should advertisements be organized by content? Should all the clothing ads be run together so readers can compare? Should advertisements appear in dedicated spaces on page 1? On section fronts? Should every newspaper have an advertising index? Should advertisements be offered only in modular units? The *News* in Boca Raton, Fla., asked readers how they used the classified ads to shop for used cars, new homes and apartments. Readers responded that they didn't like searching through columns of small text for the items that interested them. As a result, the *News* created an innovative grid that organizes apartments by geographic location and price. It did the same with homes and cars. Readers reinvented that classified section. Your readers can help you reinvent the newspaper.

10. *Respect readers' time.* Some readers have only five minutes to look over the newspaper before they rush to work. Others spend an hour or more. Unfortunately, there are more of the former than the latter. That's why newspapers need to respect readers' time by layering, the technique of providing story summaries for scanners. Another device is to provide a summary of the entire newspaper. Many newspapers, including the *Dayton Daily News,* have these one-page newspapers anchored on page 2 (Fig. 1.16).

1.16 The most common reason given by people for not subscribing to a newspaper is that they don't have time to read it. In response, many newspapers, including the *Dayton Daily News,* have created a newspaper-within-the-newspaper. Readers can scan this page and get the top news in all departments.

YOUR ROLE

Designers are key players in the new newspaper, and their role has expanded dramatically in the last 10 years.

Designers have the expertise to take advantage of the newspaper's ability as a visual medium. The best designers are, first, good journalists. They know popular culture, politics and economics. They also possess expertise in the tools of story telling: text, photographs, illustrations and information graphics. They design pages to take advantage of readership habits. They know how to use computers and appropriate software programs.

Some designers design pages for one department of the paper. Others work at newspapers that have universal desks. Those designers produce pages for any and all departments.

Because there are more jobs than designers, designers often receive premium pay. Starting salaries for beginning designers are often $5,000 to $10,000 more than beginning reporters, and many designers are able to start at larger papers than are reporters. Students who design at their college papers and who complete internships often have multiple job opportunities.

Many designers have migrated to web pages, either at the newspaper where they work or for other organizations. They use the same design skills they used in print.

Over 2,500 designers belong to the Society of News Design (www.snd.org). SND sponsors an international design contest, holds training sessions, and produces newsletters, a quarterly magazine, and an annual awards book.

CONCLUSION

The playwright George Bernard Shaw once wrote, "You see things and you say 'why?' But I dream things that never were; and I say 'why not?'" This book asks, "Why not visual journalism?" The chapters that follow explore how visual journalists working in teams rather than as individuals can ask not only "Why?" but also "Why not?," not only "How?" but also "What's the best way to tell the story?" Only then will journalists begin to achieve the potential of the medium.

Part II

Getting Started: Newspaper Layout

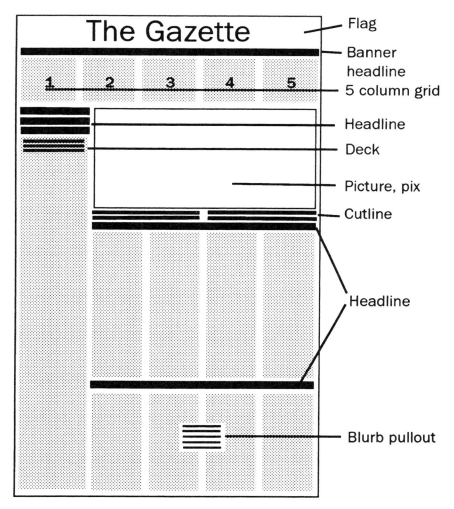

The Gazette

- Flag
- Banner headline
- 5 column grid
- Headline
- Deck
- Picture, pix
- Cutline
- Headline
- Blurb pullout

2.1 To enter the world of layout and design, you must learn a new language. Although the terms may sounds foreign to you at first, you will quickly assimilate them.

It's much smarter to plan ahead by drawing a detailed page diagram and fine-tuning each element in advance on a dummy before you begin assembling the real thing.

Design Sourcebook
The Times, Munster, Ind.

2. The Language of Layout and Design

"I need a 3-36-2 jump head."

"Should I squeeze it or take it down a couple of points?"

"Get me cutlines for these pix."

This probably sounds Greek to you. Don't worry. You're not alone. This jargon is a shorthand version of the vocabulary of layout and design editors. It is sometimes logical, sometimes illogical, and often inconsistent from newspaper to newspaper. To complicate matters, the vocabulary is a mixture of hot and cold type production systems, of dedicated terminals and of Macs and PCs. You may be more familiar with "template" than "grid," with "tracking" than "letter spacing," but you should learn all the terms.

Regardless of the production system, there is a basic layout and design vocabulary; this chapter defines some of these terms. Others are defined throughout the book, and all appear in the glossary. This chapter also teaches you how to work in picas, how to count and size headlines and how to size photographs. When you're done, you'll be ready to draw a newspaper page.

MEASUREMENTS

Although feet and inches are the basis for most measurements in the United States, designers work with picas and points. The terms may sound as if they came from Mars, but you will come to appreciate the preciseness the system offers you. Your pagination system allows you to choose between picas and inches. Picas are more exact.

Type size is measured in points; copy width is measured in picas and points. Just as there are 12 inches in a foot, there are 12 points in a pica. Although the decimal point in math indicates tenths, the decimal point in typography represents twelfths. That is why it may be more precise for you to express points and picas as 13p6 rather than 13.6; 13p6 is 13 picas, 6 points, or $13\frac{1}{2}$ picas. Working in twelfths means that you can have 13.10 and 13.11; 13.12 would be 14 picas.

Picas and points are also used to measure the gutters, the space between columns of type or pictures. The gutters between text columns usually range from 9 points to 2 picas. In the mid-1980s, most newspapers adopted a standard page width of 78 picas to make it easier for national advertisers to place their ads. This was an effort to make it easier for national advertisers to size their ads. Before, advertisers had to make ads of many different widths or permit newspapers to reduce or enlarge them, sometimes with disastrous results. Standard widths also make it easier to verify billings. These uniform dimensions are known as SAUs, or standardized advertising units. However, in the 1990s, newspapers started going their individual ways again. For instance, *USA Today* is 68p6 wide by $20\frac{1}{2}$ inches long; the *New York Times* is 76p6 by $21\frac{1}{2}$ inches long; and the *Washington Post* is 71p10 by 21 inches long. Newspapers are getting narrower to save money on newsprint.

Newspapers subdivide the space differently. When most newspapers were 78 picas wide, most of them had a six-column grid with column widths of 12p2 with 1-pica gutters. Now, at 71p10 wide, the *Post* uses six 11-pica columns with 1p2 gutters. There are several variations. In layout and design, the editor must determine horizontal widths within a couple of points. Your software will do most of the calculations for you, but here is how to do it yourself. If you remember that you are dealing in twelfths and not using the decimal system, you will realize that you can't carry over as you do in normal multiplication or division. For instance, if your columns are 12p2 and your gutters are 1 pica, to find how wide six columns are, you multiply the columns by the width and add one fewer gutters than there are columns.

$$6 \times 12p2 = 72p12 + 5 = 77p12$$

Because there are 12 points in 1 pica, you convert 77p12 to 78 picas. If you performed that multiplication using the decimal system, you would get 73.2 when you multiplied 6 x 12.2. You will find a conversion chart in Chapter 3. Elements that do not fit horizontally must be corrected, copy must be reset, and illustrations must be trimmed or resized. Such corrections take too much time. When fitting items vertically, however, the editor has more flexibility. Because copy that is too long can be trimmed quickly, vertical problems are solved more easily.

THE EIGHT BASIC ELEMENTS

The eight basic tools that editors use are text type, display type, rules and borders, photographs, artwork, structures, grids and white space. Each, except white space, has its vocabulary.

Text type

Text type is used to set the stories. It is measured in points, and most newspapers use sizes of 8 to 10 points. By comparison, books are often set in 10- to 12-point type. This book is set in 10-point type. Variations in size and legibility are discussed in more detail in Chapter 9.

The space between the lines of type is called leading, a term from hot metal days when a piece of lead separated the lines. The setting is usually expressed as 9/10, which means 9-point type with 1 point of leading or space between lines. Text can even be set with negative or minus leading (less than the size of the type being used). For example, the following copy is set with negative leading:

> This is possible because type is measured from the top of the ascender (the upper parts of letters such as d and b) to the bottom of the descender (the lower parts of letters such as p or y). Even when a descender is aligned directly over an ascender, the two do not touch, as this example, set 10/9.6, illustrates.

Most newspapers have 1/2 to 1 full point of leading between lines; there are 2 points in this book. The type size and amount of leading affect the number of lines that can be printed in a newspaper column and the legibility.

Most text copy is set flush left and flush right, or justified. That is, the copy lines up evenly on both the left and right margins. To accomplish this, the line is justified by placing small amounts of space between words and hyphenating words at the end of a line when necessary. The text in this book is justified.

> Type can also be set ragged right. Instead of hyphenating words, the computer leaves white space at the end of the line and starts a new one. Despite the irregular space at the end of the lines, ragged

14 18 24 36 48 60 72

ah ah ah ah ah ah ah ah

2.2 To lay out a page, a designer must first internalize headline sizes. One way to do this is to guess at the headline sizes in your newspaper, then use a pica ruler to find the actual sizes. With practice, you should be able to come within six points every time.

right does not take up more room. It simply transfers the extra space between words to the end. A few newspapers set all their text type ragged right, as this paragraph is.

Software programs can also be instructed to set type in a modified ragged right. That is, the computer will hyphenate words to ensure a minimum width. An editor might want to program the computer to hyphenate only when a line of type would not exceed 50 or 60 percent of the potential line length. This eliminates inordinately short lines. Newspaper text is set in columns, legs or wraps of type. A story that extends across five columns of a newspaper page is said to have five legs or wraps.

Display type

Display type or headlines are the larger version of text type. They are measured vertically in points. Headline type starts at 14 points and extends over 100 points (Fig. 2.2). Normal headline schedules start at 18 points and increase in increments of 6 points. That's because when type was metal, it was produced in 6-point increments. Now you can set type in any size you wish. However, most newspapers retain the traditional 6-point increments to help them establish headline hierarchy on the page.

The shorthand for headline instructions varies from newspaper to newspaper. One of the common systems is to designate width, size and number of lines by writing 2-36-3. This means the headline is two columns wide, 36 points, and three lines.

Various newspapers use different rules of capitalization in headlines. The least legible is all caps, or HEADLINES WITH ALL THE LETTERS CAPITALIZED. Many newspapers still use the traditional uppercase style of capitalizing the first letter of each word except articles and prepositions. The lowercase style capitalizes only the first letter of the first word of the headline and proper nouns. The lowercase style also permits more to be said in the same space.

Most newspapers position the headlines flush left; that is, the headline begins at the left margin of the copy. Other styles include centered (each line is centered in the column or columns), and stepped down (the second and all subsequent lines of a head are written shorter than the preceding one and indented under the one above it). The *New York Times* is about the only U.S. newspaper still using stepped-down style. A few newspapers, including the *Providence Journal Bulletin*, the *Raleigh* (N.C.) *News & Observer* and the *Kansas City Star* center all heads.

This headline is flush left	Each line of this sample is centered	Stepped-down lines get shorter

Headlines, regardless of where they are placed or their format, must fit. The writers can count the letters, but at most newspapers, computers are doing that work quickly and accurately. However, at newsrooms where letters must still be counted, a standardized method is needed. There are several formulas, each equally good if used consistently.

A headline "schedule" is established, in which each letter is assigned a unit of width because some letters are wider than others. The easiest, though not the most exact, way to make a headline chart is to set at least three headlines in all the sizes you will be using. Place the headlines across a full newspaper page marked off by columns. Determine the number of units, or counts, that will fit in each column width, or establish the number of counts per pica. Sometimes a headline will count shorter because it has an unusual number of l's, t's or f's, which are narrower than other letters. Here's a typical system:

$\frac{1}{2}$ unit: Punctuation, spaces, f, i, l, t, j, I, L and the numeral 1
1 unit: lowercase letters and numbers except 1
$1\frac{1}{2}$ units: uppercase letters, m and w
2 units: M and W

Not all the vocabulary that refers to special uses of headline type is standardized. However, here are the most common:

Banner: a large headline that extends across the top of the front page above the most important story of the day.

Deck: one or more lines that are subordinate to the main headline and give the reader additional information about the story. They commonly are half the size of the main head.

Summary deck: a deck usually written in complete sentences and run in sizes usually ranging from 14 to 18 points. Also called nut graphs, lead-ins and key decks.

Kicker: three or four words that are set half the size of the main headline and usually appear flush left above the main headline. Generally, the main head is indented under the kicker, which should not be smaller than 24 points. Kickers add white space.

Hammer: usually one to three words in large type. A hammer is effective in attracting attention and adding white space to the page but needs a deck to further explain the story. The hammer should be 6 to 12 points larger than a headline in the same location. The deck usually is half the size of the hammer. Hammer heads can be set flush left or centered. They are most effective in two- and three-column formats. Beyond that width, hammers usually create too much white space.

Sidesaddle: also called a side head, the type is placed at the left of the copy rather than over it. Sidesaddles are most often used in tight spaces above ads or in boxes.

Blurb: also called a pullout or pullquote, a blurb is a short piece of interesting or alluring information pulled from the body of the story and set in display type, usually 14 to 18 points.

Overline: a headline for a photograph. It appears above the photograph.

Catchline: a headline between the photograph and the cutline. Usually used with pictures not accompanied by stories.

Rules and borders

Sometimes rules and borders are used to set off headlines; they are also used around illustrations and copy. A rule technically refers to a plain line, whereas borders are ornamental, but the terms are often used interchangeably. When a rule or border is used around copy, it is called a box. Different newspapers use different-size rules for boxes, and sometimes the same newspaper uses more than one size. Most, however, use rules rather than borders to box stories. In earlier times, vertical rules were used in the gutters to separate columns; now white space commonly performs this function. Cutoff rules are lines below or alongside an illustration to separate it from unrelated material.

	1-pt. rule		4-pt. rule
	2-pt. rule		6-pt. rule
	border		border

Photographs

Photographs are also called pic (singular) or pix, and sometimes, mistakenly, art. Photographs come from staff photographers, wire services and free-lancers, non–staff members who sell pictures to a publication. The text that accompanies a photograph is most commonly called a cutline, caption or legend. When you are marking a dummy for a photograph, the first number is the width; the second is the depth.

Almost all photographs and artwork need to be reduced or enlarged before they are printed. The proportions are established by the layout editor or designer. A proportion wheel or calculator is used to determine the proper percentage of enlargement or reduction. Artwork used at 100 percent will reproduce at the same size as the original. Anything larger than 100 percent results in an enlargement; less than 100 percent provides a reduction. If you are working in a pagination system or Photoshop, you simply drag the photo to fill the space you created for it. If you are not working on a computer, you will need to calculate the change by using the standard proportion formula. You know the width and depth of the picture as is, and you know the new width you want to use because you are dummying the page. (Occasionally, you size to the depth; the formula is the same.) What you don't know is the depth. Thus, you always know three of the four dimensions. This is the formula: *Original width is to new width as original depth is to new depth.* Here's an example. Original width is 24 picas; new width is 28 picas. Original depth is 30 picas; new depth is x, the unknown. The symbol : means "as."

24:28 = 30:x

The result of multiplying the exterior numbers (24x) equals the result of multiplying the interior numbers (28 × 30). Complete the calculation as shown:

24x = 840
x = 840 ÷ 24 = 35

The original photo was 24p x 30p. The resized photo is 28p x 35p.

Artwork

Artwork is any illustration other than a photograph. Photographs used for special effects, such as silhouetting or screening to produce a different

2.3 Halftones can be shot with screens or processed in Photoshop to produce special effects. However, be careful; these techniques should be used infrequently, and then only on illustrations and occasionally on feature photos.

image (Fig. 2.3), are properly classified as art. Art that is black and white, such as a chart or a simple line drawing, is shot without a screen and is called line art. If it is the correct size, it can be affixed directly to the page from which the plate is to be burned. If it has gray tones, it must be screened (shot as a halftone).

Structures

Most newspapers use a combination of vertical and horizontal shapes to package the information. Some rely primarily on vertical or horizontal. Each approach has its advantages and disadvantages.

The *Wall Street Journal* is structured vertically. A vertical newspaper runs few headlines more than two columns wide. Stories start at the top of the page, and many run all the way to the bottom. On the inside, the vertical structure is not as pronounced because the vertical copy flow is interrupted by ads. The *Journal* has been so successful for so long that it has imbued the vertical structure with a personality that is conservative, reliable and traditional. In that sense, the *Journal* is a well-designed newspaper. Vertically structured newspapers are also quicker to lay out and compose because there

2.4   Vertical layout pushes more stories above the fold. The downside is that it inhibits photo display and usually causes more jumps from page 1.

is little for the layout editor to do but fit the stories into the holes. Other newspapers with vertical front pages include *USA Today* and the *St. Louis Post-Dispatch.*

Because one- and two-column headlines take up less space than larger multicolumn headlines, it is possible to get more stories on a vertically structured page. Consequently, the vertical format is the best choice for newspapers seeking a high story count on page 1. The *St. Louis Post-Dispatch,* a vertical paper, often offers as many as four stories and a picture above the fold (Fig. 2.4).

For some newspapers, however, the advantages of the vertical structure are also disadvantages. Newspapers that do not want a conservative, traditional image or are more concerned with visual excitement and photo display than the count on page 1 see the vertical structure as a disadvantage. This structure also works against a page design that tries to move the reader around the page. Vertical papers usually are top-heavy; the bottom half has little or nothing to attract the reader's attention, and it is difficult to keep the page from looking gray and dull.

On the other hand, the horizontal structure has several advantages, the most prominent being that most readers perceive it as more modern and pleasing (Siskind 1979). Stories laid out horizontally take advantage of the reader's inclination to read from left to right. The horizontal structure also permits the layout editor and designer to be more flexible when balancing the page and permits better display of photos. The larger, multicolumn headlines used in horizontal makeup not only attract attention but also add weight to the page (Click and Stempel 1974).

Another important advantage is the optical illusion that results when a story is laid out horizontally. A 20-inch vertical story would extend from the top of the page to the bottom. It looks long, and because of the limited number of things a designer can do in one column, it looks dull. Readers who wear bifocals have difficulty reading a vertical story because they must fold or raise the broadsheet page as they proceed down the column. The same 20-inch story run horizontally across six columns would be 3½ inches deep. Consequently, it looks shorter and may attract more readership. The *Telegraph Herald* in Dubuque, Iowa, is a horizontal paper. Although there is only one story and a picture above the fold, the photo wins excellent display, and the story is not jumped (Fig. 2.5).

One of the few disadvantages of the horizontal structure is the additional time required for layout or design. A purely horizontal page, however, is as dull as purely vertical makeup. A combination of the two is needed. A good horizontal structure needs strong vertical elements to provide contrast. Monotony is the enemy of any structure. To the editor working on a horizontal page, nothing is more welcome than a strong vertical photograph.

Grids

The grid is the scaffolding for the page. At the most elementary level, it divides the page vertically into columns. As a general rule, the more columns you have, the more elements you put on the page. Most broadsheet newspapers today use a six-column grid for most pages, but they may use five in a book section, editorial page or features, where there are fewer elements per page. They may also use between seven and nine on the sports statistics page. The basic grid for tabloids is five columns. Tabloids, too, will use fewer columns in sections where they have fewer items and want a slower pace. They will use more columns for listings.

Some newspapers have more intricate grids. The *Oregonian* in Portland uses an 11-column grid. Text normally is set two columns wide; one narrow column, called a rail, is used for such things as decks and blurbs or just white space. The *Kansas City Star* uses a six-column grid for everything but section pages and special pages, which are built on a 50-column grid.

Grids also can be used to establish a horizontal structure. A common approach is to divide the space horizontally according to the type size and leading. If 9-point type is used with one point of leading, horizontal lines are drawn every 10 points.

2.5 Horizontal layout allows the designer to display fewer elements larger. The downside is there are fewer stories to attract readers at the newsstand.

White space

All pages offer tones from black to white. Because text occupies the most space on most pages, most pages are gray. Pictures offer grays and blacks. Large headlines offer black. White provides visual relief. White space is built into a grid that specifies the space between the rule under the flag and the top of a headline or photograph; in the space between lines of display and text type; and in the margins. Designers can add white space when executing pages. White space provides a frame. Designers want to provide visual relief without bringing undue attention to the space itself.

3. Laying Out Pages

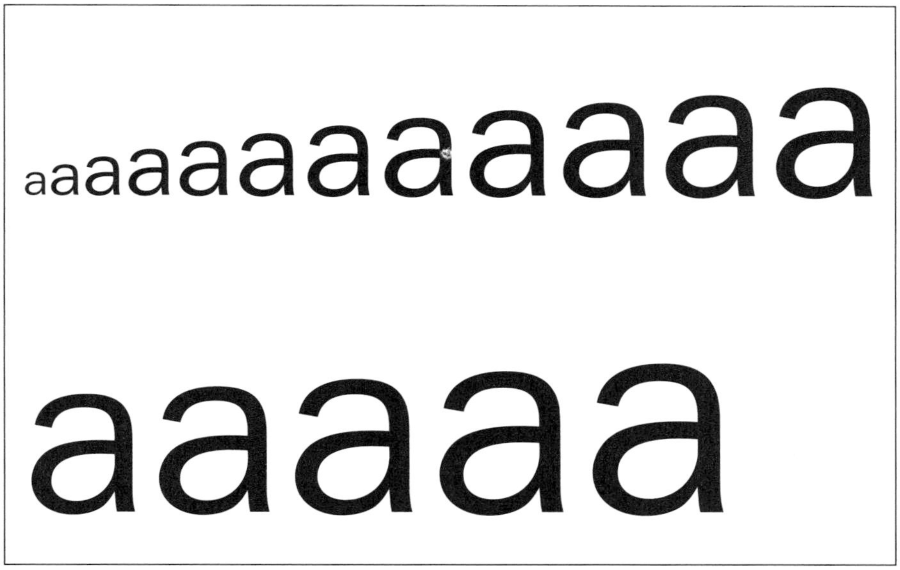

3.1 All designers must recognize type sizes with their eye if they are going to design efficiently. One way to learn sizes is to guess at the sizes of the headlines on a printed page, then measure them from the top of the ascender to the bottom of the descender.

Page design should begin with the main illustration, and its size and shape should be regarded as a fixed element to which the other display elements have to adjust.

Harold Evans
Author, *Newspaper Design, Book Five*

HOW READERS READ

1. Readers look at about three-quarters of the photos and illustrations.
2. Readers look at about half of the headlines.
3. Readers look at about a third of the briefs and cutlines.
4. Readers read about a quarter of the stories.
5. Readers are more likely to read a story if it is accompanied by a photo.
6. Readers scan pages. They decide whether to start a story based on the headlines. If they start a story, about half of the readers read at least half the story.
7. Readers spend about 25 minutes a day with the newspaper. Part of that time is spent on advertisements and comics.
8. Summaries satisfy some readers; others read them and continue to the main story.

3.2

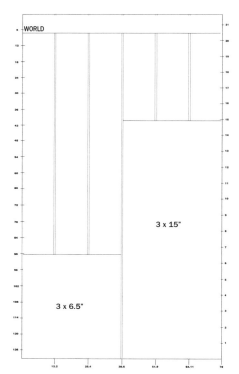

3.3   A typical inside page dummy comes to you with the advertising space already marked.

Journalism, as it refers to the reporting and writing process, has been described as literature in a hurry. Layout is design in a hurry.

Readers also are in a hurry. That is why it is important to know how readers read a page before you start arranging one. Consult the list in Figure 3.2.

Dummying is the technique of placing elements on a page. When it is done on paper, the dummy is a blueprint. On a computer, you work on a template. Normally, layout is done under deadline pressure. A designer might do one page in two or three hours, but a layout editor may need to do several. Journalists doing layout need to know how to arrange all the elements, show relationships and work in modules (discussed in the next chapter). They must also understand basic design principles. Because speed is essential for most pages in a newspaper, there is and will continue to be a need for people who know the basics of layout. Designers may work on page 1, section fronts and special projects, but most pages will continue to be drawn by layout editors. Before you lay out the page, you must make several decisions. This chapter will take you through them.

PRELAYOUT DECISIONS

Before your cursor touches the template or your pencil touches the dummy, you must make the following decisions within the philosophy of the publication for which you are working.

First, let's work on an inside page. Here are the steps:

1. Determine the amount of space left on the page after the advertisements have been placed.
2. Compile your story and illustration list. Group related stories and pictures.
3. Select your most important story. If it does not have a photograph, determine if you have an unrelated photograph that you want to place on the page.
4. Work off the ledges of the ads to create modular units.

Now let's follow these steps through to complete a typical inside page for a broadsheet newspaper. Your dummy, which shows the ads, is in Figure 3.3. Here is your list:

Killings 13″ with Map1 12p2 × 12p6 (12 picas 2 points wide by 12 picas 6 points deep) and Map2 12p2 × 12p
Tsunami 9″
Guardsman 12″ with pictures, Free, 23p × 22p
UN 8″

If you were actually working with the stories, you would have a brief description of them in the budget your wire service sends. You would also be able read the stories if they arrived via computer. Sometimes, however, you have to draw the pages before all the stories arrive.

The dummy shows us we have $5\frac{1}{2}$″ across the six columns at the top of the page and another $8\frac{1}{2}$″ in the three columns from the ad ledge down to the lower left ad. We have already grouped the elements (Step 2) by showing that the two maps go with the story slugged "Killings" and that a picture accompanies "Guardsman." The number after the slug, or the name you assign the story in the computer, is the story length in inches.

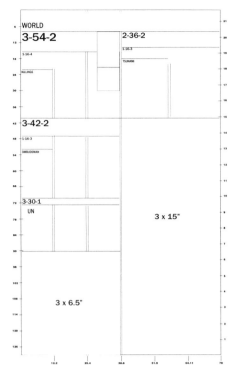

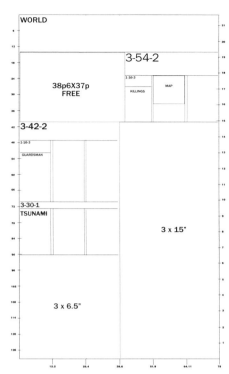

3.4 When you draw a page on paper, you indicate all the elements—headlines, decks, pullouts, pictures, cutlines and story slugs.

3.5 This is what the page dummy from Fig. 3.4 looks like when it is produced. Try to match the elements on the dummy to this page.

3.6 Even with advertising, there usually are at least two or more ways to arrange the page. This is an alternative layout to Fig. 3.5.

We have several options. As is common on tight inside pages, we do not have to use all the elements, and the stories can be shortened. For Step 3, let's select "Killings" as our lead story. We can run it either upper right or upper left on our page. However, if we run it upper left, we can use the maps to prevent tombstoning. We can enlarge the maps, but graphics, unlike photographs, should be run only large enough so they can be read easily.

In the dummy shown in Figure 3.4, we have assigned a 3-54-2 (three columns wide, 54-point, two-line headline) over the "Killings" story. The story actually runs four columns, but we are wrapping the copy under the maps, which separate the two headlines. We have added a summary deck. Even though we could run the first three columns of the story deeper, we have evened all the legs of type off at the advertisement to create a module. In the upper right, we have assigned a 2-36-2 head to "Tsunami" with another summary deck.

That leaves us the three vertical columns at the left. To the left of the large ad, we place a 3-42-2 headline with a summary deck. We also are setting it 2/3, which means two columns over three columns of space. Instead of three 12p2 columns, we are running two columns at 18p9. That leaves us a small space at the lower left to run "UN" with a 3-30-1 headline and another summary deck. The published version is Figure 3.5.

Note that we did not publish the picture. Let's dummy another page (Fig. 3.6). This page is relatively open, so let's run the picture three columns to provide a strong dominant element. When we enlarge the picture three

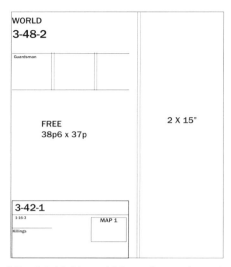

3.7 A tabloid would have fewer elements than a broadsheet. This dummy is done working from the same story list as in Fig. 3.4.

DRAWING AN OPEN PAGE

1. List the number and size of the various stories, pictures and pieces of art that will be placed on the page.
2. Decide which elements are related and how to group them.
3. Select the major display element (or elements) for the page and build the page around it.
4. Select the second major display element (or elements) for the page and put it as close to the bottom as possible and on a diagonal line from the major display element.
5. Identify the lead story. If the lead story is related to the main photograph, show the relationship. If not, disassociate them.

3.8

columns, it becomes 37 picas deep. That means we have to run it in the upper left because it extends lower than the large ad. The related story, "Guardsman," must go underneath it to show the relationship between the two. That puts "Killings" in the upper right. The headline size shows that "Killings" is still the most important story on the page.

Because of their smaller size, tabloids have less space on each page. Figure 3.7 shows a tabloid version with the elements from our story list.

If you are a beginner, the five steps in Figure 3.8 are like the formula you used when learning to write an inverted pyramid story. When you began, you mechanically went through the process of identifying who, what, where, when and why in each story and ranking them in order of importance. For the beginner in layout, it is helpful if you use these five steps. With a little experience, the process will become second nature to you. Let's take a more detailed look at each of the steps.

1. The number of elements goes a long way toward determining the look of a page. Traditionally, that decision has been made by managing editors, and the layout editors were left to find a way to make all the pieces fit. However, this method is increasingly recognized as unsatisfactory. The problem and a proposed solution are discussed further in Chapter 12. Regardless of who makes the decision, story count is critical to what can be done with the page.

   The newspaper's jump policy is also critical. If the paper is willing to continue stories from page 1 or from one inside page to the next, the story count can be higher. If the paper does not jump stories or sets a maximum number of stories that can be continued, stories will have to be shorter, there will be fewer of them, or writers will have to write to front page space and then start another story for inside display. Within the confines of the newspaper's policy, then, you determine the number of elements that must appear on the page and their size or length.

2. The second decision involves related elements. Which picture or pictures go with which story? Do any of the stories have sidebars? Is there more than one story on the same general topic, such as health or education? The process of grouping related elements forces the editor to think in terms of packages rather than individual elements. Sometimes this can result in elevating two or more less important stories to a larger package that is more significant because of its combined message, makes more sense to the reader, and is easier to handle graphically. Grouping related stories turns facts into information. Packaging puts stories in context.

3. The next step is to determine which element (or elements) will be the major display item. This is not always the same as selecting the most important story. The major display element consists of the dominant visual element. If the lead story does not have any photographs or artwork, the major display element may consist of a secondary story that has visuals. However, even if the most important story does not have any visuals, it still can be the major display element. The editor can use type and other graphic devices to create a package that adds to the information in the story and attracts attention to it.

   Usually, the major display package consists of text and illustrations. If the major display element is also the most important story, the editor's job is simplified. If it is not, the editor must lay out the page so that the most important story attracts the attention it deserves even though the page is built around the visual elements. In most cases, the page is built around the major display element, which should be placed at or near the top of the page.

4. The next decision is identification of the second major display element, which will anchor the bottom of the page. That package, which usually includes illustrations, is needed to balance the weight at the top of the page and attract the reader's eye. This creates motion on the page. The reader's eye will move from the major display elements at the top to those at the bottom. In the process, most readers scan the headlines on the page as they go. If the stories are interesting and the headlines are well written, readers may stop or return after reading other stories. If no major display element is placed at the bottom, the editors have conceded that half of the page to dullness. On inside pages, there often is no room for a secondary element.

5. The last step in preparing to draw the page is to identify the lead story. If it goes with the major display element, the editor then determines how to show the proper relationship between the story and the photo or art element. If the lead story is not related to the major display element, the editor then must determine how to disassociate them while placing both at the top of the page.

Following these steps, let's draw page 1. Here's our story list:

Suspects 12″
Speeding 12″
Show 10″ with picture Steer, 49p6 × 31p6
Pros 13″ sidebar to Show. With picture, Horse, 24p6 × 25p6
Shepard 14″

At the planning conference, the editors select "Suspects" as the lead story. That means that the major display elements—"Show" and "Pros" and their photographs—will need to be displayed so they don't show a relationship with "Suspects." The editors want both stories to appear above the front-page fold so they can be seen from newsstands.

Our dummy, Figure 3.9, leaves 14 picas for the flag and promo and 3 inches by four columns for the index and related elements. The elements that appear daily on a page often are called the furniture. You work around the furniture. One solution (Fig. 3.10) puts the lead story in the upper right

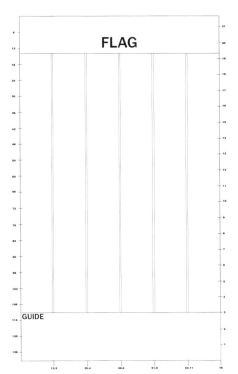

3.9 This is a typical front-page dummy. Set aside is the space for the name of the paper and the index and teasers across the bottom.

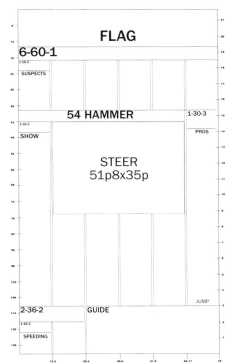

3.10 The lead story is stripped across the top; the lead package, with the "Steer" picture, sits in the middle of the page. All elements on the page are in modules. Remember that 6-60-1 means six columns wide, 60 points, one line.

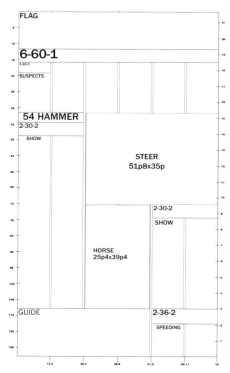

3.11 Here is an alternative to 3.10. The feature package is given all six columns for display. In the previous package, "Pros" also made it near the top of the page.

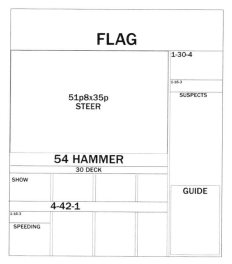

3.12 By its nature, the tabloid format is going to have fewer elements. The stories are shorter and fewer, but the display can be just as creative.

and the display package in the upper left. All stories and packages are in modules. One story jumps.

That is not the only way to do it. The dummy in Figure 3.11 shows an alternative. The dummy in 3.12 shows a tabloid version.

Selecting headlines

To draw pages, you need to be able to visualize headline sizes, know how many columns wide to run each size, and determine the depth of those headlines.

One way to internalize the size (Fig. 3.13) is to take pages from your newspaper and guess the headline sizes. Then take a pica ruler and measure the heads from the top of the ascender to the bottom of the descender (Fig. 3.14). Doing this on your own newspaper will also show you the range of headline sizes your newspaper uses. When you can consistently identify them within six points, you are ready to draw your own pages.

To match the size of the headline to the width of the story, look at Fig. 3.15. The chart is based on the number of characters that will appear in each column. For instance, if you were to run an 18-point headline two or more columns, you would have too many characters in relation to the size of the headline. The chart is only a guideline. The bolder the head, the wider you can set the type.

To figure the depth of headlines, look at the instructions in Figure 3.16. Once you understand that 72 points equals one inch, you know immediately that two lines of 72-point type will take two inches. You do not need to worry about the minimal space between the lines. It follows, then, that 48-point type is $\frac{2}{3}$″ deep and 36-point type is $\frac{1}{2}$″ deep.

As you draw pages, you will want to control tombstoning, the practice of bumping headlines against each other. Normally, you do not bump heads because the consumer might read from one head into the next. Even if the reader does not read from one head into the next, there is another reason to control tombstoning: It can create clutter by gathering too many elements and too much weight in one area of the page. Here are four ways to prevent the negative effects of tombstoning and still bump heads:

1. Run the horizontal headline one to two counts short. The white space is the most effective way to avoid the negative effects of a tombstone.
2. Run a large one-line multicolumn head against a small one-column head. It is reasonable to assume that a consumer would not read from a one-line, four-column, 48-point headline into a one-column, two- or three-line, 24-point headline. Run the one-line headline at least two counts short. The white space provides the best buffer, even when the two headlines are different fonts.
3. Vary the typeface. Using regular type against italic or bold against a lighter weight can prevent the reader from inadvertently going from one head to the other. Such techniques, however, may not avoid clutter or clustering of too much type in one place. Not every newspaper offers this option in its stylebook.
4. Start the copy under a headline and then L-wrap it under a related photo or artwork or box the stories. Copy that comes out from underneath its headline is called a Dutch wrap.

VISUAL GUIDE FOR HEADLINES

This type is 18 pts

This type is 24 pts

This type is 36 pts

This type is 42 pts

This type is 54 pts

This type is 66 pts

3.13 Most newspaper display type ranges between 18 and 72 points. Learn to recognize these sizes when you see them on the page.

MEASURING TYPE

hy 72 pts

3.14 X-height is a measurement of the lowercase x. As the x increases in size, the ascenders—the top of the h—and descenders—the bottom of the y—get short. As the x decreases in size, the extenders get longer. You measure type from the top of the ascender to the bottom of the descender.

HEADLINE SIZE GUIDE

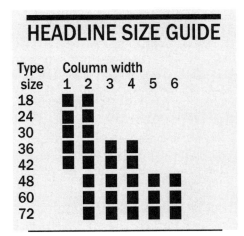

Type size	Column width					
	1	2	3	4	5	6
18	■	■				
24	■	■				
30	■	■				
36	■	■	■			
42	■	■	■			
48		■	■	■	■	
60		■	■	■	■	
72		■	■	■	■	

3.15 You can use this guide for sizing headlines with a bold headline face in columns 12-14 picas wide.

HOW TO FIGURE HEADLINE DEPTHS

1. Divide the head size by 12
2. Multiply by number of lines
3. Result is picas deep
Example for 2-line, 48-pt. head:
1. 48 \ 12= 4
2. 2 x 4 = 8 picas deep
Example for 3-line, 30-pt. head:
1. 30 \ 12= 2.5
2. 3 x 2.5 = 7.5 picas deep

3.16

CONVERTING POINTS TO DECIMALS

1 pt. = .06	7 pts. = .58
2 pts. = .17	8 pts. = .67
3 pts. = .25	9 pts. = .75
4 pts. = .33	10 pts. = .83
5 pts. = .42	11 pts. = .92
6 pts. = .50	

Always round down to the next lowest decimal. For instance, round .74 to .67 = 8 points.

3.17

COPYFITTING

Regardless of whether you are working on paper or computer, you should know how to make the copy fit horizontally. This is one truth you must remember: *You can adjust copy length to fit the elements vertically, but you must be exact when fitting horizontally.* To make sure you don't end up trying to print in the margins of the paper, you must learn how to fit copy. Here's how.

You must know three measurements of your page: the standard column width, the gutter width, and the width of your story or the package you are designing.

Most broadsheet newspapers are 78 picas wide. Most tabloids are 61 picas, 6 points (61p6) wide. To create your grid, you first subtract the number of gutters, then divide by the number of columns. Most newspapers use a 1-pica gutter. To create a six-column grid for a broadsheet, you would subtract five gutters from 78 and then divide 73 by 6 to get 12p2. *There are always one fewer gutters than columns.* To create a five-column tabloid grid, subtract 4 from 61p6, then divide 57p6 by 5 to get 11p6. Make sure that you remember you are working with points and picas, not the decimal system (Fig. 3.17).

Here are some typical copyfitting situations.

To box a story, your newspaper must determine a standard value for the box. A common standard is 2 picas when you use 2-point rules. Two picas leave space for the rule and the gutters between the box and the text or picture. For this example, you are working with 12p2 columns and 1p gutters. Using three columns, you are going to run two columns of text in a box. Here are the steps for boxing any story.

1. Determine the width of your package. 3 columns = 36p6 + 2 (gutters) = 38p6
2. Subtract 2 picas for the box. 38p6 – 2 = 36p6
3. Subtract the space for gutters. 36p6 – 1 = 35p6
4. Divide by the number of columns of type. 35p6 ÷ 2 = 17p9

If you wish to run two columns over three columns of space without the box, simply eliminate Step 2. To determine the width of a two-column picture in the box over the text, simply multiply your new column width by the number of columns and add the gutter (17p9 × 2 = 35p6 + 1 = 36p6). As you usually do, you are fitting the photo to your grid.

Here's a copyfitting situation that requires you to determine the width of the picture first. If you wish to run a picture and story alongside each other and the picture is to be a bastard (nonstandard) size, you must figure the text settings *after* you size the picture. The picture determines the text width (Fig. 3.18).

ATTRACTING SCANNERS

Most people scan a page. They look at pictures, headlines and smaller display type to decide whether to start reading the story. Many newspapers are trying to convert those scanners to readers by using more decks and pullouts. They reason that the more information you can give scanners, the better chance you have of attracting them into the story. It's not unlike when you walk down the halls of a mall. Most of us look at the window displays and the sale signs. They are designed to pull us into the stores. Our photos, headlines and pullouts are designed to pull scanners into the stories.

There's a secondary benefit to display type. It also relieves the grayness of the page. Even without pictures and graphics, editors' toolboxes are full of varying weights and shapes. Let's examine the options.

1. *Make frequent use of decks and alternate deck formats.* Headlines and decks play the most important role in attracting readers. They must tell and sell. Newspapers have been paying more attention to decks recently. Through the sixties, seventies and eighties, many newspapers decreased the use of decks. Now most researchers agree that the decks play a key role in attracting scanners.

Headlines average six words. Traditional decks, often run at half the size of the main head, also average six words. For instance:

> **Suspects in killings**
> **fighting extradition**
> Pair claim state lacks
> evidence to justify return

The main headline has five words; the deck has eight. Now let's substitute a summary deck, which is written in complete sentences. Because the size of summary decks range from 14-18 points, editors can use more lines without taking more space.

> Pair claim Missouri
> officials don't have
> enough evidence
> in murder-robbery case

This deck offers the editor 12 words to tell and sell the story rather than eight, a 50 percent increase. Given that opportunity, editors should be able to attract more readers with the summary deck.

The summary deck, also known as conversational decks, nut graphs, key decks and lead-in, isn't the only alternative deck format. Here's an example of one that appeared on the *New York Times* web site, but it can work in newspapers as well:

> **Charities use for-profit units to skirt rules**
> In this article
> • Affiliate shielded pay of top officer
> • Information scarce about businesses
> • United Way scandal highlights practice

This format is especially effective on in-depth and investigative stories. The strength of these formats is the number of words in display type. Until the 1950s, newspapers often used multiple decks, which accomplished the same purpose. Ironically, in those days, there were more readers and fewer scanners. The *New York Times* and the *Wall Street Journal* were among the few who never abandoned the formats. For instance, this headline is from the *Times*:

> **BIG SELLOFF SENDS**
> **DOW PLUMMETING**
> **NEARLY 300 POINTS**
> ———————
> A ONE-DAY DROP OF 3.41%
> ———————
> Slower Earnings Growth, Crisis
> In Asia and Strong Dollar
> Catch Up With Market

BOXING WITH PICTURES

When you wrap copy alongside and under a picture, first figure your column widths, then size the picture to your columns.

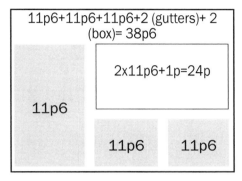

When you run a picture alongside the text, you have the option of sizing it to the columns, or of sizing the picture first, then figuring the column width.

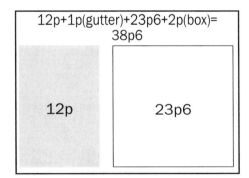

3.18

3.19 Extra white space airs out a page and gives it a non-news look and feel. The *Boston Globe* uses a lot of white space between stories in its Living Arts section to achieve a relaxed look.

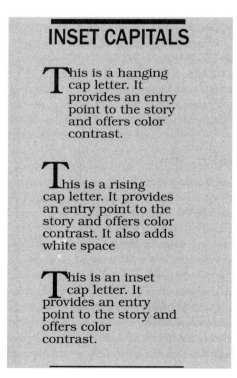

3.20

That's 27 words, significantly more than the typical headline in most newspapers. Note that the *Times* still capitalizes the first letter of each word. That, too, is a traditional approach. Most newspapers have gone to a lowercase system because it is what readers are used to and because it saves space.

2. *Use pullouts to highlight important information and tease the scanners into the story.* Pullout—also called a blurb—is a generic term that refers to information pulled out of the story and highlighted in display type. The most common pullout consists of a quote or a quote with a picture of either the person speaking or the subject of the quote. Summaries of action of meeting coverage and a list of key agenda items for advances on meetings are also good pullout material. Information the reader needs to act on—called service journalism—is also effective pullout material. Time, date and place, prices, telephone, fax numbers, postal and e-mail addresses all are elements that should be highlighted. They lend themselves to lists better than to text. Pullouts should be placed at the top of a column, or the text should be wrapped around the pullout to preserve the readers' path through the story.

3. *Consider subheads on longer stories.* Subheads are a mixed blessing. The positives are that they make long stories look shorter, which encourages readership, and they attract some readers to enter a story because they are curious about the information they find in a subhead. At the same time, they are a convenient exit point for people already reading the story. Subheads usually are bold and larger than the text type. Many newspapers leave a line above them empty to help draw attention to them. In other words, if you use 10 points of leading, you leave 10 points above the subhead.

Decks, pullouts and subheads emphasize information and relieve grayness. Other techniques provide visual relief but don't add information. White space, for instance, is an effective way to draw attention to the content. Newspapers traditionally pack pages, but that approach is counterproductive. Strategically placed, white space makes pages more inviting (Fig. 3.19).

So do inset and rising capital letters. When the first line of copy comes off the top of the capital, it is called an inset cap; when the first line comes off the bottom of the capital, it is called a rising cap. Inset caps add black tone to an otherwise gray mass; rising caps add black tone and white space where the letter extends above the copy. The size of the caps depends on the design of the package. A modest size for caps is 30 to 36 points. Some designs, usually poster sectional fronts, include caps at much larger sizes (Fig. 3.20).

Another way to provide visual relief is to vary your text settings. On a typical six-column page where the columns are 12p2, setting copy two on three produces two columns of 18p6. The contrast with the text widths around it draws attention to the story.

So does setting type ragged right or unjustified. Like slightly open venetian blinds letting light filter into a darkened room, a ragged right setting permits white space to lighten the textual gray. Ragged right does not take any more space than justified type.

Rules also provide color contrast. With the proper amount of white space above and below them, rules ranging from 2 points to 12 points bring black or a spot color to the page and can help organize the material. A light gray screen over copy also provides a different tonal quality.

You can also invent your own techniques. The possibilities are endless. One enterprising graphics editor who was working with a story that had five steps designed a series of numbered copy breakers that not only relieved the grayness but also served as a map for the reader. Chronology lends itself to the use of dates or times as copy breakers.

SEGMENTING THE PACKAGE

Some stories are like a huge banquet: There doesn't seem to be an end to the amount of food. Although we may think we can't eat it all, we might be surprised how much we can take in when it is presented in attractive courses. Breaking banquet stories into digestible bites is called segmenting. People who would not read a 40-inch story might read all or part of four 10-inch stories. People who would not read a 100-inch story might look at pictures and information graphics and read three 15-inch stories.

Segmenting begins at the stage that the story is proposed. Unless the story is compelling, reporters must recognize that most stories will get better readership if the information is presented in shorter takes. Readers unwilling to commit themselves to start reading a 25-inch story may be willing to start a 10-inch story.

The first step in segmenting is to ask the question essential to all stories: What is the best way to tell the story? One long text piece? A shorter story with sidebars? Pictures? Charts and tables? Illustrations? Diagrams? Segmenting is using all the best tools available to tell the story. The *St. Petersburg* (Fla.) *Times* used information graphics, pictures, a story and a sidebar to tell about the California wildfires (Fig. 3.21).

Segmentation should also extend to spot news stories. City council or school board stories should not automatically be 20 inches. Working from an agenda, reporters can anticipate natural subdivisions, and editors should plan two or more stories in addition to a box summarizing the action.

All of these techniques for highlighting information and providing visual relief are designed to convert scanners into readers. Designers must be aggressive, not passive.

3.21 Segmenting is the technique of taking a large story and breaking it into smaller parts so that it will not be so daunting to the reader. The package on wildfires is broken into two stories, two pictures and three graphics.

PRINCIPLES OF DESIGN

To know the principles of design is to know why you are doing what you are doing. No designer consciously carries around a list of principles. Beginners, however, use principles as guides until they are comfortable with the concepts. Although the names of the concepts may be forgotten, the lessons never are. The five principles of design are balance, contrast, focus, proportion and unity.

3.22 Not many packages lend themselves to formal balance, but the *Los Angeles Times* created an unusual package that is perfectly balanced. The illustration and heavy headlines offer visual relief to an otherwise text-heavy page.

Balance

A square is perfectly balanced, but it is also monotonous. Similarly, formal balance in newspapers is dull and predictable, as were the people described as "square" in the 1960s. Formal balance is also the ultimate victory of form over content.

Although a formal balance format does not suit a newspaper's daily needs, any given design package can use formal balance successfully. The interesting typographic treatment in the *Los Angeles Times* (Fig. 3.22) is built around the principle of balance.

Formal or symmetrical balance may be useful when building arches, but asymmetrical balance is more flexible and useful to newspaper designers. Balance is not achieved merely by using identical elements. Optical weights result from tones ranging from black to white. Tones, in turn, are provided by type in its various weights from light to bold, and by photographs and art, reverses and screens, rules, borders, and white space.

When two people are on a teeter-totter, they find the right balance by moving closer to, or farther from, the fulcrum. The weight is defined in measurable terms. Optical weight is not measured; it is observed. A small, dark shape balances a larger, lighter shape; white space in the margin balances the grayness of text type (Fig. 3.23).

Designers balance the right against the left and the top against the bottom. To achieve this, they place the major display element close to the optical center, which is slightly above and to the left or right of the mathematical center. Dividing the page into quadrants is useful only if the design does not divide itself into four equal parts. Each of the four divisions should have some graphic weight to balance the page, but the weight should not be confined to the quadrant. It should extend vertically, horizontally, or both, into other quadrants, just as the heavier of the two people on the teeter-totter moves closer to the fulcrum.

Designers working in modules have more control over weights on a page because their boundaries are defined. Meandering, irregular copy wraps make it more difficult to weight the elements visually.

Contrast

Contrast may be the single most important principle of design. Designers balance a page by contrasting weights. A three-column photograph at the upper right can be balanced with a three-column photograph at the lower left. The photograph can also be balanced with a large, multicolumn headline or white space. An 8-point rule can balance a block of text type. Designers select type to provide contrast. For instance, bold type in the main head contrasts with light type in a deck; sans serif type in the cutlines contrasts with roman type in the stories; ragged right contrasts with justified; all caps contrast with lowercase; 90-point type contrasts with 24-point type; and sans serif type contrasts with serif type.

Designers also contrast forms. Strong verticals give the impression of taller space and longer stories; horizontals appear to make space wider and stories shorter.

Dimension is an aspect of contrast too. A small photograph placed next to a larger one provides a contrast in size and adds dimension. To help children see this principle in action, Johannes Itten of the Bauhaus told them to draw an outline of their hand on a sheet of paper and next to it several pieces of fruit and a gnat. But when he then asked them to draw an elephant, they objected. Elephants were too big for a sheet of paper. So Itten encouraged them to draw an elephant so it looks big by having smaller things next to it: "Draw an old, big elephant—a young elephant next to it— the keeper . . . stretches his hand out to the elephant—in the hand lies an apple—on it sits a gnat" (Itten 1964, p. 98). From that exercise, the children learned to contrast size by using relatively large and small shapes. Publication designers use the same device.

Focus

Pages with focus clearly define the starting points and also show that an editor is not afraid to make decisions. To achieve focus, an editor has to decide which element or elements are most important or visually interesting and have the courage to let the design reflect the decision. Indecision confuses the reader and results in a meek or, worse, cluttered page.

Focus usually is provided by a dominant photograph. Three-column pictures on a six-column page are just average and have little visual impact, but pictures wider than three columns provide both focus and impact.

Type can also be used effectively to provide focus. Readers move from large to small (large photograph/headline to small photograph/headline), black to white, color to black-and-white and top to bottom. It all begins at the dominant element.

Proportion

Proportion, or ratio, has fascinated mathematicians, architects and artists for centuries. Fibonacci, an Italian mathematician of the late 12th and early 13th centuries, observed that starting with 1 and adding the last two numbers to arrive at the next created a ratio of 1:1.6 between any two adjacent numbers after 3 (1, 1, 2, 3, 5, 8, 13 ...). Fifteenth-century architect Leon Battista Alberti believed that there was a relationship between mathematics and art because certain ratios recurred in the universe.

Leonardo da Vinci, who was not only an artist but also a mathematician, collaborated with a friend on a book titled *On Divine Proportion*. To da Vinci, proportions were of basic importance "not only . . . in numbers and measurement but also in sounds, weights, positions and whatsoever power there may be."

The classic definition of *proportion* was worked out by the architect-designer Le Corbusier in the early 1900s. He drew the human form with the left arm raised above the head. He then divided the anatomy into three uneven parts: from the toes to the solar plexus, then to the tip of the head, and finally to the tip of the raised hand. From this he developed what is known as the golden ratio. The ratio is 1:1.6, the same as Fibonacci's ratio. In nature, we see the same proportion in, for instance, a daisy, a pine cone and a pineapple. The double-spiraling daisy has 21 spirals in a clockwise direction and 34 in a counterclockwise direction—a 3-to-5 ratio. The ratio of the printed surface of a newspaper page is approximately 1:1.6.

Consciously or unconsciously, designers use this ratio when working with copy shapes on a page. The wider the story runs horizontally, the deeper it can go vertically and still maintain aesthetic proportions. On a six-column page, a four-column story 56 picas wide could be 30 to 35 picas deep from the top of the headline to the bottom of the story. As it goes deeper, it approaches the shape of the less-pleasing square. Stories of one and two columns should be proportioned vertically in the same manner.

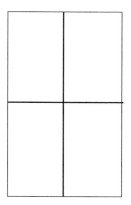

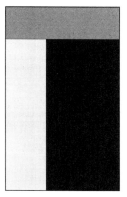

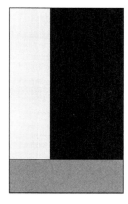

3.23 Weights on the page arise from photos (heavy), headlines (light to bold), text (gray) and white space. The designer must learn to distribute weights in the same way that children learn how to use a teeter-totter even when one child weighs more than the other.

3.24 You can describe size relationships, but you can show them even better. The designer who masters this skill will produce more effective pages.

No designer actually measures the depth of the stories to determine whether the ratio is correct. The eye recognizes what the calculator confirms. A sense of proportion is necessary for every designer.

Proportion helps convey the message in Figure 3.24. The advocates of breast screening show rather than merely tell the effectiveness of the technology they use.

In graphic design, proper use of proportion means avoiding squares unless they are required by the content. It also means being consistent about placing proportionally greater amounts of white space between unlike elements than between related elements. For instance, the designer might specify 18 points between the end of one story and the top of the next headline but only 12 points between the headline and the related story. The larger amount of space between the copy and the headline below disassociates the two when they are viewed against the lesser amount of white space between the headline and its related copy.

A good grasp of the concept of proportion is essential to anyone dealing with photographs. First, there is the proportion of the photo to the page. To dominate a page, a photograph must occupy more than half the width of the page or be proportionally sized vertically. The key is the size of the page. A broadsheet page requires one minimum size, a tabloid page another and a magazine page such as *National Geographic* still another. Smaller pages require smaller visuals, a truism that many editors have not grasped. A 40-pica picture that runs margin to margin on a tabloid would not dominate a broadsheet page. In fact, 40 picas is a modest width on a broadsheet page, but visual impact is still possible with smaller sizes.

Pictures should also be sized in proportion to each other. The 40-pica picture that looks so modest on a broadsheet page looks large when paired with one or more significantly smaller pictures. The smaller the subordinate picture, the larger the dominant picture appears. When two or more pictures are close in size, neither dominates, even if both are relatively large.

Type also looks larger as the horizontal space it occupies grows smaller. A 48-point headline appears larger in a two-column setting than in a six-column format because it is larger in proportion to the space occupied. Type size is selected in part on the basis of the length of the story. Putting three lines of 24-point type over a 3-inch story would look odd because the headline would be one-third the depth of the story. Proportionally, there would be too much headline type. Conversely, a three-line, 24-point headline over a story 18 inches long would also look odd.

Unity

The designer must unify the work on two levels: the sections of the publication and the content and form of the individual packages. Creating unity for the publication is discussed further in Chapter 18.

Designers use unifying devices in series or special packages. They should make certain that readers recognize the package whether it jumps to the inside or appears again the next day. Unifying devices include logos, consistent use of inset or rising caps, repetition of the title in smaller type with the jump, and a consistent grid.

On one level, the principles of design are esoteric; they cannot be subjected to quantitative analysis. On another level, they all have specific applications to the day-to-day operations of a newspaper. The better you understand the principles, the more confidence you will develop in your own judgments about design.

4.1 Modules are rectangles or squares. When you work in modular layout, each package sits in the same module. That is, you can draw a box
around it, and all the related elements would be inside the box. Weights
vary among modules because of pictures, white space and headline sizes.

Even the ads in many papers make the news design look
shabby. But sometimes newspapers stack up ads for a
dreadful appearance.

Frank Ariss
Designer

This is the age of modules—modular homes, schools, furniture and electronics. This, too, is the age of modular page design.

A module is a unit, a subdivision of the whole. As applied to page design, it is a rectangular or square unit. It contains anything from a single story to a package that includes a story, sidebar and illustrations. Pages are formed by assembling modules. If they are put together in a pleasing arrangement, the page is well designed.

The *San Jose Mercury News* is one of many newspapers whose editors work in modules. The front page shown in Figure 4.2 has six modules and 12 elements. In Figure 4.3 you can see the modules in a blueprint of the page. The page is clean and organized. Most readers probably will look first at the large photo, then move to the story or list in the box. Photos draw the most attention, followed by headlines and pullouts. Most people scan a page before stopping to read, although a story of particular interest to them may stop them at any time.

4.2 Each package on this page is modular. The main module contains a picture and three text elements. One advantage of modular layout is that you can react to breaking news easier. For instance, if McGwire hit his 70th homerun after the page was drawn, the designer could substitute that story for another in that spot.

4.3 This blueprint of the San Jose page helps you visualize the modules. By comparing the two, you can also see the weight distribution.

An alternative to the modular page is one in which copy wraps irregularly around related or unrelated stories and pictures. Copy in irregular shapes is said to dogleg. Few newspapers still use this method. Most of those that do are papers that depend on street sales. The doglegs allow them to jam more items above the fold, where people looking at them on the newsstand or in a vending machine can see them. Like many of these papers, *USA Today* often runs a headline over an unrelated story (Fig. 4.4).

Beginning in the early 1960s, many newspapers went to the simplified modular style and eliminated column rules, fancy borders and decorative type. By 1974, when the *Louisville* (Ky.) *Times* sponsored a watershed experimental newspaper design seminar, nearly all the proposed redesigns were modular. Newspapers did not suddenly invent the concept of working in modules. Magazines had been doing it for years, with good reason. Most of them sold advertising in quarter, half and full pages. The result was an editorial space blocked off in squares or rectangles. Most newspapers still do not have that advantage. The Standard Advertising Unit (SAU) system permits 56 advertising sizes for the broadsheet page.

ADVANTAGES OF MODULAR LAYOUT

In addition to its clean, simple look, modular layout saves time in the production process, adapts quickly to technological changes, permits better packaging of related elements, provides the opportunity for contrast on the page, and serves reader preferences. Irregular wraps are more time-consuming in both traditional paste-up and electronic pagination systems. Corrections are also more quickly accomplished on modular layouts because lines can be added or subtracted more easily in modules than in irregular wraps.

Production time is also saved when editors have to substitute stories on a modular page. A layout editor can easily pull out a module and substitute another without disturbing the entire page or a large section of it. Such changes are more difficult on a page with several uneven wraps. If the new story is shorter, the editor can insert two stories; if it is longer, the editor can eliminate two or more modules. In either case, the editor does not have to disturb a substantial portion of the page to make a change. This flexibility is especially attractive to papers with multiple editions. Working in modules also forces the layout editor to group related stories, pictures and artwork for the reader's benefit. The basic principle is that all related material should be in the same module. Readers want to know which stories are related and prefer to have similar stories grouped by subject matter (Clark 1979, p. 30). Proper use of modules accomplishes this in a strong visual message.

Modules also make it easier for the editor to provide balance and break up the grayness that results from unrelieved areas of textual matter. Dividing the page into modular units forces the editor to work in specified subdivisions of the page, and the final product usually has better contrast throughout. Breaking up the broadsheet into smaller, more manageable areas allows the reader's eye to deal more effectively with the space.

The last and most important advantage of the modular format is the favorable reaction of the readers. Respondents to a survey in the early 1970s told researchers they preferred newspapers with a modern design, which is characterized by modules, an optimum six-column format and horizontal layout. In fact, the authors concluded that the findings were a "ringing endorsement" for such newspapers (Click and Stempel 1974). Sissors (1974) sampled young, college-educated readers to determine format preferences. Reactions to the four front pages were mixed, and even though a traditional page edged out a more modern design, the clearest finding was the extremely low rating given to the only page not done in a modular format.

Until research is done using modules as the only variable, it is impossible to say flatly that modular layout is preferred over irregular wraps. It is unlikely that people in all communities will prefer one over the other. Most of the research, however, lends support to modular formats. Designers who are trying to achieve a clean, uncluttered appearance and are conscious of legibility research prefer to use the modern formats.

4.4   Many metropolitan papers run a large headline across the top of the page that leads to a story in the far right column. However, when the photograph doesn't go with the headline, there is always a chance it will confuse the reader. *USA Today* attempts to handle the possible confusion by boxing the Sinatra picture and story.

ADVERTISING STACKS

It is a challenge for editors to accommodate the reader's desire for uncluttered design on pages that contain both news and advertising, because some advertising formats work against good design. There are two basic advertising configurations: the pyramid stack and the modular layout.

Most newspapers use the pyramid, in which ads are stacked toward the top left or top right. This permits the news department to use either the top right or left of the page for a package that will attract readers as they look

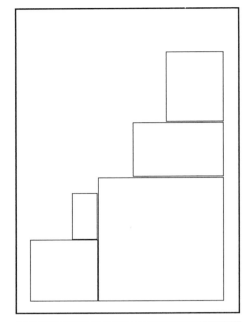

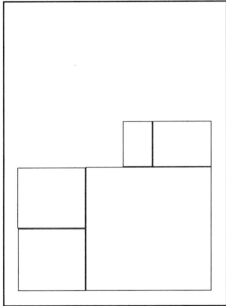

4.5 A pyramid stack leaves ledges on the page. Even within a pyramid stack, you can decrease the number of ledges by the way you pair advertising.

through the publication. A modified pyramid stack is one in which ads of various sizes are stacked to decrease the number of advertising ledges jutting into the editorial space (Fig. 4.5). The modified pyramid stack creates only one ledge, whereas the pure pyramid of the same ads creates four ledges.

The pyramid stack places news copy adjacent to the advertisements. Newspaper advertising departments have long sold the idea that readership of advertising that touches editorial copy is higher than readership of advertising that does not touch editorial copy, such as a shopper. However, a 1989 study did not support this contention. In addition, the author of the study reported that readers found the pages with modular advertising stacks and modular layout to be more attractive (Lewis 1989, p. 73). Although the intent of the advertising arrangement is to serve the reader, the arrangement of the news and advertisements may be counterproductive. As one reader told a researcher, "I was reading this story and it was interesting, but then I turned to where it was continued and all I could find was a big ad for discount drugs or liquor or something which occupied most of the page" (Clark 1979, p. 19).

From both economic and readership standpoints, advertisements are important. A newspaper without advertising sells far fewer copies than a newspaper with ads. Papers that do not have a good selection of grocery ads, for instance, are harder to sell than papers that do. Classified ads attract strong readership because advertisements carry information that readers want. Consequently, it is important that advertisements and editorial copy work in tandem. Although readers object to searching for copy buried among the ads, they also object to editors using space alongside large ads for uninteresting stories. A well-designed advertisement can attract readership on its own and does not need the perfume of news copy.

In the 1970s, modular advertising formats were adopted by many newspapers, including *Newsday* (a tabloid), the *Chicago Tribune* and the *Los Angeles Times*. Smaller newspapers may have trouble selling the concept to local advertisers because a purely modular advertising system restricts ad sizes to an eighth, a quarter, a half or a full page (Fig. 4.6). However, smaller papers can adopt a modified modular system by selling all the traditional sizes and stacking the ads so that they are blocked off.

WORKING WITH ADS

Editors of newspapers that do not use modular advertising stacks must learn to work with advertisements instead of against them. The problems the pyramid stack poses are not insurmountable. The editor can create modular units with the space remaining on the page by working off the corners of the ads. In Figure 4.7, lines are extended from the corner of the stacked ads. The lines represent headlines or the edges of photographs or artwork. By working off the ledge, you create a modular unit. Each of these units can be subdivided into more modules. The number and shape of possible modules are limited only by the editor's imagination.

Any reasonable designer and editor would be quick to acknowledge that the content cannot always be accommodated in a modular unit on an inside page. Often this is not possible because there is room for only one story, and the editor cannot break off the ad stack with headlines for secondary stories. In all cases, logic must temper layout decisions.

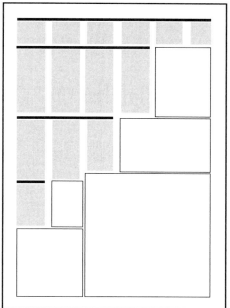

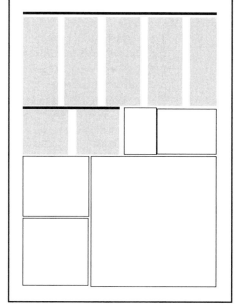

4.6 A modular advertising stack is more harmonious with the editorial copy. The modular stack also allows the designer more options with the editorial space.

4.7 When you have advertising ledges, you run headlines or align photographs off of them to create modular units in the editorial space. In most cases, you will have at least two options by the way you use the ads.

4.8 The main module contains the text, three pictures and the display type. Three more modules align across the bottom of the page.

MODULAR OPEN PAGES

Although it is much simpler to work in modules on pages with no advertisements, editors are obligated to arrange the elements on these open pages in a pattern that enhances readability.

The designers at the *San Francisco Examiner* worked in modules on the "Flour power" page (Fig. 4.8). Four modules containing nine elements fill

4.9 The front page contains more elements. This page contains seven modules and 14 elements. Examine the main package on the GOP to see how five elements are packaged.

4.10 One way to show a relationship between a headline and a picture is to run the headline over the picture. However, in this case, the headline and the picture were not related. The result was probably embarrassing to the newspaper and the people pictured.

the page. The *Boston Globe* uses seven modules to display 14 elements (Fig. 4.9). It offers vertical and horizontal shapes. Both of those pages have a low story count, a function of the page content, not of modules.

SHOWING RELATIONSHIPS

Working with a modular layout is relatively easy, but using modules to communicate relationships can be complicated. The effort is necessary, however, if publications are to serve the best interests of readers. Grouping elements in an orderly fashion adjacent to each other helps the reader understand the relationships, but putting all the elements into a single module makes it easier for the reader to see the relationships. Working under deadlines, editors often unintentionally place unrelated elements together and create a funny or embarrassing package. That was the case when the headline about the sex education class ran over an unrelated picture of youths at a baseball party (Fig. 4.10).

Five ways to show relationships

When multiple elements are put into the same module, a relationship is established. That's not always enough. Editors have five ways to establish relationships even within the module (Fig. 4.11). Here are the details:

1. *Placing related elements in a vertical module.* The natural order is photograph, cutline, headline and story. The eye is first attracted to the photograph. Most readers come out of the bottom of a picture to look for cutline information. The natural move is then to the large headline under the photograph. To show the relationship successfully, the headline should begin at the lower left hand corner of the picture and extend the width of the picture. The relationship between the two photos and the GOP story is established using this method (Fig. 4.9).

2. *Boxing related elements.* Elements within a box must be on the same topic. As fences define the boundaries of a yard, boxes define the boundaries of the related elements in a package. A box that pulls elements together also separates. For instance, it is inappropriate to run a main story and box a sidebar outside the module of the main package. Short sidebars can be boxed if they are contained within the larger unit, as in Figure 4.12. But if the same story runs outside the package, the box disassociates the two stories.

3. *Running the headline over related elements.* We have already seen the confusion, and sometimes embarrassment, that can result when a headline runs over unrelated elements. That ambiguity occurs because readers have been taught that the headline creates relationships among the elements under it.

4. *Running the story alongside and under related elements.* Sometimes you do not wish to run a headline over a story and picture because of other elements surrounding it or because the story deserves only a one- or two-column headline. Your solution then is to L the story under the related picture.

5. *Using icons, color or other elements to show relationships.* When you work in modules, stories stacked on or alongside each other are technically in the same module even when they are not related. To show the relationship of adjacent stories, you can use a repeating element. Icons, a small graphic representation such as a check mark, can be inset into the beginning of related stories. Same-color bars can be repeated with related stories. In fact, any repetition of design elements helps communicate relationships.

HOW TO DISASSOCIATE ELEMENTS

Just as important as showing relationships is signaling readers when elements are not related. When you are trying to disassociate elements, avoid putting elements together in the five ways just described. But additional steps need to be taken to disassociate elements. There are three ways (Fig. 4.13):

1. Boxes associate; they also disassociate. When you work in modules, you are going to have stories alongside each other. One way to show readers that they are not related is to box one of them.

2. Vertical and horizontal rules are like fences; they separate stories. The risk you run is having the reader overlook them. Look

SHOWING RELATIONSHIPS

Vertical package with copy the same width as the picture

Box all related elements

Run a headline over the copy and related picture

"L" the copy alongside and under the related photo

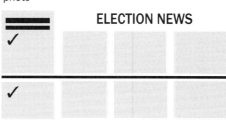

Use logos or icons to show relationship

4.11

THE BOX WITHIN

4.12 Although a box separates, if the box is surrounded by the larger story, readers will understand it is part of that package. A box to the side, however, looks unrelated.

DISASSOCIATING ELEMENTS

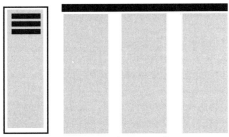

The box disassociates the one-column story from the three-column story

The vertical and horizontal rules help separate unrelated stories

One way to show a photo is not related to the stories underneath is to box the photo

4.13

closely at Figure 4.13. Notice the vertical rule between the unrelated stories. If the rules are used consistently, regular readers will understand them. If they are used inconsistently, readers may not understand. Horizontal rules are called cutoff rules. That's because they are intended to cut off the reader from reading from one element into the next.

3. Almost all newspapers run stand-alone pictures. Unless the picture is sitting on the bottom of the page, it immediately creates a challenge to disassociate the copy that appears under it. Many newspapers properly box stand-alone pictures. That may not solve the problem. The rule may not be heavy enough. If you show a relationship between a picture and story by running a headline from the lower left hand corner of the picture the width of the picture, it follows that you should not run a headline the width of the picture if they are not related. In the last illustration in Figure 4.13, the two stories under the picture are not related to the picture. The box separates the photo from the unrelated stories underneath. Also, because no story starts at the lower right and extends the width of the picture, readers are less likely to be confused.

PROTECTING COPY FLOW PATTERNS

Modular copy gives the reader a fixed starting point, a principle long prized by legibility experts. In Figure 4.14, even though there are four wraps of copy, readers return to the same height or starting point each time they finish a column of type. Little is lost with an L-shaped copy wrap (Fig. 4.15), where the jumps from the end of each column are the same. The L-shaped wrap also requires that the reader make less of a jump to columns B, C and D than many other alternatives, such as the reverse L (Fig. 4.16). The jump from column A to column B is longer, more difficult and more time-consuming.

Usually in an effort to break up the grayness of the text, editors sometimes create copy flow patterns that challenge readers to follow. In the first illustration in Figure 4.17, readers are required to jump over a pullout quote to continue the story. The second illustration in Figure 4.17 presents a solution: Wrap the copy around the pullout. Larger illustrations create

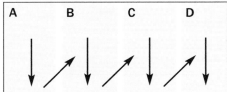

4.14 One advantage of modular layout is that the reader can easily find the next column because it usually is the same height as the previous column.

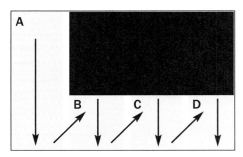

4.15 An L-wrap around a picture effectively ties the story and picture. You can run either a one-column headline or a four-column headline with this package.

PROTECT COPY FLOW

Don't break across more than one column

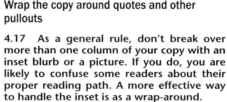

Wrap the copy around quotes and other pullouts

4.16 The reverse L-wrap is not as effective because you will now have to deal with disassociating the picture from whatever goes beneath it.

4.17 As a general rule, don't break over more than one column of your copy with an inset blurb or a picture. If you do, you are likely to confuse some readers about their proper reading path. A more effective way to handle the inset is as a wrap-around.

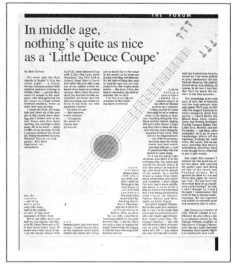

4.18 Had there not been copy below the illustration in the first two columns, this inset might have worked. However, some readers are going to bounce to the second column when they reach the guitar only to find that they are lost. Respect the reader's time.

more serious problems. To read the article in Fig. 4.18, readers have to jump the illustration three times to follow the copy trail. Reading shouldn't be as difficult as running a triathlon.

That problem could be avoided by following a simple rule: Never break across more than two columns of your setting with anything. Don't run pullouts, maps or pictures through the middle of two or more columns. Place these elements on the top of columns or at the bottom of the package, or wrap the type around them. When you break across columns, you invite some readers to detour to the top of the next column. There they discover they made the wrong turn, and they may not care enough to turn around.

5.1 Photojournalists tell stories with pictures. This aerial view requires a large size so the reader can see the detail. Because it is a view that only pilots can see, it tells part of the story that words cannot.

Documentary photographs are most memorable when they transcend the specifics of time, place and purpose. When they invest ordinary events and objects with enduring resonance. When they illuminate as well as record.

Naomi Rosenblum
Author

5. Using Photographs

The body of an American soldier is dragged with ropes through the dusty streets of war-torn Mogadishu last Monday. The dead soldier was one of 15 Americans who were killed or have died as a result of last Sunday's assault on warlord Gen. Mohamed Farah Aidid's military command. The family of Army Staff Sgt. William David Cleveland Jr. believes he is the soldier in the photo, although his body had not been officially identified as of Friday.

THE IMAGE THAT BROUGHT THE TRAGEDY HOME

5.2 The power of the still photograph to move people emotionally is proved daily for better or worse. Readers in several U.S. communities reacted angrily at newspapers for publishing this photograph of a U.S. soldier's body being dragged through the streets of Somalia.

When newspapers and newsmagazines ran a photo of a wounded American being dragged through the streets of Somalia like a trophy, Americans reacted with outrage—as much at the publications for running the picture as at the Somalian mob (Fig. 5.2). A typical reader protest appeared in the *Indianapolis News*: "How would you react if he were your brother, father, son, husband or friend? I'm sure those pictures . . . will haunt the people who loved him for the rest of their lives. You are no more civilized than the desecraters. I'm appalled!"

The reaction testifies to the power, even in the video age, of still photography. The ability of photographs to attract readers' attention and report the news remains the great untapped resource of journalism at many newspapers. The successful use of photographs and words in tandem is a realization of the powerful potential of the newspaper as a visual medium. Photographs are the stop signs in the designer's traffic pattern. Photographs are the most-looked-at items in newspapers (Garcia and Stark 1991). Stories with pictures command better readership, hold the reader's attention longer, and result in greater recall and comprehension than stories without pictures (Lee 1994, Bain and Weaver 1979).

We have come a long way since 1893, when the editor of the respected magazine *Nation* asserted that pictures appealed chiefly to children and were beneath the dignity of good newspapers. Even though *Look* and *Life* magazines pushed the still photograph to new limits, and *National Geographic* dramatized its potential as a reporting tool, it was not until the 1960s that a significant number of newspapers started integrating the photograph into the news product instead of using it as a decoration or to break up type.

Many editors still consider the photograph a supplement to words rather than a form of reportage. That is not surprising because most newspaper managers were reporters first. Consequently, photographers are still fighting for first-class citizenship in too many newsrooms.

Once there is an understanding of the role of photography in telling stories, layout editors and designers must be trained to use them correctly. At large newspapers, a photo editor, usually a photographer by training, is responsible for the selection and display of all photographs and artwork. At small and medium-size papers, the layout editor, who is usually a former copy editor, does that job. Editors who would be aghast at having a photographer run the copydesk think nothing of having copy editors edit, crop and display photographs. Photographers need to be photojournalists; copy editors need training in photography. Both need to know not only how to use photographs but also how to recognize when an ethical line has been crossed. This chapter will help you participate in the editing discussions and provide guidance on using photos on the page.

THE PHOTO SYSTEM

One of the most important steps to getting better photography is to foster a system wherein everyone from assigning editors to designers understand that photographers are journalists with cameras. If we understand that, we will shoot, select and publish photos based on their information and aesthetic value, not just to improve the looks of a page or to break up headlines. One characteristic of a system that produces good photography is a photo request form. It's a *request* instead of an *order* form when the photo editor has the authority to reject or negotiate the request. There are several reasons why a request might be denied. The most common would be that the situation would not yield good photographs. For instance, where a reporter might request a picture of an awards ceremony at which a volunteer will be honored, a photographer would rather shoot the honoree doing her volunteer work. Ideally, the photographer and reporter would work together on a story. The photographer should be willing to include the people and places the reporter thinks are important; the reporter should be willing to include the people and places the photographer believes make good pictures. Sometimes the photographer shoots to the story; sometimes the reporter writes to the pictures. When journalists don't work as a team, it's impossible to produce a package. For instance, at one daily when an early-morning fire raced through a barn and destroyed several valuable horses, assigning editors sent a reporter and photographer to the scene straight from their homes. Both worked alone. When they returned, the photographer didn't have a picture of the dejected owner who led the story. And the reporter didn't have any quotes from the dejected owners whom the photographer had interviewed and shot. Words and pictures can't work together if journalists don't work together.

When the reporter and photographer can't work together, or when there is no story planning conference, a photo request is necessary. The story, even if only in rough draft, should accompany the request. If no draft is available, the request should include a synopsis of the story. It should also include such other basic information as when, where, the reporter's name and phone number, the source's name and phone number, time and date the photos are due, and whether they are to run in color or black and white. The photographer should also know where the stories and pictures are expected to run. Photographers shooting for news pages know that it is difficult to get space for more than two pictures, but they will shoot differently if it is for a feature package.

EDITING PHOTOS

The best photo editors have a sense of news as well as balance and flow. Like reporters, photographers often are the best judges of their own work. They do some physical editing while shooting and some mental editing on the way back to the office. However, also like reporters, they occasionally are too close to the story to see the significant or the unusual. Sometimes a second editor can catch the overlooked frame.

Picture selection depends on the space available and whether there is an accompanying story. Photos that stand alone must capture the essence of the story; photos with text can concentrate on a part of the story. The successful wedding of pictures and words sometimes requires that photos be selected to follow the text and sometimes that the text be written to focus on the dramatic angle developed by the photographers. Consequently, it is important that the photographer and reporter work together on assignments. Such teamwork can produce startlingly good journalism. Photo editing can be an enormous job. Photographers at the *Lexington* (Ky.) *Herald-Leader* annually shoot as many as 10,000 frames of the Kentucky Derby and then used approximately 60 of them in a special section.

In the rush of daily editing, will you find the photograph that tells the story? When a bomb demolished the Oklahoma City federal building, scores of photos moved on the wire. *USA Today* and dozens of other news-

5.3   Many U.S. papers published this photo of an officer handing a baby to a fireman after the bombing in Oklahoma City. Yet, in retrospect, it was not the best photo of that incident.

5.4   This photograph of the firefighter looking down at the baby has become the icon of the Oklahoma City bombing. Whenever a publication does a retrospective story, it reruns this photo. What emotion does this photo show that the one in Fig. 5.3 doesn't?

5.5   If the point of the story and pictures is size, then select the photos to show size relationships. This package clearly demonstrates the size of the miniature soldiers in three of the four photos. If the one in the upper left had been run alone, we would not know the size of the soldiers.

papers published a photo of a rescue worker handing a baby to a fireman (Fig. 5.3). The *Kansas City Star,* among many others, published another photo taken a second later of the same fireman looking at the child in his arms (Fig. 5.4). That photo, not the other showing the handoff, has become the lasting visual image of the bombing. Why? Opinions vary, but advocates of the picture point to the empathy evident in the second photo as the fireman makes eye contact with the child. The Associated Press later quoted the baby's mother as saying the firefighter showed compassion in the picture. Perhaps he felt a special empathy because he had a 2-year-old of his own. The lesson for the next time you are selecting pictures is the same lesson that writers learn: Focus on the individual. Allow the reader to reach out and touch someone. In the handoff picture, the baby is a thing. In the second picture, the baby is a human being.

There are other common situations. When the point of the story is size, select photographs that show size relationship. When the *Chicago Tribune* published a feature about the Military Miniature Society of Illinois, the photos that accompanied the story concentrated on images that depicted the sizes of the miniature soldiers. The photographer showed the size of the miniature soldiers by having the creators hold them (Fig. 5.5).

Editing for sequence is another common situation. When the *Wichita Eagle* covered the demolition of an important downtown building, it devoted its entire front page to the sequence of photos showing what words couldn't begin to tell (Fig. 5.6).

Most of the time, however, you are editing for a package that includes words. When you find the photograph or photographs that tell the story, make certain the accompanying words tie the picture to the story, as the *Star Tribune* did with a picture of the president visiting the Twin Cities (Fig. 5.7).

A good photo editor is like a strong city editor who can find the story line in a reporter's notes and help the reporter organize the story. A good photo editor recognizes possibilities in the photo that others may not see. Photo editors can turn tepid shots into red-hot drama by cropping tight for impact and backing off for content and form, or by cropping to eliminate distractions in order to focus attention on the point of the picture. For instance, in Figure 5.8, you see a loose crop of a group of men talking. The tighter crop has more impact and allows the reader to focus on the main character (Fig. 5.9). Similarly, the *Philadelphia Inquirer* chose a loose

5.6   Editing and displaying sequence shots is another skill designers must acquire. Sometimes all the pictures will be the same size in a sequence, but more often, you select one to show the key moment.

5.7   Selecting and displaying the photograph are the first two important steps. The third is writing the right words to make it a package. This appeared in Minnesota, whose state's motto is "Land of 10,000 lakes."

5.8   Crop tight to focus on key points. This frame is loosely cropped even though the point of the picture is the only person whose face we can see.

5.9   By tightening the crop, we enlarge the main character's face and force the reader's eye to the point of the picture.

56Chapter 5

crop to provide context when Michael Johnson broke the world record in the 200-meter race (Fig. 5.10). By contrast, the *Virginian-Pilot* chose to crop tightly to focus on the record breaker (Fig. 5.11). Which has more impact? Cropping is an art, but it is an art built on principles. You are trying to exclude people and things not germane to the point of the photo while trying to include enough context to understand the photo. Cropping will change if there is more than one photo of the same situation because then you can show close-up and context in different frames. Cropping that creates interesting horizontal and vertical shapes is appropriate when the action is essentially horizontal or vertical.

Size makes a difference to photographs. Some photographs can still be read when they are small; others need size to show the detail and to increase the impact. The editors of the *Virginian-Pilot* decided that the full 78 picas was needed to show the enormity of the blast and the details of the destruction (Fig. 5.12). That picture could not be read easily if it were three columns. A close-up of a ring on a finger could be read at one or two columns. Enlarging it would not add impact.

PHOTO ILLUSTRATIONS

When a photographer can't get a literal representation to accompany a story, a decision must be made whether to order an artist's drawing or a photo illustration. For instance, a photographer can't always be at an undercover investigation, but an artist can effectively re-create a scene, such as an exchange of drugs or money in the shadow of a doorway. A photographic re-creation of the scene would be misleading; readers would immediately recognize that the drawing was a re-creation. Stories that discuss ideas and concepts sometimes lend themselves to photographic illustrations, which are pictures staged with people and/or props that represent ideas rather than literal scenes. Most often, photo illustrations

5.10 Sometimes the decision how to crop can go either way. It depends on the story you are trying to tell. The *Philadelphia Inquirer* included the runners behind the triumphant Johnson to provide context.

5.11 The *Virginian-Pilot* elected to come in tight on Johnson to emphasize his reaction to his winning time.

run in food and fashion sections (Fig. 5.13). However, it is risky to try to use a photo illustration with people for stories on emotional and highly charged issues such as abortion or gun control. Some readers may misinterpret the illustrations as a documentary photograph.

To produce an illustration, a photographer needs time, props, facilities and a thorough understanding of the story being illustrated. Ideas for illustrations are often produced in conferences involving the reporter, story editor, design editor and photographer. It is a time-consuming process, but it pays visual dividends. The photographer who received the request to illustration a story on nylons obviously worked with the designer. The headline probably was written before the illustration was shot (Fig. 5.14).

A photo illustration should not be used as a substitute for documentary photography because an illustration lacks immediacy, spontaneity and, to some extent, credibility. It is, after all, a made-up situation. It should be labeled as a photo illustration. These days, photo illustrations are as likely to be created on a computer as they are in a studio. It becomes even more important that readers understand what is happening. It may not be enough to put "photo illustration" in small type under illustrations done on a computer, because they look so real. If there is any chance readers will be deceived, information about how the illustration was produced should be included in the cutline.

USING TWO OR MORE PHOTOGRAPHS

The one-frame mentality that dominates the thinking of many editors inhibits good photo selection and use. Although a reporter can cover several disparate topics in a single story, a photographer can usually capture only one segment of a story in a single frame. Much of the drama is left in the photographer's discarded contact sheets when the editor says, "Give me your best picture to go with this story." However, the best picture may be a two-picture package. Here are some common situations.

1. *Contrast.* Look for dissimilarities in like subjects and subtle similarities in unlike subjects (Hurley and McDougall 1971, p. 5).

5.12 Like the flooding picture that opened this chapter, this photograph of the bombing needs size to communicate the enormous destruction. Most photographs have more impact as the size increases, but some photographs demand more size so they can be read.

5.13 Used carefully, photo illustrations have a place in newspapers. Because this appeared in a package on food and because it clearly is a setup, there is little chance readers will confuse it with documentary photography.

5.14 The illustration is humorous, the type is playful, the words are funny. The package clearly is built around an illustration, not a documentary photograph.

5.15 Be alert to two-picture situations, even when space is tight. This package works because the two pictures are not redundant. The smaller photograph is needed because the woman pictured is a key character in the story. She was the logical choice for the smaller picture because there are only two people in the picture. The large picture could not be read easily if it had been run the size of the smaller of the two.

5.16 The headline and deck tell a story about a woman who is a Sunday School teacher and a belly dancer. This cries for a second picture of her teaching Sunday School.

2. *Close-up and context.* When the photographer has to back up to show where the action is occurring, the picture makes a general statement. A second shot can give a close-up look at a small portion of the overall scene.

3. *Sequence.* One frame captures just one moment in the series; two or more frames permit the action to unfold. However, when displaying sequences, keep the same vantage point in the cropping.

4. *Avoid redundancy.* If the context photo includes a small image of a key person, you may need a second frame for a close-up, but if the person is featured in the context photo, a close-up is redundant.

In photography, one and one make three. Although each photo has its own story, pairing offers a third story that results from the interplay of the two photos. That happened when the *Jacksonville* (Ill.) *Journal-Courier* ran a context shot of a group eating dinner. The secondary picture showed a close-up of the woman who takes the men into her home. Combined, they visually report the point of the story (Fig. 5.15).

Properly used, the pairing principle tells a story quickly and dramatically. However, when the words say two and there is only one picture, there is an obvious hole in the package. That was the case in the package on a woman who is both a belly dancer and a Sunday school teacher (Fig. 5.16). The story needs two pictures to show her in both roles.

A feature story on a rail transient is told through an environmental shot of the subject far down the tracks and a close-up that shows him smoking a cigarette (Fig. 5.17). The larger picture communicates the loneliness and solitary nature of his life. The close-up permits readers to see him.

The pictures in both examples are adjacent, complement each other and are dominant-subordinate. Those three points are important to remember whether two or several pictures are being used. The first ensures that the reader immediately grasps the relationship between the pictures. The second ensures that there is focus to the package in the same way that a writer must focus on one aspect of the story. And the last, the dominant-subordinate guideline, ensures that one picture is significantly larger than the other.

If a package contains three or more pictures, there are four additional guidelines: interior margins should be consistent, excess white space should bleed to the outside of the package, sizing should be proportionate to the space of the total package, and there should be a variety of shapes. Figure 5.18 shows the use of these guidelines. One photo clearly is dominant, and it provides focus for the spread. There are a variety of shapes, and the interior margins are kept consistent by allowing the excess white space to bleed to the outside of the pictures.

To be dominant, a picture must be large in proportion to the page, or portion of the page, it occupies. For instance, in *National Geographic,* a picture 20 picas wide will dominate the page. In a tabloid newspaper, however, a dominant picture needs to be 40 picas wide, and in a broadsheet newspaper, 50 picas wide. The size of the dominant picture should be proportionate to the total space available, but the size of the subordinate pictures should be proportionate to the dominant picture. The difference in size between the dominant and subordinate pictures should be obvious to the reader's eye.

Experience in the use of photos permits possibilities beyond these guidelines. Some situations require two large photos of equal size. A sequence or story about a man who is a banker by day and a farmer by night might have more impact with two equal pictures. Knowing how to handle these exceptions comes with experience. A common exception occurs when newspapers are printing weddings and engagements, which usually run the same size. In these and similar situations, follow the principle of clustering and alignment. To help the reader, it is important to place the copy with the picture. But to organize the page, it is also important to run the photos in

5.17 The photograph of the solitary figure on the railroad tracks offers both contrast and excellent graphic qualities. However, because we can't see the person the story is about, a second picture is needed.

5.18 This page illustrates the basic guidelines for designing a picture page: One photo is dominant, there are a variety of shapes and sizes, and the interior margins are consistent. The extra white space sits at the outside of the package.

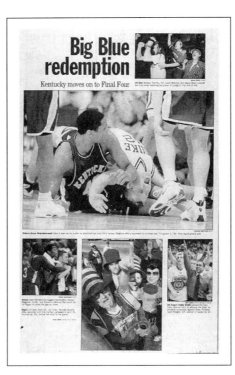

5.19 When you are dealing with multiple pictures of the same or nearly same size, cluster them. When you create common alignment, you organize the page.

5.20 A collection of pictures can be an essay or a story. This is a story because of the chronology.

5.21 This is an essay, a collection of pictures based on a theme. It is a Labor Day feature about working people.

groups and to use common alignment (Fig. 5.19). Whenever you print two or more head shots in the same package, make the heads the same size.

THE PICTURE PAGE

A page of pictures does not make a story, but a page of pictures with continuity does. Selecting and displaying a group of photographs is similar to writing a major story. When the material is selected and arranged in a coherent and entertaining manner, it has impact. If poorly done, the information is submerged in the resulting clutter. The difference between a picture story and a picture essay is like the difference between a news article and interpretive reporting (Hurley and McDougall 1971, p. 69). The picture story is a narrative. The essay expresses a point of view. Both require focus, a strong opening and a strong closing. Unfortunately, too many groupings of pictures are just collections of related events. Such groupings are similar to stories that ramble, and they should be rejected.

"Big Blue Redemption" illustrates a picture story. It consists of a series of photographs that tell the story of a basketball victory and the reaction of fans, players and the coach (Fig. 5.20). As is the case with most stories, the story is built on chronology. By contrast, "Bodies of Work" is an essay on working. The news peg was Labor Day. There is no story line, but all the photos are built on the theme of working (Fig. 5.21).

When creating picture pages, consider the following:

1. The telling of a story through pictures begins before the shooting, when the photographer and reporter plan the project. Even if the photographer is doing both pictures and text, planning is important. It makes the difference between a story and a collection of facts.
2. The pictures and text must work together. If the text is going to tell a story by focusing on one person, the photos should too.
3. The title of the page must capture the essence of the story. The display type is essential to the success of the page because the title is the quick explanation of all the pictures and text. The title and dominant picture should hook the reader.

When selecting and displaying pictures, include these steps:

1. Select as few pictures as possible (most picture pages have too many pictures) so that the ones that are used can be sized adequately. Do not use a full page if the material is not worth it. Skilled photo editing saves space.
2. Omit redundancies. If the story is told with as few pictures as possible, redundancy will not be a problem. Unfortunately, we are always tempted to repeat ourselves photographically, both in full pages and in lesser packages.
3. Run one photo significantly larger than the others. That photo should be the dramatic moment or emotion, the essence of the story.
4. Maintain consistent interior margins. White space is trapped when the margins are not consistent, and the reader notices it for itself rather than as a feeling of airiness. Let the extra white space bleed to the outside of the package.
5. Write a cutline for each picture and place it under the picture. Ganged cutlines make readers work extra hard.
6. After you have selected the pictures and determined the length of the text, set the photos before you. The story line and the flow of action should determine the arrangement of the pictures on the page.
7. Place the copy in a modular block. The title doesn't necessarily have to go directly over the copy, but if it doesn't, a subhead over the copy is useful.
8. Write a title or headline that plays off a photograph and place the title directly over or, preferably, under that photograph.

No list of guidelines can prescribe the proper way to produce a successful page. Such guidelines can only steer the beginner away from pitfalls that others have experienced.

CUTLINES

Cutlines, or captions, may be the most overlooked element in the paper. Journalists, not readers, ignore them. Readership of cutlines is 10 to 15 percent higher than that of stories. This figure alone suggests we should write better cutlines and use them to attract readers to stories.

Writing better cutlines requires changing the system in most newspapers so that the person who edits the story and writes the headline also writes the cutlines. At some newspapers, people write cutlines without even seeing the photographs.

The goal should be to create a package whose parts complement each other. The photograph and headline both tell and sell part of the story; these are the two elements most readers see. The cutline not only should tell readers what they need to know about the photograph but also include something from the text to tease them into reading the story. What we pull should not already appear in the headline or pullouts.

One-line cutline formats usually are too restrictive. A few photographs need only a line, but every newspaper also needs a text cutline format. A text cutline is used when a photograph needs a longer explanation. Here are 14 things to consider when writing cutlines (for more details, consult McDougall and Hampton [1990], who have excellent instructions and examples on cutline writing).

1. Cutlines can convey nonvisual senses better than photos: hearing, touch, smell, taste.
2. Cutlines can tell time, temperature and size better than photos.
3. Cutlines can identify people and their relationships. Photos can't.
4. Cutlines can explain the causes or consequences of what the photos show.
5. Cutlines can prevent possible misunderstanding of photos.
6. Cutlines can call attention to something that might be overlooked in the photo.
7. Cutlines should explain any techniques used to create special effects. Even if it's a natural phenomenon, such as a light source, explain it.
8. Cutlines should entice people to read the accompanying story but should not repeat information in the headline or pullouts.
9. Cutlines should match the mood of the photo.
10. Cutlines should be accurate. Check the names, address and numbers in cutlines against the story. Compare the number of names in the cutline against the number of faces in the photo.
11. Crop the photo before you write the cutline. It will save you the embarrassment of identifying someone not in the photo.
12. Don't state the obvious: "kisses the trophy," or "grimaces."
13. Don't editorialize, don't attribute human characteristics to animals and don't put words into people's mouths or thoughts into their heads ("Jones must have been unhappy . . .").
14. Be succinct. Use "from left" instead of "left to right." Omit needless phrases, such as "pictured here" and "above."

Journalistic tradition calls for cutlines to be written in the present tense to convey a sense of immediacy. It may be time to question that tradition because it must be obvious to any reader that the action is over. It also leads to awkward and grammatically incorrect sentences when writers use the present tense with a date: "Jones scores a basket Sunday . . ." Writers are to use the past tense in the sentence in which the date is reported, but many forget. Even if they follow convention, the cutline becomes a mix of present and past tense.

When a picture stands alone, it often has a catchline or headline over the cutline. Depending on the newspaper's headline style, the catchline is either flush left or centered. Some newspapers also put headlines over page 1 photographs that extend so far below the fold that they cannot be read without opening the paper. The goal, of course, is to get enough of the photograph above the fold so that readers looking at it in vending machines can read it.

Cutline text type should be larger than the text type and should offer contrast of race—serif or sans serif, for example, or at least form. Because text type in newspapers is usually serif, sans serif works well, but italic and boldface of the text font will also differentiate the story and cutline text.

The newspaper should have standardized text cutline settings for the width of the picture. Text cutlines in the 10- to 12-point range generally should not exceed 25 picas in width. One way to build white space into the paper is to set cutlines narrower than the width of the picture. This permits extra white space at either side of the cutline. A one-line format often is a larger version of the cutline text face; 13- or 14-point type works well. In this size, there are no gutters; the cutline can extend the width of the picture.

Although cutlines should appear underneath the related photo, occasionally they are placed to the right or left. In such cases, they should line up with the bottom of the photo to make it easy for readers to find it. Placing cutlines anywhere except underneath the photo should be an exception. Readers read out of the bottom of the photograph in search of the cutline. Grouped cutlines irritate readers because they have to work harder to match the text information with the appropriate photograph. Most won't work that hard. Grouping more than one cutline in a copy block may make the page look neater, but it does not help readers.

And speaking of not helping readers, no amount of cutline writing instruction would stop this cutline, which apparently was written as an in-house note but got published in the *Lincoln* (Neb.) *Journal-Star:* "Wava Staab (left) and Rosie Dauner, both of Omaha, board a Fun Tours bus, while Rosie Dauner stands behind. Both are from Omaha. (The other lady (in blue on the right) is Ruth Nelson, but she's dead now. It might be better to crop her out of the picture.) (I need this picture back.)"

PHOTOGRAPHIC ETHICS

Ethical questions fall into two categories: definitions of manipulation and questions of taste.

Manipulation

It used to take time and effort to alter a photograph. All that has changed. Thanks to computers, photo editors now can change photos digitally, so the opportunity for mischief is greater and easier than ever. The first computer photo software had just been installed when there were celebrated cases of questionable photo manipulation.

On its February 1982 cover, *National Geographic* moved a pyramid so the photo would fit better in a vertical format. Rich Clarkson, then director of photography, explained: "It's exactly the same as if the photographer had moved the camera's position. I have a hard time thinking that's a clear-cut issue. But people say, 'My God, you moved a pyramid! Then you can move anything!' Also in that picture was a camel train. There's suspicion that the photographer convinced them to move the camel train to that area. He also used a filter to change the sky. The scene you'd see if you were there is not the scene the photographer took. But it's a beautiful photo" (Reaves 1987, p. 32). Many in the industry were disturbed at the *Geographic*'s disclosure. But the word did not get to everyone.

5.22 Our ability to combine separate photographs into a single unit brings into question our ethics. Should we show Clarence Thomas and Anita Hill in the same frame when they were never photographed together? Will casual readers realize this is a computer-generated composite?

Where do correcting and manipulation intersect? Many newspapers used their computers to "correct" the blue in the historic Associated Press shot of the space shuttle Challenger exploding. Is that unethical? Photographers have always corrected color, burned and dodged in the darkroom. Should there be different standards for electronic retouching? Computer software permits us to alter far more than we could in the photo lab, and the computer enables us to do it quickly and with such attention to detail that it is difficult to detect. *TV Guide,* for instance, electronically placed Oprah Winfrey's head on Ann-Margret's body—and dress—for a cover photograph. Who blew the whistle? Not Winfrey. Not Ann-Margret, but Ann-Margret's dress designer. During O.J. Simpson's murder trial, both *Time* and *Newsweek* ran his police mug shot on the cover. However, there was a significant difference. On *Time*'s cover, Simpson's skin was significantly darker. *Time* apologized for altering the photo. *Newsweek* failed to learn from its competitor's mistake. In its cover photo of Mr. and Mrs. Kenny McCaughey, parents of septuplets, *Newsweek* improved the appearance of Bobbi McCaughey's teeth. The editors attributed the manipulation to their attempt "to lighten shadows." In its apology, the magazine said, "While we often correct color values and contrast levels in pictures we use, it is not *NEWSWEEK*'s policy to change or misrepresent the subject matter in any way."

Some editors say that although they would never manipulate news photos, they have different standards for feature photos. Some draw the line only at photo illustrations, which are a made-up situation anyway. Sheila Reaves of the University of Wisconsin gathered a cross section of views on the limits of photo manipulation. She concluded: "Will readers be able to make distinctions between a newspaper's handling of feature photography and news photography as easily as some editors do? If not, newspapers may risk losing the public's trust in all photography" (Reaves 1987, p. 32).

Some editors suggest that some manipulation could be done if it were noted in the caption. One problem is explaining to readers. *Newsweek* found in 1990 that less than 40 percent of the public had even heard of "digital enhancement." Newspapers in some Scandinavian countries use a small logo in the corner of a photo that has been changed electronically. The Associated Press' policy is clear: "The content of a photograph will NEVER be changed or manipulated in any way." In a survey that posed increasingly more intensive levels of manipulation or retouching, editors involved in photo selection were not unanimous in almost every situation (Reaves 1992). Here are five of them.

1. Okay to remove a telephone wire from the background? *Yes, 29 percent; no, 70 percent.*
2. Okay to zip up a child's pants? *Yes, 27 percent; no, 71 percent.*
3. Okay to move subjects closer together to fit a layout? *Yes, 6 percent; no, 83 percent.*
4. Okay to eliminate some extraneous people to improve the graphic effect of the picture? *Yes, 11 percent; no, 87 percent.*
5. Okay to eliminate a distracting person in the background? *Yes, 10 percent; no, 89 percent.*

Some editors also have no problem with combining photos to create a photo illustration. Is the combination in Figures 5.22 and 5.23 a photo illustration or news photography? Anita Hill accused Clarence Thomas, then a nominee to the U.S. Supreme Court, of sexual harassment. Neither *USA*

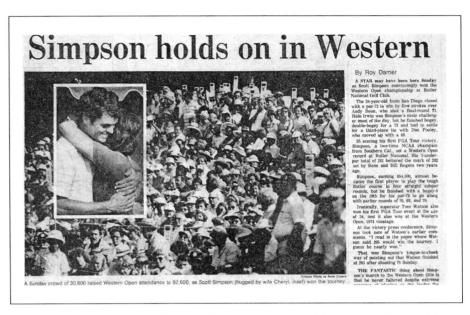

5.23 The "tear" down the middle communicates the split between Thomas and Hill—she accused him of sexual harassment. Will some readers think this is a single photo?

5.24 Designers must be careful when insetting one photo into another. This inset interferes with our ability to read the larger photo.

Today nor the *Boston Globe* had a picture of the two of them together, so they created a composite. *USA Today* created a blue background grid, presumably to signal to readers that it was a composite. The *Globe* created a rip. Neither told readers how the pictures were produced.

At stake is the credibility of photographs. As readers realize what can be done with photographs, will they ever again trust what they see? As soon as they see a photograph they don't believe or don't want to believe, will they accuse the publication of lying? Each publication needs to address the issue and produce written guidelines. The *Atlanta Journal-Constitution*'s policy prohibits manipulation of "any photographs, for any reason." This policy does not preclude using silhouettes, but if two or more photos are combined in a silhouette, the cutline must state that the images are from separate photographs.

Integrity of the photograph

Changing the facts in a photograph or deciding whether to publish pictures of victims involves ethical and legal questions. Techniques such as mortising, insetting, overprinting and silhouetting involve the integrity of the photo.

Mortising, which is the overlapping of two or more photographs, or of type and a photograph, is rarely effective. A preferable technique is an inset, a picture placed entirely within another photograph. This technique is successful when the inset adds information to the dominant photo, is effective in a small size and does not detract from the large image. The technique fails in Figure 5.24 because it obliterates part of the main picture. By

5.25 These insets work because the background offers the designer space to fit them without ruining the larger photo.

contrast, the multiple insets of the Olympic images work because they are small, easily read and nothing is lost from the dominant picture (Fig. 5.25).

The guidelines for overprinting headlines or text on a photograph are similar to insetting: Overprint only if you don't interfere with the content of the photograph, and overprint only if there is a continuous tone. Black type can be printed against a light area such as the sky, or type can be reversed to run against a black background. This guideline protects legibility. By reversing type over a time-exposure picture of coal mining at night (Fig. 5.26), the designer was able to echo the environment of the story without interfering with the message. However, the Saturn package (Fig. 5.27), although dramatic, is too difficult to read because there is so much small text type. (See Chapter 9 for legibility considerations.) Reversed display type works when there are few words and the type is large. Text type should be larger than normal (at least 11 points) and used in small amounts. Designers often use sans serif type for text in reverses because it is easier to read. In small sizes, reversed type often loses its serifs.

Silhouettes are effective when the contrast between the silhouetted object and the background is substantial. For instance, a person wearing light clothes should never be silhouetted against a light background. Silhouettes currently are popular in front-page teasers, but most newspapers restrict silhouettes to non-news sections. The *St. Petersburg Times* used silhouettes so they could substitute the images for words (Fig. 5.28).

TASTE IN EDITING

Designers must be sensitive to the issue of whether to use photos showing victims grieving, dead bodies, people in compromised positions and other instances of questionable taste. The profession has many examples of intense negative reader reaction when photos of victims or of grieving relatives have been published. More than 500 readers objected with phone calls, threats and letters when the *Bakersfield Californian* ran a photograph on page 1 of a family grieving over the drowning of a 5-year-old son and brother. The victim's face was visible from the half-open body bag. John Irby, then editor of the paper, said part of the reason for running the photograph was to increase awareness of the danger of drowning. Not only were there several cancellations, but the paper also received a bomb threat. The paper later apologized in a column for running the photograph (Lund-Seeden 1996).

Sandra Rowe, then executive editor of the *Norfolk Virginian-Pilot*, reported a similar reaction from readers when her paper printed a page 1 photograph of three young victims of a car accident (Fig. 5.29). The father, a police detective, told the paper, "Three of my children

5.26 The designer has the same obligation to be careful when placing type on photographs. Look for a consistent tone—dark or light—so readers can read the type and find a place that does not interfere with the photograph.

were still in hospital beds. I had no idea a picture like that was going to be in the newspaper. I was hurt. I was upset" (Thornburg 1986).

Both photos won awards. Both photos evoked a public outcry. Journalists must be aware of community standards. The decision may be made to print regardless of the public's attitude because it serves a greater public good, such as intensifying a drive for safer swimming or driving conditions. Or the decision may be made that although the photograph is exceptional, it is not suitable for a general-circulation newspaper.

An even more complicated situation occurred when the Pennsylvania state treasurer called a news conference to respond to stories that he had accepted bribes. With video rolling and still cameras clicking, he shot himself. The pictures were extraordinary, sensational, repulsive and historic. The Associated Press moved pictures of the treasurer pulling out the pistol, handling it, placing it in his mouth, slumping to the floor after firing, and lying dead on the floor. A survey of newspapers in New York, North Carolina and Pennsylvania found that only 17 percent of the 114 respondents ran the picture of him with the pistol in his mouth, and only 5 percent ran the photo of him dead. In Pennsylvania, however, of the 57 respondents, 25 percent ran both pictures along with others (Kochersberger 1988).

Many memorable pictures are offensive. Lasting images of the Vietnam war include the photographs of a naked child running screaming down a street after her village was napalmed, and of a South Vietnamese general shooting a prisoner in the head. These types of photographs are always tough calls. In hindsight, it is easier to make the call on classic photographs. However, no picture is a classic when it arrives at deadline. The soldier being dragged through Somalia's streets may be the lasting image of our involvement in

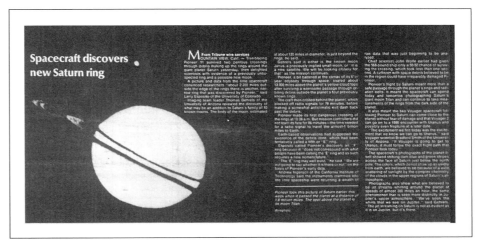

5.27 Reverse display type is easy to read because it is large. However, reverse text type slows reading speed by about 20 percent.

5.28 Silhouettes can work as they do here. First, we are not in the news, business or sports sections where you depend on documentary photography. Second, the silhouettes support the tone and context.

5.29 Some of the best photographs are also some of the most controversial. Editors should know that readers think we are invading privacy when we show grief. However, that does not mean we don't publish these pictures. It does mean you make the decision to publish with the knowledge that it will offend some people. It may also mean that if you publish, you tell readers why you are doing so.

that country, but at the time it arrived, it was just another dramatic picture that raised questions of taste (Fig. 5.2). The photograph ran on page 1 of scores of newspapers. The *Tennessean* in Nashville circulates at Fort Campbell, Ky., where the soldier was based. It did not publish the picture. The *Clarksville Leaf-Chronicle* also circulates there. It ran the picture on page 1. The editor received at least 100 calls and had about 50 cancellations. The editor said that as time passed, some people who were initially angry came to understand the reason for publishing it (Fitzgerald 1993).

There is no "right answer." As ethicist Deni Elliot says, "There always are pictures where reasonable people will disagree and both be ethical. The ethics is not that you print, but how you come to the decision" (Kalfus 1991, p. 30). Here are some criteria against which to measure your decision.

1. *Proximity.* A picture of local people has more impact than showing the same incident miles away. Readers are less offended by pictures of war or starvation abroad but react strongly to a picture of death at home. An image of death or suffering from another city in the same state would generate less reaction than the same image taken in your community.
2. *Dead bodies.* Dead bodies seem to be acceptable to readers in some instances. But when the face is showing, the reaction is usually stronger and longer.
3. *Accident victims.* A picture of an accident victim who will survive is accepted more readily than one of a victim who may later die. The problem is that the outcome often is not known at publication time. If the victim is in serious or critical condition, readers will normally react negatively, especially to a photograph showing the face.
4. *Suffering.* Many readers consider it an invasion of privacy to show the suffering of people.
5. *Size.* If a photo is exceptionally good, the first impulse is to run it large. Many readers accuse the paper of sensationalism when it runs large pictures of tragedy.
6. *Location.* It is natural to put such photos on the front page. The same picture is less offensive inside.
7. *Purpose.* Last, but most important, ask yourself whether there is a real or only an imagined public benefit to be derived from publishing the photo.

None of these criteria is meant to suggest that controversial photographs shouldn't be run. Some should; some shouldn't. What is important is that journalists not make knee-jerk decisions. A newspaper should have written guidelines for handling pictures involving death, injury, suffering, nudity and offensive cultural elements. The discussion should include the photographer, a photo desk representative, the ranking news executive available and the section editor where the picture would run. If the decision is to run, editors should carefully write a cutline and headline and review the page proofs. In some situations, the editors may want to explain the decision to readers and invite their reactions. Whether the picture is published or not, steps should be taken to guard against future possible misuse of the photo if it is going to be placed in archives. The staff should also be informed of the decision.

MAINSTREAMING MINORITIES

Designers and photo editors must reflect the entire community the newspaper serves and avoid dealing in stereotypes. A National Association of Black Journalists' study in 1991 of one week's papers from four cities showed that the number of minorities in photographs fell far below the representation of those minorities in the readership areas. Reporters, photographers and graphic journalists must consciously mainstream minority coverage. Ray Wong, former design editor at the *Nashville Tennessean*, says he doesn't define mainstreaming as publishing pictures of African-American athletes or entertainers. "However," he adds, "a successful African-American businessman (and we're not talking about just another minority success story), Asian-American triplets at college orientation, a Hispanic-American Girl Scout or an African-American mother who bakes bread as a food page feature are good examples of mainstreaming."

Avoiding stereotypes requires everyone in the chain to ask questions about the fairness of the photos and illustrations. Mike Martinez, senior photo editor for training at the Associated Press, said that when he worked at *Detroit News*, staff members spent weeks working on a series on crack babies. Two days before the series was to run, an editor looking at the photographs asked, "Why are all the photos of black women?" The newspaper held the story for two weeks until the photographer produced pictures of black and white mothers of crack babies. That question needs to be asked often and routinely.

GoingOut

The long & short of it

Meet Khan

8'0" TALL

Residence: Miami, Fla.
Full name: Aurangzeb Khan

100" ARM SPAN

Motto: "God makes some people tall and he makes some people small, just to show us all the wonderful things he can do."

53" CHEST

48" SLEEVE

52" WAIST

Background: Born to average-sized parents in Punjab, Pakistan. Emigrated to America when he was unable to find a job to suit his stature. Worked as a bouncer in Chicago before joining Ringling Bros. last year. His wife, Irum, who is of average height, works in the circus nursery.

41½" INSEAM

Long-term goal: To work in movies and other entertainment.
Questions he hears most often: "How tall are you? Are those (his legs) really real?"
Stock answer: "I am 8 feet tall, and yes, these are my real legs, they are not stilts."
Best part about his job: "Meeting the kids at the show. Their eyes grow very big when they see me."

size 20 SHOE

380 lbs WEIGHT

Step right up!
Ringling Bros. and Barnum & Bailey Circus has reverted to its retro roots. The '98 edition of the Greatest Show on Earth is rounded out with a sideshow of captivating curiosities with tongue-twisting titles.
Here's the long and short on the tallest and smallest celebs of the 128th edition of the circus. Khan and Michu and company will be at the United Center in Chicago from Nov. 17 through 29. Tickets begin at $13.50 and are available at the box office and all Ticketmaster outlets.

Meet Michu

Real name: Mihaly Michu Messaros
Residence: Has a home in Los Angeles and another at Michael Jackson's Neverland ranch. "Michael is a very good friend."
Background: Born in Hungary to midget performers with Budapest's Lilliputian Theatre. Attended a state-run circus where he learned juggling, acrobatics and pantomime. Circus promoters Irv and Kenneth Feld signed him in 1973 after a two-year search for a man shorter than the legendary Tom Thumb (Michu is 7 inches shorter). His resume includes the title role in the TV series Alf, films and a dozen music videos.

33" TALL

5" HAND SPAN

Motto: "Laugh, enjoy life. It is short!"

29" CHEST

29" WAIST

Long-term goal: "The circus is where I belong, where I am respected. I love to perform. I love the applause."
Questions he hears most often: "How tall are you? Are you grown up?"
Stock answer: "I am grown up, just not tall."

15" INSEAM

childs 5 SHOE SIZE

50 lbs WEIGHT

6.1   You can tell that one man is larger than the other, but the *Weaton Sun* was able to show the difference. This graphic is a story.

---

*Design is about **how to**. But first you have to understand **what is**.*

Richard Saul Wurman
Information Anxiety

6. Understanding Information Graphics

Information graphics are the ultimate combination of words and visuals. Take a fresh look at the charts, maps and diagrams the next time you pick up a newspaper or magazine. How much would you understand if you eliminated all the words? Richard Saul Wurman reminds us in *Information Anxiety* that all description is words, pictures and numbers. The entertaining and informative graphic that opens this chapter (Fig. 6.1) is a classic combination of words, a picture and numbers. The picture and words wonderfully illustrate proportion. You get a mental outline when a writer tells you that Khan is three times as tall as Michu, but the picture fills in the outline. A writer could tell you that Michu's belt would only go halfway around Khan's waist, but the picture shows you. Writers are advised to show, not tell. Information graphics show. When every journalist, whether reporter, editor, photographer or designer, knows the range and best uses of graphics, readers will be treated to information in a format that is understandable and visual.

While information graphics as a genre are centuries old, their frequent use in mass media is relatively new. First, *Time* magazine and then *USA Today* started using them in the early 1980s. Because both are national publications, journalists saw them and added them to their own story-telling toolboxes. In October 1987, when the Dow Jones average fell 508 points, it's possible that more newspapers published more information graphics on front pages than on any day in history. Graphics were used to chart the fall of the Dow Jones average. Again, in January 1991, graphics dominated newspaper front pages when the United States attacked Iran to open the Gulf war. This time it was because no action photographs were available. Now graphics are as likely to be on page 1 as they are on business or feature pages.

In addition to locally produced graphics, there are several sources of syndicated graphics, such as the Associated Press, Gannett Graphics Network and Knight-Ridder Tribune. Information graphics are recognized for their ability to show visual relationships among numbers or locations and to attract more readership than text. Properly done, information graphics, like stories, convert data into information and information into understanding. Information graphics are here to stay.

THE RANGE OF GRAPHICS

Information graphics (a compound noun often stated—incorrectly—as informational graphics) encompass a wide range of story-telling devices. If used correctly, all of them show relationships between two or more items. Charts are pictures of numbers. Maps not only locate Peoria and New Delhi but also show elevations, underground rock formations and cancer clusters. Diagrams explain a space shuttle and how to play hockey.

The industry assumed that graphics were useful for communicating certain types of information, but it didn't really know. In the early 1980s, statisticians and psychologists performed most of the research on information graphics. Much of the material tested was too complicated to run in the mass media. Researchers at journalism schools are scrambling to catch up, and the early returns support the initial enthusiasm. Several small tests have been conducted. In general, these are the findings (Ruel 1993, Stark 1992, Lott 1993, Vessey 1991, Ward 1992, David 1992):

1. Numerical data is comprehended better in graphics than in text.
2. Readers are more likely to read and remember data in graphics than in stories.
3. Information graphics attract slightly higher levels of readership than stories.
4. Readers have a low threshold for "chartjunk," the artwork some artists build into the data lines. Readers lose the data in the art, and the art sometimes distorts the data.
5. Charts allow readers to grasp trends among numbers more quickly, but comprehension of the numbers in tables is higher than that of charts.
6. People read charts on two levels. One is the visual level—a quick scan that picks up trends or relationships. The second level comes from those who examine the graphic closely, look at the numbers, the trends, and second and third levels of information.

HELPING READERS UNDERSTAND CHARTS

The term *charts* encompasses bar charts, line or fever charts, pie charts and tables. To help readers understand charts, journalists have developed some aids. Two of the most important are the headline and copy block (Fig. 6.2). The headline tells readers and scanners the most important information in the graphic. Unlike a label or title, the headline has a subject and verb and completes a thought. "City budget" is a label that doesn't tell the reader the important news; "City budget up 10%" is a specific statement. The copy block should fulfill some or all of the following functions:

1. Add details to support the headline. "The City Council adopted a budget Wednesday that increases spending $500,000. Most of the increase is for police and fire protection."
2. Tell the reader what can't be or isn't contained in the graphic. "The budget will require a tax increase of 50 cents per hundred dollars evaluation."
3. In charts reporting poll results, support the headline and give readers the information they need to evaluate the survey: how many polled, when and how the survey was conducted and the margin of error.
4. Call attention to something that might be overlooked in the graphic.
5. Tease or direct the reader to the story for more information.
6. In stand-alone charts, explain the causes or consequences of the information.

The headline and copy block serve the same purpose as the headline and lead paragraph in an inverted pyramid story. All information graphics also should contain a source line, the equivalent of attribution in a story.

FOUR KINDS OF CHARTS

Before you worry about what kind of information graphic you will create, you should ask the reporter, other editors or yourself these questions:

1. What is the point of the story? Some graphics are stand-alone elements. Even when it accompanies and supplements a story, the graphic should also make sense by itself. Some readers who look at the graphic will not read the story.

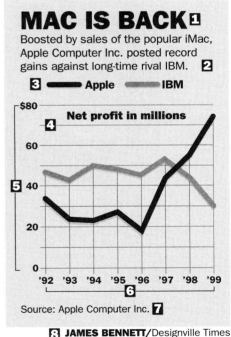

ANATOMY OF A CHART

1 Headline: Use a subject and a verb just like any other in a newspaper.

2 Copy block: Explains the most important point in the chart and puts the data in context with background information.

3 Key: Identifies parts of a chart whenever direct labeling is impossible.

4 Tick marks: Help label values or time. They must be evenly spaced.

5 Y-axis: Dependent variable.

6 X-axis: Independent variable.

7 Source line: Lets readers know where the data came from.

8 Credit line: The graphic's "by-line" is optional according to newspaper policy.

6.2

2. Do the story and graphic agree? At design conferences, anecdotes abound about graphics that were created using a different time period than the reporter, and about graphics with data that didn't agree with the reporter's data.
3. Ask, "So what?" Just because a story involves numbers doesn't mean it needs a graphic. If the point can be explained in a couple of lines in a story, it's a waste of space and time to create a graphic.
4. Ask, "Compared with what?" Too often reporters use a set of numbers in stories and expect them to be graphed when they haven't finished their reporting. For instance, when the local schools annually report the results of the ACT tests, among the first questions a reporter should ask is "Compared with what?" That question could lead to ACT figures for the state, region and nation, and the inclusion of those figures would result in a better story.

There are four kinds of charts: column and bar, line, pie, and tables. Both column and line charts have an x axis, or horizontal scale, and a y axis, or vertical scale. The x axis contains the independent variable, and the y axis, the dependent variable. Thus, when charting inflation rates over time, the rates—the dependent variable—appear on the y axis. Time—the independent variable—appears on the x axis.

You should ask a number of questions about each chart:

1. Are the right numbers used? For instance, if you were reporting on the performance of newspapers, would you compare circulation or penetration? Penetration is the comparison of number of copies sold to the number of households in your circulation area. A newspaper whose circulation is rising might be falling behind if the population is growing faster.

You are using the wrong numbers if you are using nominal dollars instead of real or inflation-adjusted figures. A rule of thumb is to adjust the dollars for inflation if you are using numbers five or more years old. Even at a modest 3 percent annual rate of inflation, $1 in 1995 would be worth only 84 cents in 2000. Another way of looking at the impact of inflation is to take a city budget that is $1 million in 1995. If the budget increased just to cover inflation, the city would be spending $116 million five years later. Your chart would show a spike in spending. If you adjusted the numbers for inflation, the visual message would be that spending stayed flat. If you charted both nominal and real dollars on the same graph, you would improve the reader's understanding of the numbers.

The Bureau of Labor Statistics publishes the Consumer Price Index, which tracks the cost of goods and services. It is used to deflate dollars. When you're working on national stories, you would use the national CPI. There are also urban and rural CPIs, and CPIs are available for specific product categories, such as meat, poultry and fish, household furnishings, shoes, and medical care, to name just a few. The bureau also publishes CPIs for regions, and the figures are also available on a monthly basis. You can get the latest CPI by going to the BLS web site at http://stats.bls.gov/cpi-home.htm. Historical figures are contained in the Statistical Abstract of the United States. You can also allow News Engine's web site (www.newsengin.com) to adjust for inflation for you. Select Free Tools on the main menu. If you need help figuring percentages, News Engine will also calculate those for you.

2. Are the tick marks on the line chart spaced equally, and do they represent equal amounts or time periods?

3. Do the length of the bars and portions of the pie chart accurately reflect the numbers?

4. If any of the lines or shapes are canted, are the data distorted? Canting is the technique of giving lines, bars or pies a 3-D effect.

5. Is the choice of chart appropriate for the content? Software charting programs allow you to type in the numbers and then select the type of chart. Just because you have all those choices doesn't mean they all work well. The content determines the form.

6. Is the headline specific and does it focus on the key point of the chart?

7. Does the copy block explain other findings in the chart and/or give readers information they need, such as polling data, to evaluate the chart?

8. Is there a source line?

9. Does it use space efficiently? Charts do not have more impact when they get bigger. They only need to be large enough to be read easily.

10. If art is included, does it obscure or distort the data?

11. Has the story been edited with the graphic in mind? Do the numbers agree? Is there unnecessary redundancy?

Jonas Dagson, graphics editor for Knight Ridder Tribune Europe, whittles the questions down to two: "What facts do I want to tell the readers in this graphic? In what way can the visual form present this information better than text?" (Dagson, 1998).

Column and bar charts

A column chart has vertical columns, and a bar chart has horizontal bars (Fig. 6.3). Journalists commonly refer to both as bar charts. Think of column and bar charts as still photographs. The format freezes and emphasizes the numbers. By comparison, a line chart is like a video; it maps trends, it shows action. Besides emphasizing the numbers, column and bar charts are useful when you have missing years in your data. A line chart requires an unbroken string of data at even intervals. When some data is missing, when data is not available in even intervals, or when the data could have changed significantly between time intervals, a bar chart is more accurate than a line chart.

Column and bar charts are strongest when they compare two or more items. For instance, you could compare the price of a steak, a gallon of gas and a movie ticket at intervals over several years. If you wanted to emphasize the specific numbers, you would use a column or bar chart rather than a line chart. If the y axis interval values are so large that it becomes difficult to determine the exact value of the bar, you may wish to print the numbers at the end of each bar. Bars can be arranged by size, alphabet and location, to mention only a few possibilities. However, once you have established the order, each cluster should be consistent. Column charts, rather than bar charts, should be used when you are showing deficits because the vertical presentation is easier to understand.

One variation of the bar chart is the two-layer or stacked bar chart, which shows two layers on one column (Fig. 6.4). It's a space-efficient way to present data. Another variation is the hi-lo chart, used for such

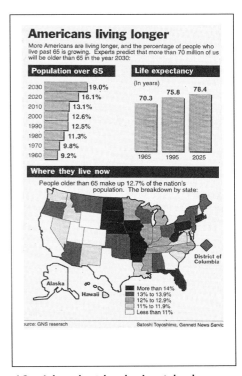

6.3 A bar chart has horizontal columns; a column chart has vertical columns. Both are commonly referred to as bar charts. More important, they freeze the numbers. The map is called a data map because it shows the distribution of numbers geographically.

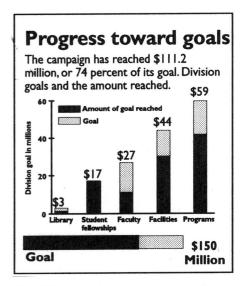

6.4 The layered column or bar chart saves space because two measurements are contained in a single bar. The dark color should be kept at the bottom of the bars because heavier weights always go at the bottom.

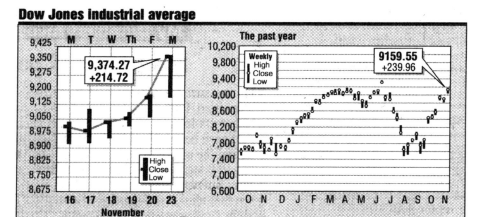

6.5 The hi-lo chart is an efficient way of presenting ranges such as stock market prices and temperatures. The top of the bar shows the Dow Jones high; the bottom of the bar shows the low. The horizontal line shows the closing price.

A penny more

A look at postal rates from 1885 to Sunday, Jan. 10, when the new rate of 33 cents takes effect:

Cost per ounce

Rate adjusted for inflation

In current dollars

Jan. 10
33¢

45¢
40
35
30
25
20
15
10
5
0

July 1, 1885
2¢

'90 1910 '30 '50 '70 '90

Source: AP research   **AP**

6.6 The line chart—also commonly referred to as a fever chart—shows numbers changing over time. The emphasis is on the trend; the bar chart emphasis is on the numbers at one particular moment. This one compares the postal rate increases, current dollars to real dollars.

things as showing the high and low of stocks or temperatures on a given day (Fig. 6.5).

Line charts

A line chart shows variations in numbers over time (Fig. 6.6). It is also popularly known as a fever chart because it has been used to chart hospital patients' temperatures. Like a video, it shows numbers moving, although it doesn't show individual numbers as well as the bar chart. Nor does it work well when there is too little variation in the figures, because the line appears flat. Sometimes, when there is too great a variation in the numbers, the line may rise or fall so much that too much space is required and there are large gaps between numbers. A single line across the chart often indicates that the data could be told in a couple of sentences. For instance, a single line showing DWI arrests in five-year intervals for the last 25 years isn't complete. The arrests should be compared with something, such as arrests in similar jurisdictions or other kinds of arrests. If the change is significant, the numbers should be adjusted for population changes. One of the most important concepts to remember in dealing with numbers is that a single number or a single data set is difficult to understand. If you tell readers that your city had 50 homicides last year, their first question is likely to be, "Is that good or bad?" To make the number understandable, you need comparisons. The number of homicides during each of the last five years would be one way to translate the numbers. Another would be to convert them to murders per capita and compare them to the per capita homicides in other cities.

Too many lines are confusing. Color permits you to use more lines because each can be identified more easily. When you must work in black and white, it is better to restrict yourself to two or three lines, particularly if they cross.

Pie charts

The pie chart is used to show parts of a whole (Fig. 6.7). It is usually, though not always, circular. The divisions are usually expressed as percentages. The pie chart has limited usefulness. It does not work well when there are too many divisions: They are hard to see, hard to label and hard to differentiate, especially in black and white. On the other hand, a pie chart showing only two divisions is often a waste of space; the numbers would take a single sentence in a story. Pie charts show proportions, but they aren't numerically precise because they don't show strict measurements. When you want to show visually the proportional parts of the whole, a pie chart is the right choice.

If you are using more than one pie to show comparisons, be sure to keep the order of the elements the same. If you are using color, use the same color code for each pie.

A first cousin of the pie chart would be any representation showing parts of a whole. Thus, to show market share for the automobile industry, a car could be divided into appropriate shares and labeled. Be careful, though; the form can easily overwhelm the content. Pie charts are inflexible. They can show only parts of one number. Because pie charts show percentages, the number the percentages are based on should appear in the copy block.

If you are using adjacent pie charts to show year-to-year changes, use the same key to identify the same categories and keep the categories in the same order.

Tables

Like Rodney Dangerfield, tables don't get no respect. Yet readers can understand them more easily than other types of charts. Tables appear every day as television grids. Sports agate is full of tables, from the standings to performance reports on players. Tables are columnar listings of names or numbers or both and can organize and relate several categories of information. Use tables when there are too many numbers to chart, the data is too disparate (for instance, comparing a group of schools by more than one measurement, such as math and verbal scores), or it is necessary to see the exact numbers, such as in an income tax table. When there are few numbers or when the numbers show a definite trend, a bar or line chart may be preferable.

Tables often are not used to their potential. You can list items by rank, size or alphabet, but the decision should be based on how you expect readers to use the list. If the list is short, rank or size can work. If the list is long, you may want to consider listing them alphabetically because readers will more easily be able to find the entries they are interested in. You can add another column to show rank or size. When you have more three or more columns and a row of 10 or more entries, you need to help readers follow a line horizontally. One way is to add a space after every three entries. That allows the items to stay on the line because they will be following the top, middle or bottom of the three-entry cluster. Another way is to highlight every other line with a screen or tint.

Tables are grids used to organize information into rows (vertically) and columns (horizontally). If you want to compare the services and costs of day-care providers in your city, readers can access a table more easily than a story. Many publications use tables to compare and contrast candidates' stands on key issues (Fig. 6.8). The format offers readers a quick and understandable summary before they vote.

DATELINES

History tends to conceal relationships; datelines reveal them. When you create a dateline, you can see patterns

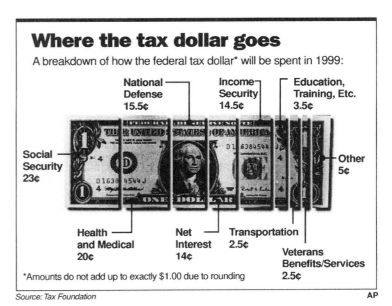

6.7 Pie charts show parts of the whole. Although they get their name from the shape of a pie, any item that is sliced to show parts of the whole, such as the dollar in this chart, is a pie chart.

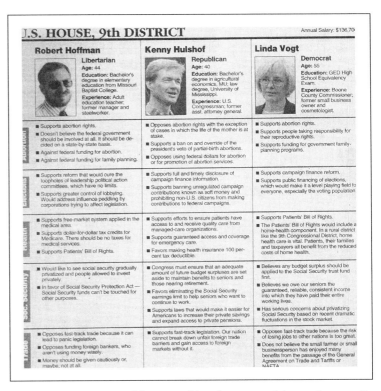

6.8 Tables can be used for everything from organizing voting results by wards to creating grids for entertainment listings. Here one is used to show candidates' positions on issues. Readers understand tables better than any other information graphic format.

Colombia moves towards peace after three decades

Colombians hope that peace talks can end a 34-year-old conflict between the government and rebel forces.

1984: Rebels and the government declare a cease-fire after **President Belisario Betancur** sent emissaries to a FARC stronghold in southern Colombia.

June 1991 (Venezuela) and **March 1992** (Mexico): Peace talks take place between FARC and Colombian **President Cesar Gaviria.** Talks fail amid fighting in Colombia and the peace envoy's withdrawal.

1964 ◀▶ 1980 | 1985 | 1990 | 1995 | 1999

1964: FARC founded by communist peasants demanding land reform and an end to government repression.

The conflict claims thousands of lives every year. FARC is at its strongest ever and growing. Its estimated 15,000 regulars control 40 percent of the countryside.

1985: A FARC faction agreed to disarm and form a political party, but in the ensuing decade 3,000 party activists and two presidential candidates were assassinated by right-wing death squads.

1990: An army offensive routs the FARC from its rear-guard retreat in the southern town of Uribe, but the rebels regroup and grow to 15,000 fighters.

July 1998: President-elect Andres Pastrana meets with top FARC leader Manuel Marulanda. The two agree to begin peace talks, and Pastrana facilitates these by withdrawing all troops from a rebel-dominated region. Peace talks began Thursday, **Jan. 7.**

Pastrana   Marulanda

Source: AP research   AP/Wm. J. Castello

6.9   Datelines are effective visual formats to show the progression of events over time. This one shows events in the country of Colombia from 1964 to 1999.

or relationships among events. If you were to create a dateline identifying developments that have affected newspaper design, you might include many different factors: the development of type and typesetting, machinery, presses and photography, even the price of newsprint. The increase in transmission speeds of word and pictures. Creation of the Society of News Design. When these are arranged chronologically, you can begin to see how a development in press plates, for instance, affected the design of the times.

The dateline concept can be combined with line charts and bar charts (Fig. 6.9). Copy blocks can identify events that may have affected the numbers being graphed.

SEVEN KINDS OF MAPS

Maps, which put us in touch with our world, are being used more and more. The *New York Times* nearly doubled its cartographers, from seven to 13, between 1961 and 1993. At the Associated Press, 14 artists create 5,000 maps a year. The mass media use several kinds of maps, and only two of them—the transportation map and locator map—are used to show location. Several other kinds of maps—data maps, distribution maps, geologic maps, topographic maps and land use maps—offer journalists formats with which to tell stories. Cartographers use even more formats, but the following list includes those readers can most easily understand.

Locator maps

Every newspaper ought to have a file of base locator maps, outlines of political subdivisions such as the ward, city, county or parish, state and nation. With base maps, you can quickly add the type needed to locate action in an accompanying story (Fig. 6.10).

All of us grew up with transportation or road maps. We learned the coding: the larger the type, the larger the city; different icons and colors to identify interstate highways, state highways and county roads. These codes are useful when making maps because your readers also know these codes. However, it is a mistake to adhere to them when you are not creating a transportation map. For instance, you may be creating a map to locate a disaster in a rural area several miles from the city in which you publish. Transportation map coding would require you to put the name of your city in large type and the location of the disaster in small type. That would defeat your purpose, which is to focus on the disaster area.

There are several things to remember when making locator maps (Fig. 6.11):

1. Identify north.
2. Include a mileage scale.
3. Create a type hierarchy that focuses on the important location rather than on the cities around it, even if they have larger populations.
4. Include enough of the surrounding territory to identify the location.
5. Eliminate unnecessary detail, including cities and streets that aren't needed to locate the place featured.
6. Include a small secondary map window to locate the exploded area within a larger division.
7. Keep map symbols to a minimum.
8. Curve the type along curved features, such as rivers.

Data maps

Besides showing location, maps can show the geographical spread of data. The geographical distribution of data reveals what numbers alone can't. Data maps show patterns and trends. Are citizens in some parts of the country more likely to have cancer, on a per capita basis, than those in others? Do some states or regions have higher divorce rates than others? What is a bank's real estate loan pattern throughout a city (Fig. 6.12)?

Base map

6.10 Base maps, such as this one showing the counties of Missouri, are invaluable time savers.

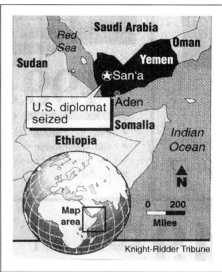

Knight-Ridder Tribune

6.11 Locator maps show the location by showing the context. The globe shows the location in the world. That allows the artist to give more detail on the close-up of the region.

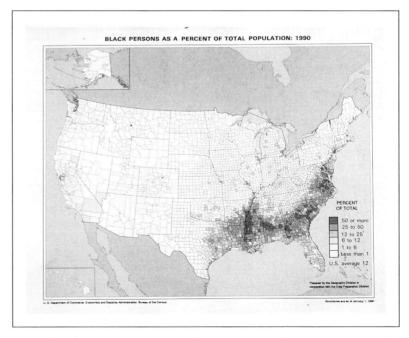

6.12 This data map, prepared by the Department of Commerce, shows the number of African-Americans and where they are living. The key shows that the denser the color, the higher the population.

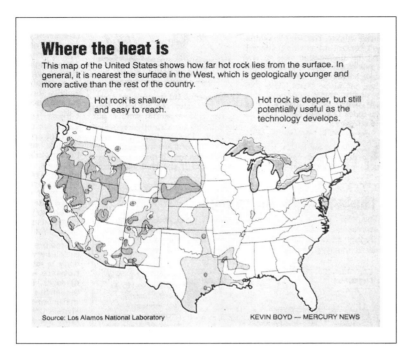

6.13   A distribution map shows the location and depth of items, in this case, the location and depth of hot rocks underground.

Distribution maps

The first cousin of the data map is the distribution map. Instead of showing the distribution of numbers, it shows the distribution of items, such as natural resources (Fig. 6.13).

Geologic maps

Geologic maps show the area underneath the ground layers of soil, rock formations, and even underground streams (Fig. 6.14).

Topographic maps

Topographic maps show land formations above the surface and usually include elevation information (Fig. 6.15).

Land use maps

Land use maps show how a given area is being used. It can show zoning designations or actual use within the zoning classification (Fig. 6.16).

Weather maps

Few newspapers prepare a full-scale weather map locally. Most use a map from the Associated Press or

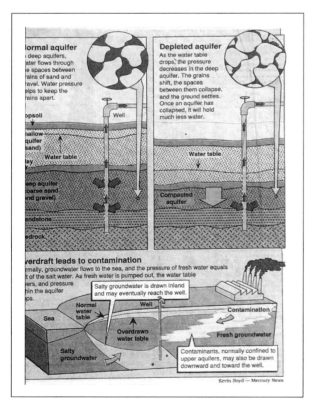

6.14   Geologic maps show what's under the ground. The cutaway allows us to view the earth's subsurface.

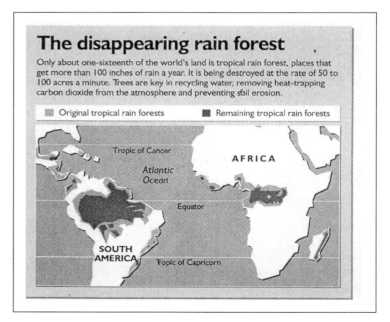

6.15   Topographic maps show what is above ground. The key shows that the gray areas indicate the original rain forests; the dark areas show the existing rain forests.

buy one from a service. However, even when the map is obtained from another source, many newspapers fail to include the key. Even though readers have seen map symbols for years in newspapers and on television, many cannot identify the symbols that indicate cold, warm and stationary fronts (Fig. 6.17).

DIAGRAMS AND ILLUSTRATIONS

Diagrams can take many forms; like pictures, they can be worth a thousand words. Some of them use thousands of words. They also use artwork and photographs. They may even incorporate some charts. Diagrams often use several formats to tell a story, ranging from the simple to the complex. All take time—time to gather the information and time to create the graphic. You can explain in a story how hockey is played, or you can explain by drawing it (Fig. 6.18). You can describe a chase scene, accident or race routes, but you might be able to communicate more effectively by drawing them. You can write about the difference of antacids and H2 blockers, but you can explain more

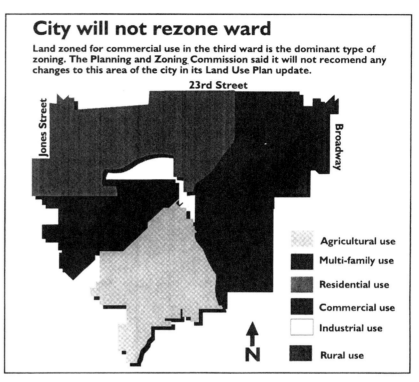

City will not rezone ward

Land zoned for commercial use in the third ward is the dominant type of zoning. The Planning and Zoning Commission said it will not recomend any changes to this area of the city in its Land Use Plan update.

6.16 A map showing the zoning for any political division would be an example of a land use map.

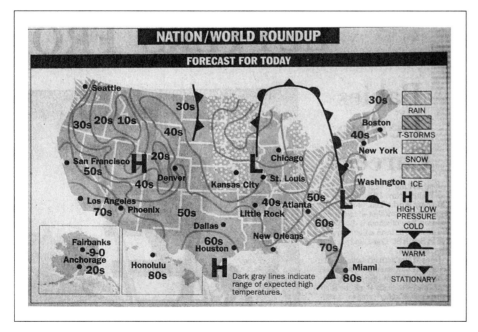

6.17 The weather map is one of the most common seen in newspapers, but despite its wide usage, journalists should remember to include the key on the map.

6.18 This illustration is a hybrid between art and text story. It's another story-telling device in the arsenal.

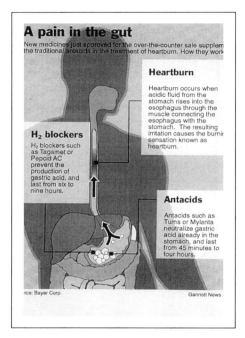

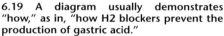

6.19 A diagram usually demonstrates "how," as in, "how H2 blockers prevent the production of gastric acid."

6.20 This illustration not only shows what the dinosaur looks like, but also compares its size to other dinosaurs.

clearly in a diagram (Fig. 6.19). When a North Carolina museum bought the fossil of a dinosaur, the *Charlotte Observer* used the power of illustration to show the skeleton, what the dinosaur would have looked like and compare the sizes of different kinds of dinosaurs. The visual presentation helped explain what visitors to the museum would see (Fig. 6.20).

Like charts, diagrams should have headlines. Some graphic journalists, in fact, write the headlines before they start work. This forces them to focus on the main idea in the diagram. Whether there needs to be a copy block depends on the diagram. Some don't need it because there are text blocks throughout the diagram. Ironically, the danger in these large-scale projects is that the information becomes too complex. The goal, as always, is to make complex things simple.

MINORITIES IN GRAPHICS

Graphic journalists have an obligation to see that people who appear in charts and illustrations reflect the multicultural community the newspaper serves. Sadly, many don't. A study of 50 lifestyle sections entered in the Penney-Missouri lifestyle section contest in 1990 turned up 194 illustrations with 381 people depicted. Of those, only 5 percent were identifiable as minorities. Of the 22 people shown in charts, none were identifiable as minorities.

Some newspapers aggressively try to reflect their communities in their photos and graphics. At the *Nashville Tennessean,* for example, artists are encouraged to reflect the racial makeup of the community in all graphics and illustrations. To ensure representation in photographs and drawings, editors must indicate in their budgets whether the story or illustrations include minorities. A newsroom committee reviews the papers each month and reports on how well they have done mainstreaming minorities into the coverage.

Every graphics department would do well to make a conscious effort to mainstream minorities into daily illustrations.

CREATING A STYLE SHEET

To achieve uniformity and to cut production time, each publication needs a graphics style sheet and templates (Fig. 6.21). The style sheet identifies typefaces, sizes and formats. It also identifies the color palette (see Chapter 16).

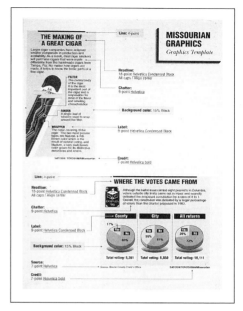

6.21 Style sheets and templates ensure consistency and save time.

7.1 Information graphics have become a common story-telling device for newspapers, and the graphics show up on page 1 frequently. Now journalists—both those who produce the graphics and those who edit and publish them—must demand a high level of accuracy.

Graphical excellence is that which gives to the viewer the greatest number of ideas in the shortest time with the least ink in the smallest space . . . and graphical excellence requires telling the truth about data.

Edward R. Tufte
Author, *The Visual Display of Quantitative Information*

7. Creating Accurate Information Graphics

Information graphics create even stranger bedfellows than politics. The creators combine text (story), mathematics (numbers) and art (form). In academic circles, both journalists and artists are often known as "math avoiders." Too many of us fear numbers; we think figuring simple percentages is advanced algebra and deflating dollars is harder than getting to the moon. The results are evident daily in both stories and graphics in the mass media. These examples are all real:

— numbers that show the dramatic increase in city spending during the last 15 years but do not account for either inflation or population increases;
— numbers that compare violent deaths in the United States with several other countries but do not account for population differences;
— numbers that compare crimes over time without taking into account changes in population or laws.

Fortunately, most chart errors are unintentional and can be corrected with a little education. A few of the errors may be intentional, in the same way that a few journalists commit plagiarism, make up quotes or ignore information that doesn't fit a story. Those are exceptions. If we pay more attention to the numbers and recognize the causes of distortion and inadvertent deception, we can correct unintentional errors. We can make our graphics meet and surpass the same standards of honesty and completeness that we impose on stories.

SEVEN COMMON ERRORS

Readers read graphs on two levels. One is the visual message embedded in the rise and fall of a line, the differences in heights of bars and different proportions of a pie. The second level is the verbal messages embedded in the words and numbers. To avoid misleading readers, we must make our charts accurate visually and verbally. The first step to ensuring chart accuracy is to recognize the potential problems. There are seven common charting errors:

1. Using the wrong chart form
2. Using uneven intervals along the x or y axes on a line chart
3. Distorting the chart format
4. Using wrong or incomplete numbers
5. Comparing data in charts with different y-value intervals
6. Creating a visual inaccuracy
7. Failing to offer enough historical perspective

Using the wrong chart form

Matching the correct chart form to the data is more art than science. While tables score highest on comprehension tests, no research exists to show that comprehension is higher for some types of data in a certain format than others. Still, common sense based on knowing the strengths and weaknesses of various chart forms should lead you to select carefully the appropriate format for your data.

Line charts connect data between time intervals with a straight line. When the data is compiled annually (crop production, automobile fatalities) or when the information changes slowly, the straight line is fine.

However, some types of data are so volatile that the straight line may show a trend that doesn't exist. Sometimes you don't want to break down the time intervals because it would take too much space or because you don't have the data for the time between intervals. The solution is to use a column chart. For instance, voters are notoriously fickle in their preferences for candidates during a campaign. In Figure 7.2, not only do the straight lines purport to show something that isn't known, the time intervals are not equal. It appears that Clinton enjoyed a steep and continuous rise in voter preference between June and July. He may have, but the newspaper doesn't know because there were no polls between those two dates. One solution is to use column graphs to show the polling results over time.

If you have missing data points, column or bar charts are a better choice than a line chart. If you use a line chart, you can break the line at the missing data points and explain the omission.

Line charts are most effective when you want to emphasize change over time. Bar and column charts are most effective when you want to emphasize the numbers at a given moment. Line charts show trends; bar and column charts show the numbers at a given moment. If the time intervals for your data are not the same, you will need to use a column or bar chart.

Comparing uneven intervals

Readers who will examine a chart closely enough to detect data charted during unequal time periods or to detect tick marks unevenly spaced are rare. When the time periods are unequal, quite often it is because the data are not available or not obtainable on deadline. Informing readers of the discrepancy will work if it could be assumed that the uneven time period does not change the visual picture. If there is doubt, a column chart should be used. An accurate line chart requires equal time periods. In Figure 7.3, the line chart has four intervals of 10 years, and one of seven. The discrepancy is not called to the readers' attention.

Even more serious is when chart makers do not space the tick marks evenly. Graphing software is not precise, but it is close enough to prevent visual distortion in line charts. However, when graphic journalists create a chart freehand, they sometimes do not pay enough attention to the precision with which they locate the tick marks.

Distorting chart shapes

Whenever a line chart has one axis longer than the other, the picture created can be misleading. In newspapers and magazines, this occurs frequently because of the restrictions of

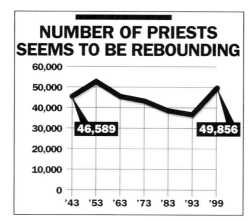

7.3   When you are comparing data, you normally use equal time periods. However, if you are showing 10-year figures and have only the last nine years of the current period, you must indicate to the reader that the time periods are unequal.

It is important to use the right kind of chart for the right kind of data.

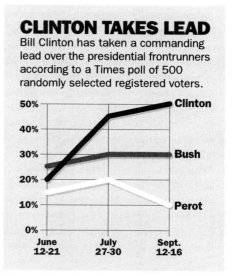

The graphic above inappropriately uses a line chart that appears to chart public opinion over three months. In fact, it only has data for three days within each of those months.

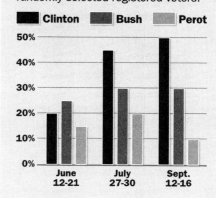

The second graphic uses bar charts to give a snapshot of the campaign on the dates available. Some of what happened over the three months is shown, but it doesn't make assumptions about what happened to public opinion in between the polls.

7.2

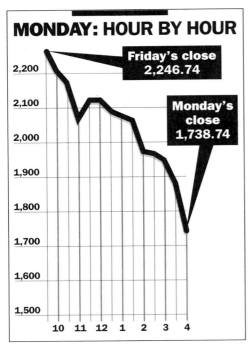

7.4 The farther you deviate from a 1:1 ratio in the length of the x and y axes, the more you distort the visual message. By putting this information in one column, the y axis becomes much longer, and that makes the decline look even more pronounced.

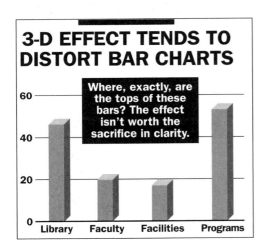

7.5

column widths. Squeezing a chart into one column can distort the data when the y axis ends up significantly longer than the x axis. In Figure 7.4, the 508-point decline in the stock market is graphed in one column. The y axis is about 2.25 times the length of the x axis, creating an image of disaster. The decline was significant enough without help from the chart format. The goal is to get the vertical and horizontal axes somewhere between 1:1 and 1:1.5. When the format is corrected, the picture changes from disaster to steep decline. The shorter the period charted, the more distorted the information will become.

An even more common form of distortion occurs when chart makers cant, or turn, the graphic. The intent—to create a more aesthetic graphic—is benign, but the result is a visual inaccuracy. Column, bar and pie charts that are canted to create a three-dimensional effect distort the information. In pies, the pieces of the pie are distorted because the area is expanded or compressed by the angle. To check the distortion on a canted pie chart, use a protractor. Because there are 360 degrees in a circle, each percentage point represents 3.6 degrees. Multiply each figure in your chart by 3.6 and compare with the percentage to assess the distortion. When column and bar charts are canted, readers don't know whether to read the front or back of the bar. Even if the bar is labeled with the exact value, the visual message remains distorted (Fig. 7.5).

Using wrong or incomplete numbers

When wrong numbers are used, it usually reveals a lack of understanding of how to tell stories with numbers. If journalists remember to ask themselves "Compared with what?" they will begin to help readers understand the numbers. A single number, or a series of single numbers reporting the same phenomenon, is the most complicated number or series in the world. Numbers beg for context. "Information is not knowledge," Theodore Roszak wrote in *The Cult of Information: The Folklore of Computers and the True Art of Thinking*. "You can mass-produce raw data and incredible quantities of facts and figures. You cannot mass-produce knowledge, which is created by individual minds, drawing on individual experience, separating the significant from the irrelevant, making value judgments." Context converts data into understanding. Telling readers that General Motors has lost $17 billion on its North American operations in the last 10 years is meaningless until you add other things about the company, such as its annual revenues, its net profit or loss during the same period, its net operating revenue or Ford's performance during the same period.

Using numbers without comparing them to anything is an error of omission. If you chart graduation rates for your state, you need more than the rates for your state over a period of years. Understanding results from a comparison of those numbers with others: the rates for the nation, the rates for comparable states or the rates for other regional states. Understanding also results from listening to the experts describe the causes: increasing juvenile crime rates, less spending per pupil (on an inflation-adjusted basis), higher student-teacher ratios, and so on.

If you are going to wade into the swamp of percentages, be aware that the bottom is quicksand. Here are three recommendations that will help you find solid footing: (1) Use a constant base; (2) when you don't have a constant base, convert to rates; (3) don't confuse percentages with percentage points.

When percentages figured on a changing base are charted, we are comparing apples and oranges. If you report that on a percentage basis, the United States ranks behind France, Belgium, Sweden and Switzerland in use of nuclear energy, you are right, but because of the differences in the size of the countries, relying on percentages is misleading. Although only 20 percent of the energy in the United States is produced from nuclear power, the United States produces more than five times as much energy by nuclear power than France, the next-highest country. Even the gross numbers are inappropriate in this comparison. The U.S. population is much larger than that of any of the other countries. The appropriate numbers to chart represent per capita production.

If you don't think a different base has a significant impact on the figures, consider this. Say you are making $30,000 and a colleague is making $40,000. The salary is the base. Your employer awards you a 5 percent increase and your colleague a 4 percent increase. Before you begin feeling too good about the honor, consider that your raise is $1,500 ($.05 \times 30,000$) and your colleague's raise is $1,600. Your colleague won a bigger raise, and the gap between the two of you grew from $10,000 to $10,100.

When you have a different base upon which the percentage is figured, convert to rates. That's what you would do when you are reporting on any story involving spending over more than five years. In most cities, the budget changes yearly. That means the base for the percentage changes yearly. A typical solution is to convert from percentages to rates. You do that by getting the population figures for each of the years and figure the spending per citizen. That way, you avoid the distortion created by the changing base.

Last, if you aren't alert to the difference between percentage and percentage points, you are going to make errors. Assume that 15 percent of your colleagues are history majors and 20 percent are journalism graduates. That's a five-percentage points difference but a 25 percent difference ($20-15=5$; $5 \div 20=25\%$).

Percentages work if the base on which the percentage is figured remains constant. That's why pie charts, which show a portion of one number, can use percentages. Column and bar charts can also show percentages with a constant base. The base, however, should be revealed in the copy block.

Population and dollars change with time, and both should be factored into a study of those changes. Inflation changes the value of money. Nominal dollars should be converted to real or inflation-adjusted dollars (see Chapter 6).

Another set of numbers all journalists need to understand are polling statistics. Polls are reported in newspapers daily, and the stories and graphs are full of errors and omissions. Graphic journalists need to be alert to the pitfalls.

The Associated Press Managing Editors Association prepared a checklist of the information you should share with your readers about any poll you are reporting. The list includes:

1. *The identity of the sponsor of the survey.* This is important because sponsors can produce the results they want by the way they select

the respondents and how they word the questions. For instance, a newspaper ran poll results from Performance Research showing that 71 percent of NASCAR fans said they were likely to buy sponsors' products, while only 28 percent of Olympics fans were likely to buy sponsors' products. One suspects that Performance Research took the poll to help sell advertising for NASCAR. Regardless, what the graphic journalist needed to add to put the numbers in context is the number of fans of each sport. Twenty-eight percent of the Olympic fan base is much larger than 71 percent of the NASCAR fan base. Sometimes, the journalist has to dig. The identity of the real sponsor can be hidden by the name or subcontracted to a polling firm. Sometimes when you find out, you decide not to publish the results because the results have been skewed. Sometimes you publish but identify the true sponsor. At all times, identify the sponsor in the graphic.

2. *The exact wording of the questions asked.* How questions are worded greatly influences the results. Because of the detail, normally this would be contained in the accompanying story, not the graphic.

3. *A definition of the population sampled.* If you are talking about voter preferences for candidates, did the pollster ask everyone old enough to vote? Just those registered to vote? Just those who said they intended to vote in the next election? Try to include this information in the graphic copy block.

4. *The margin of sampling error.* All polls have a sampling error, which is an acknowledgment that no poll is accurate because it is a sample. That error typically is expressed as plus or minus (x) percent. The error usually ranges between 3 and 5 points. Here is the application: If 42 percent say they will vote Republican and 44 percent Democratic and the margin of error is +/- 4 points, it means that between 38 and 46 percent say they will vote Republican and between 40 and 48 percent say they will vote Democratic. Although many newspapers would say the Democrats have a slight edge, it would be accurate to say only that the race is too close to call. The margin of error should be identified in the copy block. If the results with the error margin overlap, the copy block should say that that the race is too close to call. Especially be alert when you are charting subgroups. For instance, if you were asked to chart how the women sampled intend to vote, you are now dealing with a sample about half the size of the larger one. That means the margin of error probably will jump to nearly 8 points.

5. *The sample size and the response rate.* The margin of error is based on the sample size. The larger the sample, the lower the error rate. You need to know how many people actually participated in the poll.

6. *How the interviews were collected—in person, by phone or by mail.* Reveal this in the copy block.

7. *When the interviews were collected.* People's attitudes change, and sometimes they can change overnight. During a campaign, opinions are volatile. A candidate may state a position, her opponent may make a charge, or a newspaper may reveal the results of an investigation into the candidate's background. To evaluate the poll results, readers need to know when the questions were asked. This should also be included in the copy block.

When you are running multiple charts from a single poll, you may be able to combine all this information in a single pullout.

Comparing charts with different y interval values

Charts that are accurate take on a different meaning when placed next to others to compare the data. If comparisons are to be made, the y axes must have the same value line. When they don't, casual readers—and sometimes even careful readers—will get the wrong message. In Figure 7.6, the y axis values top off at 250 million in the Missouri chart, 1,400 million in the Illinois chart and 8 billion in the U.S. chart. Each chart is accurate by itself, but stacked next to each other, the visual message is that Missouri produced more corn than Illinois in 1987. In fact, Illinois produced nearly five times as much. It also appears that the United States produced only slightly more corn than Illinois. The Missouri and Illinois charts could be adjacent if the y values were the same. Remember that the first level of chart reading is visual. Only those who read the words carefully would detect the differences in y axis values.

Creating a visual distortion

Author Edward Tufte calls graphics that are overwhelmed by decoration "ducks," after a building constructed in the shape of a duck. "Chartjunk" reverses the process of decorating a building to building a decoration (Tufte 1983). The artwork incorporated into the chart in Figure 7.7 makes it difficult for the reader to determine how much was earned. A smaller illustration that provides context but does not obscure the data is usually a better solution. Art, in the form of an icon, can be used to create the environment for the chart without overwhelming the message.

Nigel Holmes, who pioneered the use of information graphics at *Time* magazine, often used art in his charts. Later in his career, he acknowledged

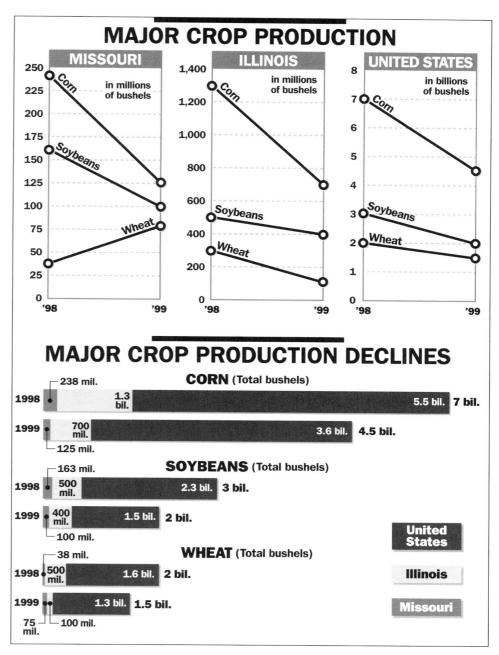

7.6   Graphic artists have to wrestle with problems caused by y values that vary greatly from one chart to another. If you put them alongside each other, many readers are likely not to notice the y values are different and will compare them. (Note range from 8 million to 1,400 million bushels.) A better solution is a bar chart. If you can't find another solution, then you should stack them vertically so the reader doesn't have a horizontal alignment.

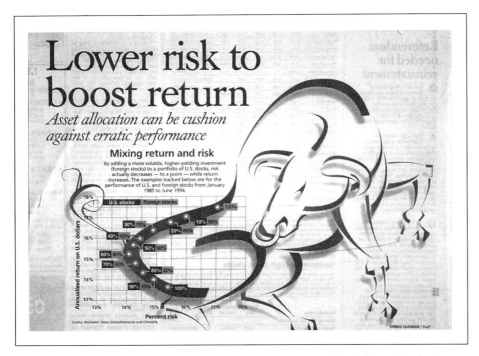

7.7 When you build the numbers into the art, it is very easy to lose information in the art. A preferable approach would be to use the art as a smaller icon on the graph.

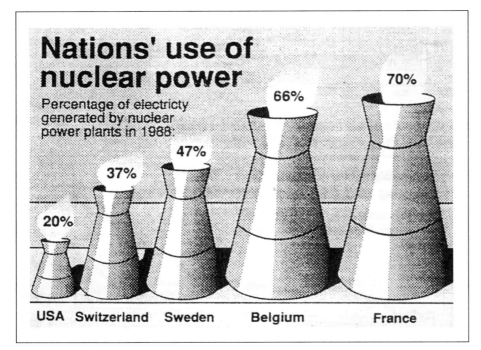

7.8 When you substitute art for the bars, you distort the size as you increase the artwork because it grows wider as it gets taller. As a result, the visual message doesn't match the numbers.

that he may have overdone it. "There is considerable value in a picture, as opposed to a daunting set of statistics," he said. "I purposely avoid the word 'boring.' Statistics are not boring—they are daunting. People are scared of statistical displays, they don't have the time to study them and don't think they will understand them. So, a picture may help. I don't think that's patronizing. The value of the picture, as opposed to decoration, is to help people understand. But, if the picture takes over and obscures the information, then it would be better not to have it at all even if you risk losing the reader."

Holmes continued, "This is where my thinking has changed. Before, I would have said it is paramount to get the reader interested and then deliver the information. Now I think that if you risk losing the reader because you've given him too much picture, then it's better not to give him the picture in the first place."

Adding art to the chart is one thing. Substituting the art for the bars is another. Art expands proportionally. The surface area expands geometrically while the height grows mathematically. When cooling towers were substituted for bars, consultant Loren Needles pointed out the visual distortion (Fig. 7.8). Although 70 percent is 3.5 times larger than 20 percent, the surface area of the French cooling tower is about eight times larger.

Another way to distort the visual image of the data is to amputate the zero base on the y axis. On column charts, when the base does not start at zero, the space between the top of the bars inaccurately reflects the proportion. In Figure 7.9, the zero baseline shows one relationship; the nonzero baseline makes the difference look almost three times as large. A nonzero baseline usually works on line charts because the visual message is in the line or between the lines, not between the x axis and the line.

Failing to offer enough historical perspective

Whenever there is a significant rise or fall in the stock market, front-page headlines proclaim the news in large, bold type usually accompanied by a chart. Often the chart shows the hour-by-hour Dow Jones averages for that day; sometimes the chart shows the swings for the week. In either case, the time frame is too short to provide meaningful context for understanding the gyrations. In October 1987, the stock market dropped 508 points to close at 1738.74. That's a 23 percent drop. Those publications that offered only a short time span in the charts may have unnecessarily scared readers because they didn't offer context. Yes, the drop was significant and worthy of page 1 display, but a longer time frame for the chart would have shown that the market was still higher than one year earlier and much higher than two or three years earlier.

In 1997 the Dow dropped 554 points in one day. Because the market was up to 7715.41, the drop was only 7.2 percent. Still, some newspapers offered a visual image of disaster (Fig. 7.10); others offered a more meaningful time frame and, thus, a more accurate visual picture (Fig. 7.11).

Historical perspective is context. Context leads to understanding. If you are charting crimes for your city, convert them to per capita rates and chart them for several years. You may find that while the gross number of crimes is up, on a per capita basis they may be lower than 10 years earlier. It is important that you help your readers understand the data.

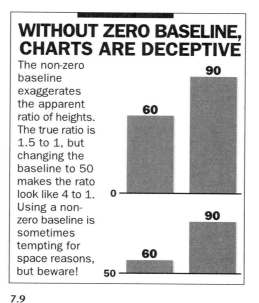

7.9

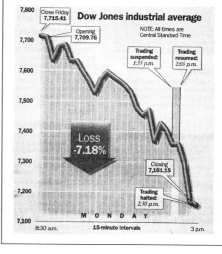

7.10 A one-day look at the performance of the stock market emphasizes the blip over 24 hours.

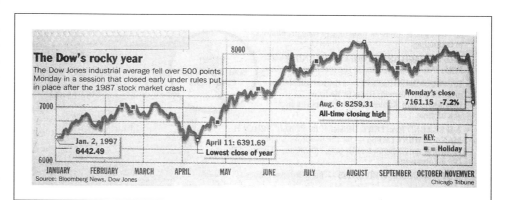

7.11 When you look at a longer time period for the stock market, you can see that although the market dropped dramatically, it is still higher than it was just five months earlier. The facts didn't change; the context did.

8.1 Understanding the differences in letterforms allows the designer to choose the fonts successfully to create an atmosphere that is appropriate to the message. A good way to study the serifs and bracketing in letters is to look at them in reverse. This is a Bookman *g*.

LETTERS are to be read, not to be used as practice models for designers or to be molded by caprice or ignorance into fantastic forms of uncertain meaning. They are not shapes made to display the skill of their designers; they are forms fashioned solely to help the reader.

Frederic Goudy
Typographer

8. Understanding Type

8.2 It may not be everyone's choice, but if you are going to use only type on your page, this is an excellent way to do it. This German paper carefully controls the leading, letter spacing and white space to enhance the readability of the page.

Type is to the reader what the interstate highway is to the trucker. The better the highway, the faster the trucker goes. With a sound typographic infrastructure, readers can quickly and easily absorb the information.

Because approximately 80 percent of the editorial matter in a newspaper consists of type, its selection and use are critical to successful communication. Yet, perhaps because it is so pervasive, type is often overlooked for the flashier tools of the designer: illustration, white space and color. The headline face, the text type and the design of the advertisements, which are primarily type, give each publication a personality. The classic look of the *Frankfurter Allgemeine* is constructed only of type and white space (Fig. 8.2). Despite the importance of type, there are few typographers working for newspapers or magazines. Consultants and designers perform this function on a hit-or-miss basis, but often the day-to-day use of type is left to personnel with inadequate training. Even so, given the proper type and instructions on how to use it, local staff members should be able to produce a daily or weekly product that is fundamentally sound typographically. Designers who handle type every day should understand the basics of its use. This chapter, the first of three on typography, discusses the design, language, grouping and identification of type. Chapter 9 reviews legibility considerations, and Chapter 10 shows how to use type.

TYPE DESIGN: A BRIEF HISTORY

Here's 550 years of typography in four minutes.

Although the Chinese and Koreans first invented movable type, Johann Gutenberg was the first Western printer to use it. Furthermore, Gutenberg solved the problem created by the different widths of letters. Understandably, his first typeface was a modified reproduction of the handwriting used to produce sacred works such as the Bible. From that point, printers modified type to reflect their tastes and cultures.

Although type was the first mass-produced item in history, nearly four centuries passed after Gutenberg produced his type before a typecasting machine was invented, and it was not until the end of the 19th century that the entire process became automated. By then, many of the great typefaces still commonly used today had already been designed.

William Caslon, for instance, was an English typographer who lived from 1692 to 1766. The rugged but dignified Caslon typeface has staying power. It was used in the American Declaration of Independence and the Constitution. More than 100 years after it was cut, it became popular again following its use in the first issue of *Vogue* magazine. In 1978 designer Peter Palazzo brought it back once more in modified form when he redesigned the *Chicago Daily News*. In 1750 another Englishman, John Baskerville, designed a face known by his name and still commonly used today. Giambattista Bodoni, an Italian printer, developed a face in 1760 that was the standard headline in American newspapers from the post–World War II era through the 1970s. In 1896 another Englishman,

William Morris, reacting to the conformity brought about by the Industrial Revolution, produced *The Works of Geoffrey Chaucer*. The Chaucer type he designed, combined with specialized initial letters and artistry in design and printing, reawakened an interest in printing as an art form. Because his typefaces are highly stylized and personal, they are not used today for mass-circulation publications, but his work influenced more than a generation of designers.

One of the people Morris influenced was Frederic Goudy, the first great American type designer. Goudy, founder of the Village Press, cut 125 faces, many of which are still used today. Goudy lived until 1946. At one time, the types he designed, including the one carrying his name, dominated the American press. They fell out of favor after World War II, but when the 1980s brought a revival of the classic faces, Goudy was dusted off.

The 1900s brought a host of typefaces. Some were new; others were modifications of classic faces. Century Expanded was cut in 1900, Cheltenham in 1902, Cloister Old Style in 1913, Baskerville Roman in 1915 and Garamond in 1918. The interval between the wars produced two startling new faces. Paul Renner designed Futura in 1927. Stanley Morrison produced Times New Roman for the *Times* of London in 1932. In 1972 the *Times* switched to Times Europa because it printed better on the newsprint it was using. Because of offset printing and improvements in the typeface from digital typesetting, the newspaper switched back to a revised Times New Roman in the mid-1980s. In 1991 the *Times* changed once again, this time to Times Millennium. Futura, a geometric sans serif face that is monotone in cut, ushered in an era of sans serif faces that brought us the popular Univers and Helvetica in the mid-1950s. Hermann Zapf is our most successful contemporary designer. In the 1950s, he designed both Optima and Palatino, the face used in the classic redesign of the *New York Herald Tribune*.

Most typefaces commonly used by newspapers and magazines today were designed before World War II. Tastes in type run in cycles, and some faces that are more than 200 years old are brought back periodically and modified to take advantage of technological innovations and modern tastes. The "modern faces," such as Helvetica, Univers and Optima, already are more than 40 years old, but they are mere infants in the life span of a typeface. The newspapers that rushed to embrace the modern look of Helvetica in the 1970s found themselves slightly out of step with fashion in the 1980s when the country began to turn back to traditional values. If the ubiquitous Helvetica is put on the shelf, it will be dusted off again later—maybe in 20 years, maybe in 50—just as the Caslons, Goudys and Bodonis keep reappearing.

The introduction of photocomposition essentially halted the design of new typefaces for use in general-circulation publications. Foundries were busy converting their libraries to negatives for the new photocomposition machines. Most of the work involved modifying existing faces to take advantage of the new technology but still adhere to copyright laws. Some of the alterations have distorted the type and lowered the quality. Digital typesetting ushered in the present era. Now that the old faces have been digitized, waves of new typefaces are washing over our computers. Software programs allow even amateurs to design typefaces or create hybrids out of existing faces. As could be expected, when amateurs gain access to the technology, the results are inconsistent at best, horrible at worst.

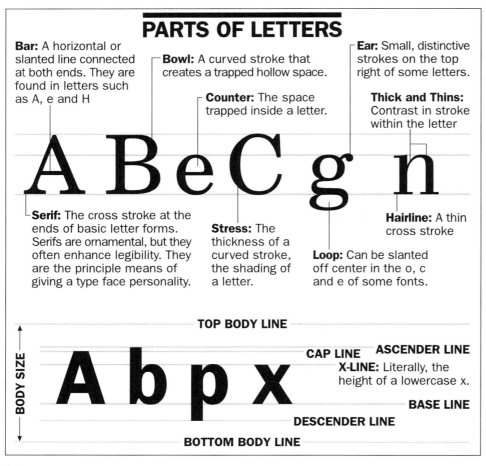

PARTS OF LETTERS

Bar: A horizontal or slanted line connected at both ends. They are found in letters such as A, e and H

Bowl: A curved stroke that creates a trapped hollow space.

Counter: The space trapped inside a letter.

Ear: Small, distinctive strokes on the top right of some letters.

Thick and Thins: Contrast in stroke within the letter

Serif: The cross stroke at the ends of basic letter forms. Serifs are ornamental, but they often enhance legibility. They are the principle means of giving a type face personality.

Stress: The thickness of a curved stroke, the shading of a letter.

Hairline: A thin cross stroke

Loop: Can be slanted off center in the o, c and e of some fonts.

BODY SIZE

TOP BODY LINE

CAP LINE   ASCENDER LINE

X-LINE: Literally, the height of a lowercase x.

BASE LINE

DESCENDER LINE

BOTTOM BODY LINE

8.3

Which brings us to you. If you're going to be a writer or editor, you must learn grammar. If you're going to be a designer, you must learn typography. This chapter is a start.

PARTS OF LETTERS

The basic unit of all type designs is the individual letter. Just as we classify trees by the bark, leaves or needles, and shape, we classify type by its individual parts. Here is a visual explanation of type (Fig. 8.3). From it, you can learn the basic vocabulary:

With these terms in mind, let's look at Bodoni. Bodoni is most easily recognized by the distinctive tail of the Q, which drops from the center and slopes to the right. The serifs join on the diagonal stroke of the W. The T has drooping serifs. The O, U and C are symmetrical; there is no distinctive loop. The strokes are composed of consistent thick and thin lines to give each letter a precise, balanced quality. The stress of such letters as O, G and P is vertical rather than rounded. The serifs attach to the strokes at right angles. Because of its classic and elegant feel, Bodoni appears often as the display type in fashion stories and advertisements.

QWTOUC
Bodoni Type

THE LANGUAGE OF TYPE

The basic vocabulary of type doesn't end with the individual letters. You'll also need to be familiar with the following terms:

You say capitals; typographers say *uppercase*. You say small letters; typographers say *lowercase*. Why? When type was set in wood and later even in metal, type was kept in drawers, called cases. The capitals were kept in the top or upper case; the small letters were kept in the lower case. The shorthand for this designation is "u&lc."

Some *fonts,* a complete set of characters in one style and size, come with a set of *small caps* or small capital letters, usually about 75 percent of normal. You have REGULAR CAPS & SMALL CAPS.

When you speak of type, be sure you differentiate between text and display. *Text* refers to type below 14 points; *display* type refers to type 14 points and larger.

For text and display type, but especially for text, you must control spacing between lines, letters and words to make the text easy to read.

Leading is the horizontal space between the lines. It is usually expressed as 9/10, which means 9-point type with 1 point between the lines; 10/12 means 10-point type with two points between the lines.

Letter spacing is the distance between letters. You control this with the tracking function. Normally, tight letter spacing increases the speed of reading and saves you space. You do not want to make the letters so tight that they become hard to read, however. Tracking controls the letter spacing in blocks of type; kerning controls the spacing between irregularly shaped letters (see Fig. 8.4). When you install your software, the default setting will give you precisely equal spacing between letters based on the farthest right hand part of the letter to the farthest left hand part of the next letter. However, some letter combinations appear to be farther apart than others, so kerning corrects this optical illusion. You should be especially careful to adjust the letters in display type to optical spacing because what appears to be irregular spacing is so obvious in large sizes. Most publications will create default settings in the kerning table for all text and display type that is regularly used. When you use another typeface that hasn't been adjusted, you will need to kern letter pairs individually.

Some fonts offer *ligatures,* two or more characters designed as a single unit. Common ligatures include the combinations of ff, ffi, fi, ffl and fl. A ligature has to be created by design, not by kerning. Here are some of the most common pairs that require kerning:

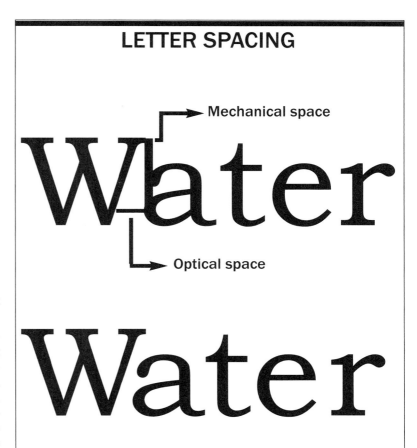

LETTER SPACING

Mechanical space

Optical space

8.4 Ironically, mechanical spacing is exactly the same but looks wrong. Optical spacing is uneven but looks right. Some letter combinations need to be moved closer together because the construction of the letters makes it appear that the space between them is not consistent with other letter pairs.

Yo We To Tr Wo Tu Tw Ya Te P.
Ty Wa yo we T. Y. Ta Pa Wa

Text has *color,* which is determined by the design of the text type. Type with uniform stroke weights will be darker than type with variation in stroke widths, called thicks and thins, which look grayer in large amounts of text type. Leading, letter and word spacing all affect the color. The less space you use, the darker or denser the text will look.

When you are debating which text type to select, one consideration is the amount of space it takes. You have already seen that the x-height is the size of the lowercase x. Because of variations in the length of the extenders, type in the same point size, shown here, can appear larger or smaller than another.

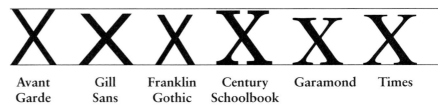

| Avant Garde | Gill Sans | Franklin Gothic | Century Schoolbook | Garamond | Times |

Typefaces also vary in width. To determine the width of a type, you check the *lowercase alphabet length* (LCA). The length of an entire lowercase alphabet of a single type size is called the lowercase alphabet length. The width of a type determines how many letters and words you can fit on a line, an important consideration at any publication. The LCA is figured on a character per pica (CPP) basis and computed by counting the average number of letters that will fit in a given horizontal space and dividing by the number of picas. Thus, if the average number of characters that will fit on a 10-pica line is 32, the CPP is 3.2. Unfortunately, even though the method of computing the alphabet lengths and CPP is standard, the results are not because of the way type producers have altered the face and spacing between letters. The CPP for Baskerville with italic when manufactured by Linotype in 10 point is 2.68; manufactured by Intertype, 2.35; and manufactured by Monotype, 2.48. When comparing the CPP counts of typefaces, it is critical for the designer to know the type manufacturer. Here is a visual demonstration of the differences in font widths. All these are 10-point samples:

abcdefghijklmnopqrstuvwxyz   Times New Roman
abcdefghijklmnopqrstuvwxyz   Century Schoolbook
abcdefghijklmnopqrstuvwxyz   Bookman Old Style

These are all set at normal width. However, fonts also come in narrower and wider versions. To describe variations of the *width* of a font, typographers use the terms ranging from condensed to expanded. In this computer age, the terms *compressed, narrow, thin* and *wide* sometimes are applied.

This is Helvetica regular
This is Helvetica narrow
This is Helvetica Expanded

In QuarkXpress, you can condense or expand type with the horizontal/vertical scaling function. While this is okay for a single title in a design, you should not use it frequently. The horizontal/vertical scaling function distorts the type. Each font, whether condensed or expanded, roman or italic, has its own proportions. When a software program is asked to condense or expand, it simply squishes or stretches the type. None of the proportions or niceties of the typeface are preserved.

Type also varies by *weight,* the degree of thickness of the letter strokes. Weights range from light to black. Popular types will offer several weight choices. Book weight is so named because that is the weight the designer intends for mass use in text sizes. Here is a sample of typical weight differences:

This is Franklin Gothic Book
This is Franklin Gothic Medium
This is Franklin Gothic Demi
This is Franklin Gothic Heavy

When you read type, you usually are viewing it as a *roman*. That's a *form* of type that means the letters are straight up and down, as this text is. You can also use *italic, letters slanted right*. Sans serif type, which means without serifs, also has an italic, although the technical name is **oblique**.

Now, let's see what happens when you put all the variations of width, weight and form together:

Garamond condensed bold
Garamond condensed italic

TYPE GROUPING

To enable typographers to communicate about type and ensure harmonious use, type has been organized into races, families and fonts. Race is the broadest system of categorization.

Unfortunately, typographers do not agree precisely on the number of categories. Having too many categories leaves typographers splitting hairlines, but having too few forces them to lump dissimilar type into the same race. The discussion in this book follows the guidelines of the authoritative *Composition Manual*, published by the Printing Industry of America. The six races are Roman, square serif, sans serif, text letter, cursive and ornamental.

Roman

The lowercase roman refers to the straight up-and-down design of the type as opposed to the italic or slanted-right version. Originally, that was an incorrect use of the term, but it has became so common that it is now widely accepted. For the purpose of identifying races, Roman with a capital R is also a classification of type that has serifs and thick-and-thin curved strokes, which distinguish it from another serif race, the square serifs. Some typographers believe Roman is too general a designation and refer instead to five categories within the race: old style, modern, transitional, clarendon and glyphic. For starters, it is enough to recognize the Roman race.

Bodoni is from the Roman race

Square serif

On square serif type, the strokes are nearly monotone in weight, and as the name suggests, the serifs are rectangles. Many of the square serifs have Egyptian-sounding names, such as Karnak and Egyptienne, because the design reflected the influence of hieroglyphs. Square serifs were first designed about 1815 to be used in advertising. They preceded sans serif by about 30 years.

Bookman is from the square serif race

Sans serif

Befitting the mood of the day, the 1850s brought sans serif type. *Sans* is the French word for *without,* and the type is without serifs. The type is easily identified not only by the lack of serifs but also by the uniformity in the strokes. Sans serif type became popular in the 1920s. The purpose of the design was to eliminate all flourishes, including serifs, and produce a type that served the function of communicating without any of the aesthetic benefits that serifs offer. In the United States the sans serif race was also referred to as gothic. The most popular sans serifs are Helvetica, Futura, Univers and Franklin Gothic.

Franklin Gothic the sans serif

Text letter

This race, also called black letter, has type that is medieval in appearance. It is the style that Gutenberg used to print the Bible. Its designers were influenced by Gothic architecture, which was popular at the time. Cloister Black, Old English and Goudy Text are examples of this race.

FetteFraktur is text letter

Cursive or script

This name is also self-descriptive. The type is a stylized reproduction of formal handwriting and is most often found in formal announcements of events such as weddings, anniversaries and graduations.

ExPonto Regular is from the cursive race

Ornamental or novelty

This race is a catchall for type that has been designed to portray a particular mood or emotion and is so unusual it cannot be used for other messages. The type is most frequently used in posters, movie advertising, cartoons and display advertising. Newspapers occasionally use a novelty type on features to reflect the content.

Mistral is from the ornamental race

FAMILIES

Like most families, type families share the same last name. Although they share genetic similarities, each family member also has unique characteristics. The differences are based on width, weight and form. Some families have several members; Caslon has at least 15, Cheltenham at least 18, and Univers nearly 30. The widths range from condensed to expanded; the weights from light to black. Most types have two different forms—roman and italic. When the type is available in special form, such as an outline or shadow version, it generally is classified under the novelty race.

Helvetica
Helvetica Black
Helvetica Light
Helvetica Narrow

FONTS

A font is a complete set of one member of a family. Nearly all families have fonts that include uppercase and lowercase type, punctuation and symbols; some include an alphabet of small caps. Some also have ligatures, such as ff, ffi, fi, ffl, and fl. Others have special symbols.

ABCDEFGHIJKLMNOPQRSTUVWXYZ
ABCDEFGHIJKLMNOPQRSTUVWXYZabcdefghijklmnopqrstu
vwxyz1234567890!@#$%^&*()_=[]{}\|;:'",<.>/?`~

IDENTIFYING TYPE

The Printing Industries of America has compiled the following list of 10 ways to identify typefaces:

1. Serifs. All type immediately breaks down into serif or sans serif, but the differences between types with serifs can be startling.

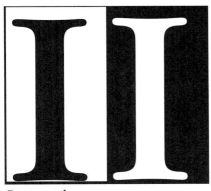
Garamond

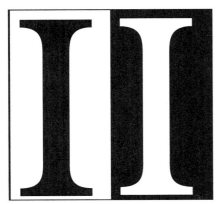
Bookman

Times

2. Terminations on top of the strokes of E, F or T. Note the differences in the terminations between Century Schoolbook and Times Roman:

EE, FF, TT

3. Weight of strokes. Are they thick or thin, and how much contrast is there?

Thick and thin <small>Bodoni</small>

Thick and thin <small>Bookman</small>

4. Shape of the rounded characters BCGOPQbcgopq. Are the bowls symmetrical or balanced diagonally? How is the weight distributed?

Bog Bog

Garamond   **Times New Roman**

Bog Bog

Palatino   **Bookman**

5. Length of descenders. Note the difference between Avant Garde and Futura in the same point size:

Avant Garde hy hy Futura

6. Formation of terminals on J and F. The curves or angles are good clues to the identity of the font.

Times Roman JF JF Garamond

7. Formation of the ears of the letters. Look particularly at the r.

Franklin Gothic r r Futura

8. The shapes of key letters of the font. Look at a, e, g, r, m and H.

Franklin Gothic/Futura

aa ee gg rr mm HH

9. General proportions of the letter. Is the bar of the H located above, below or at center? Are the letters equally proportioned or do they tend to be condensed or extended?

Futura H **H Techno**

10. Overall appearance on the page when the type is massed. What is its personality?

Most graphics editors and designers have a working knowledge of six to 12 typefaces. For additional faces, they consult a type book or look at fonts on the web. It is not necessary to memorize large numbers of typefaces, but you should become acquainted with those most commonly used in newspapers and, especially, the publications you read regularly. The popular sans serif Helvetica, for instance, is identifiable by its uniform but dignified cut. It has short extenders, a square dot on the lowercase i and j, a distinctive capital G and a straight tail on the capital Q, which is slanted and starts on the inside of the bowl. The stem of the a curves at the baseline.

Compare **Helvetica** to Franklin Gothic. Franklin Gothic to Futura.

Unfortunately, type identification is becoming increasingly difficult because of the barely distinguishable alterations performed for computer fonts. There is no effective protection for new typeface designs in the United States. The popular Helvetica, for instance, is produced with little or no variation under the names of Vega, Boston, Claro, Corvus, Galaxy, Geneva, Triumvirate, Helios, Swiss, American Gothic, Ag Book, Newton and Megaron. Optima is marketed by different manufacturers under the name of Chelmsford, Oracle, Orleans, Musica, Orsa and Zenith. Palatino also has several imitators, including Palateno, Elegante, Patina, Andover, Palladium, Pontiac, Michelangelo and Sistina. By whatever name they are known, however, they are still Helvetica, Optima and Palatino.

x-he**i**ght

9.1   All the letters in the word *x-height* are the same point size, but optically, they vary greatly. In this chapter you will learn how to account for x-height as you select type.

Reading is the most important part of the whole design. If you limit this—if you slow down the speed of reading— I think it is wrong.

Hermann Zapf
Typographer

9. Legibility of Type

For more than 70 years, researchers have been studying the variables that affect legibility. The findings have been enlarged significantly since Miles Tinker's pioneering studies in the 1920s. His work in later years, notably with D.G. Paterson, added significantly to the body of knowledge about legibility. The Merganthaler Linotype Company published *The Legibility of Type* in 1936 and a similar volume in 1947 in an attempt to distribute the research findings from the ivory tower to the grass-roots level. G.W. Ovink published *Legibility, Atmosphere-Value and Forms of Printing Types* in 1938. Sir Cyril Burt published the landmark *Psychological Study of Typography* in 1959. Tinker's 1963 *Legibility of Print* pulled together hundreds of studies that he and others had conducted. Bror Zachrisson and his colleagues at the Graphic Institute in Stockholm spent 10 years researching legibility variables and published the results in *Studies in Legibility of Printed Text* in 1965. Rolfe Rehe compiled the results of hundreds of tests in his 1979 book *Typography: How to Make It Most Legible*. The studies continue, but dissemination of the results to the people working with type daily in American newspapers still lags far behind the research.

For too long, knowledge of legibility has been buried in academic journals or limited to the province of professional consultants. The men and women who work on newspapers every day must have the opportunity to learn and understand the factors that affect legibility. The daily examples of type printed over an illustration, reversed, or set too small, too narrow or too wide indicate that many editors have still not awakened to the need to remove typographic barriers between the reporter and reader.

Perhaps the reason that many editors are just beginning to inquire about the proper use of type is that they now have more control over typesetting and the flexibility to be creative. Designers can directly control everything from letter spacing to line spacing, from weight and width choices to line length. Designers can wrap copy in any shape imaginable. This control is both liberating and daunting. It's liberating in that designs are exploding off the page with vigor. It's daunting in that designers must remember that their goal is to communicate, not to decorate. If readers can't follow the type or if the design slows reading appreciably, the designer has failed. Unread type is expensive. A new era has begun, and editors are asking the right questions. The new graphics design editors will need to have the answers.

This chapter distills the results of hundreds of legibility research projects, but it is not a substitute for reading the original research. Several studies and books referred to in this chapter are listed in the bibliographic sections at the end of the book.

LEGIBILITY CONSIDERATIONS

Legibility and readability are often confused. Legibility is the measurement of the speed and accuracy with which type can be read and understood. Readability is a measure of the difficulty of the content. Legibility research has been conducted by typographers, educators, journalists, printers and ophthalmologists, all of whom have a stake in the printed word.

Some research methods are more useful for testing legibility factors than others. Visibility measurements, for example, test reading speed by controlling the amount of light. This is useful for measuring the effect of contrast. Another method resembles the familiar eye test and measures what can be read at various distances. This test is most useful for work with large advertisements such as posters and billboards. Many other testing methods have been used through the years, but the most effective has been to measure reading speed while controlling all but one variable, such as line length.

Researchers have also been able to track eye movement by using still cameras, video cameras and various electrical devices. The results show that we read in saccadic jumps, the movements from fixed point to fixed point. For a split second when the reader pauses, reading occurs. The reader scans shapes, not individual letters, and fills in the context. The right half and upper portion of the letters are most helpful in character recognition. To illustrate how readers fill in the forms, one researcher gave this *xa*ple of * se*te*ce *it* mi*si*g l*tt*rs.

The results of all these tests are not uniform. Some of the discrepancies are attributable to incomplete control of the variables, others to the different measuring methods used. The measurement of legibility is an inexact science, but there are some general principles that can be extracted from the great body of research.

Legibility is determined by at least eight factors: (1) type design, (2) type size, (3) line width, (4) word spacing and letter spacing, (5) leading, or line spacing, (6) form, (7) contrast, and (8) reproduction quality.

In real life, the reader's reading ability and interest in the text also affect the speed of reading, but these variables are separate from the selection and display of the type. In testing, reader interest is controlled by comparing results against a control group. By the same token, the quality of reproduction, which depends on the paper and printing process, is important. In tests, researchers can control reproduction quality carefully. Editors, unfortunately, can't. The newspaper is printed on an off-white, flimsy paper called newsprint. The texture is disagreeable, and the resulting contrast between the black type and the background is not as good as that found in magazines using coated paper. However, other variables that contribute to legibility can be manipulated with little or no expense to the newspaper. The most important factor to remember is that no one variable can be taken by itself. For instance, leading requirements change as the type and line width change; if the type size is changed, several other variables must be altered also.

Type design

For text, the basic type choice is serif or sans serif. It is not a choice to be made lightly. In recent years, several newspapers have had to spend thousands of dollars changing their text font after readers complained loudly. A study conducted in 1974 for the American Newspaper Publishers Association by Hvistendahl and Kahl (1975) found that roman type was read seven to 10 words a minute faster than sans serif type. The serif body typefaces that were used included Imperial, Royal and variations of Corona; the sans serif faces were Helvetica, Futura, Sans Heavy and News Sans. The researchers found that the subjects in the study read the serif text faster, and two-thirds said they preferred it. This study confirmed the earlier work by Tinker and Paterson (1929), who found that a sans serif face was read 2.2 percent more slowly than a roman face (Dowding 1957). Robinson et al. (1971) found it took 7.5 percent more time to read sans serif than roman type. Serifs help identify small letters.

This limited research does not mean that newspapers should never use sans serif in text. Some newspapers and magazines use sans serif through-

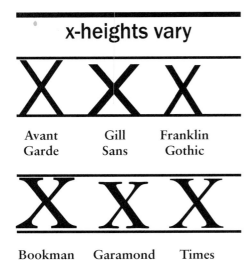

9.2 The point size is the same, but the x-height is different. The x-height is what gives the font the appearance of its size, and it is more important than the point size. The x's in this example are all the same point size.

out. It does mean, however, that editors might want to consider restricting its use to special sections or features. For instance, some newspapers that use a serif for most text use sans serif in the personality, people or newsmaker features. It is also used successfully in cutlines.

Weight should be medium or slightly heavier. Readers do notice the difference. The *St. Louis Post-Dispatch*'s ombudsman wrote, "Probably the most frequently heard request is for darker print. Many of you tell me you have to carry the paper into brighter light—maybe to a window—in order to read the text of news stories. The printing is so light as to be hard on the eyes, I keep hearing, even to the point of threats of cancellation, sometimes" (Fiquette 1993, p. 2).

Mass circulation publications use only a handful of the serif text faces. Corona, Ionic No. 5, Imperial, Times Roman and Excelsior have proved themselves on newsprint. The *Los Angeles Times* once used Paragon. The *St. Louis Post-Dispatch* used Dutch811 from Bitstream in its 1997 redesign. Bookman is a distinguished text type, but some typographers shy away from it because it takes more space than most of the other commonly used faces. Other text possibilities include Utopia, Poynter, Cheltenham, Newton, Plantin and Century.

Like all type, most of these text faces have been marketed by different companies under different names. To guide your type search, here are some of the common synonyms:

- Ionic No. 5, News No. 9, No. 10, Regal and IC
- Times New Roman, Times 2 New Roman, English Times, Times Roman and TR
- Excelsior, Paragon and Opticon, News No. 14, Regal and EX
- Corona, Aurora, Crown, Nimbus, News No. 2, No. 3, No. 5, No. 6, Royal and CR
- Imperial, Bedford, New Bedford, News No. 4 and Gazette
- Book Antiqua, Palatino and Zapf Calligraphic

Type size

The proper size of type is closely related to the line width and subject matter. Tinker (1963) found that moderate type sizes (9 to 12 points) are the easiest to read. A discussion of type sizes in points, however, can be misleading. The x-height is a more accurate measurement of the actual size of the type (Fig. 9.2). When testing legibility, Poulton (1955) had to use 9.5-point Univers and 12-point Bembo to equalize the x-heights. Another researcher found that 60-point Univers Bold, 72-point Caslon Bold and 85-point Bodoni Bold were needed to get an x-height of 12.6 mm. The x-height of Linotron's 9-point Helvetica is 4.8 points, but its Caledonia is 3.8. The difference is in the length of the extenders. If there are long extenders, the distance between the base line and x-line is smaller; if there are short extenders, the size of the bowl is larger and the type appears larger. X-height, then, is the critical determinant of type size.

A smaller type size can be used for reference material such as sports scores, box summaries or classified ads because readers don't read large amounts of it. When the columns are wider, as for editorials, a larger type size may be appropriate. Depending on the x-height, 11- or 12-point type is appropriate for material set wider than 18 picas. *A rule of thumb is that type can be used twice the width of its size.*

In 1980 one-third of U.S. and Canadian newspapers were setting text type less than 9 points. Even though most newspapers are now using type at nine points or larger, more needs to be done. Editors reluctant to lose space to larger type are ignoring a significant portion of the potential audience. Poindexter (1978) found that 8.5 percent of the nonreaders did not read newspapers because of poor eyesight. A Gannett researcher found that 16 percent of the subscribers wanted larger type and that the percentage was even higher among people over 50, who are among the most loyal newspaper readers. Another newspaper found that one-third of its readers wanted larger type (Curley, J. 1979). Newspapers, which use column widths ranging from 11 to 15 picas, should use type between 9 and 10 points with a good x-height.

One of the most popular text faces is Times, also known as English Times, Times Roman or New Times Roman. It is popular because it often is included in pagination software packages. Times has a modest x-height but uses space economically. It is a good compromise between x-height and character width. However, Times is more legible at 10 points than at 9. By contrast, Corona, Olympian, Utopia, Nimrod and Ionic have larger x-heights and are adequate at 9 points. Depending on the age of the audience, however, any editor should consider setting text type closer to 9.5.

Line width

In newspapers, column widths range from slightly less than 9 picas to 15 picas, but all run bastard settings even wider. Some newspapers do not have a standard setting for pages without ads. The *St. Petersburg Times* permits settings between 11 and 22.6 picas for its 9-point Century Schoolbook.

Newspaper column widths have historically been shaped by advertising rather than by legibility considerations. Advertising is sold by the column inch, and eight columns produce more column inches than five or six columns, even though the total space on the page doesn't change. Consequently, newspapers were loath to change to a six-column format even when it became commonly known that it produced a more legible line length. Such a change also required a sizable increase in advertising rates on a column-inch basis to maintain the same income per page. As a result, some newspapers converted to a nine-column advertising format and a six-column news format.

The six-column format was an improvement over the eight-column format because the line widths are between 12 and 14 picas for most newspapers. Tinker and Paterson (1929) found that a line width of 18 to 24 picas provides the easiest reading when 10-point type is used. This width provides 10 to 12 words per line, which they found to be the optimal number. Because most newspapers use type of about 9 points, the 12- to 14-pica range produces nearly the same number of words per line. Hvistendahl and Kahl (1975) found that the highest reading speed was obtained when they set serif type in 14-pica columns.

In the 1980s advertising again forced a change in column widths. In its first-ever attempt to standardize columns to attract national advertisers, the industry settled on a format that reduced column widths to about 12.2 picas in the six-column format. That width is nearly the same as it was when newspapers had eight columns but wider pages.

All newspapers use bastard settings. Any setting is legible in small amounts, but when stories go beyond approximately 10 inches, the designer

SPACING

Regular spacing: The spacing between letters also affects the speed of reading. By tightening letterspacing, more words can be printed in the same amount of space. With proper handling, this can increase reading speed. Condensed type in particular, whether text or display, should not have a large amount of letterspacing.

Set too tight: Up to the point that the letters lose their shape, the closer the letters are, the faster we will read them because we will take in more of them during eye pause. However, every letter needs some space around it, or it loses recognizable form.

9.3 When you don't allow enough space between letters, the eye cannot quickly recognize the shapes of the words. However, the standard letter spacing that exists in your software often is looser than it needs to be.

should consider changing the size and leading to accommodate a setting wider than 18 to 20 picas.

Word and letter spacing

We read by perceiving shapes and groups of words. If words are widely spaced like this, it slows reading speed considerably. More stops are necessary, and words must be read as individual units rather than as parts of phrases. For newspaper purposes, type is read most comfortably when word spacing is between 3 to the em and 4 to the em. An em is the square space of the letter m in the type size being used. The term *3 to the em* means one-third of an em spacing. Word spacing should not be greater than the leading.

The spacing between letters also affects reading speed. Tight letter spacing allows more words to be printed in the same amount of space. With proper handling, this can increase reading speed. Condensed type in particular, whether text or display, should not have a large amount of letter spacing.

Up to the point that the letters lose their shape, the closer the letters, the faster we will read them because we will take in more of them during each eye pause. However, every letter needs some space around it, or it loses its recognizable form (Fig. 9.3).

Leading

The correct amount of leading depends on the width of the line and the size and design of the type. Unleaded material generally slows reading speed (Becker et al. 1970), but too much leading can have the same effect. For newspapers that have columns in the 12- to 15-pica range and use 9-point type, Tinker (1963) found that 1-point leading is desirable. He also found that 10-point type set solid (no leading) was read faster and was more pleasing to readers than 8-point type with 2-point leading (Fig. 9.4). However, newspapers can easily use a half point of leading, which saves space without significantly reducing legibility. Less leading, however, does change the color or airiness of the page.

There are some situations in which the designer will have to apply common sense because research does not answer all the questions. For instance:

1. Type with a large x-height generally needs more leading than type with a small x-height. The large x-height has shorter descenders and gives the impression of less space between lines.
2. Sans serif type generally needs more leading than serif type because sans serif has a strong vertical flow, and leading will counteract this. Serif type with a strong vertical stress, such as Bodoni, also needs more leading.
3. Leading for headlines can be much tighter than for body copy because the type is large and consists of only a few words. In fact, some newspapers have gone to minus leading in headlines. For instance, try setting 24- and 30-point headlines at minus 2-point leading; type above 36 points can be set at minus 4-point leading.

Form

The design of the type and how it is used affects legibility. For newspaper and magazine purposes, editors are primarily concerned with the legibility of text type between 9 and 12 points. Readers prefer moderate designs—neither too condensed nor too extended—for textual material. The shape of the bowls and, for serif type, the design of the serifs are also factors. The space within the bowls determines legibility (Roethlein 1912), which is why boldface is slower to read in large quantities. Boldface type has heavier lines and less white space within the letters (Fig. 9.5). If you compare a typewritten page from a typewriter that has not been cleaned against one that has, you'll see that it's far more difficult to read a page when the letters are filled in. If the serifs are too fine, they may not reproduce well on newsprint in small sizes. That's why some modern serif types such as Bodoni, with its thin serifs, are not used as text type. Among the sans serif types, the differentiation among letters is even more important than it is for serif faces. News Gothic has been successful in this regard (Poulton 1955).

Once the typeface is selected, the editor must decide how emphasis will be added. **Boldface in small amounts is a good method;** *italic type is another.* But both of these forms are harder to read in volume. Tinker (1963) concluded that "the use of italics should be restricted to those rare occasions when added emphasis is needed." In display use, however, bold and italic forms do not affect legibility because of the size and number of words involved.

Text or headlines in all-capital letters should be avoided, except as special treatment, because it slows reading and displeases readers. Because readers perceive shapes, IT IS MORE DIFFICULT TO READ ALL-CAP MATERIAL. THE SHAPES BECOME UNIFORM, AND THE READER IS FORCED TO LOOK AT INDIVIDUAL LETTERS RATHER THAN AT WORDS AND PHRASES. A headline style that requires capitalization of the first letter of the first word and proper nouns only is more legible than one

LEADING

9 pt. with no leading

FranklinGothic
The amount of leading required depends upon the width of the line, x-height and design of the type. For newspaper purposes, 9-pt. type set at 12 to 14 picas should have about 1 pt. of leading.

Bookman
The amount of leading required depends upon the width of the line, x-height and design of the type. For newspaper purposes, 9-pt. type set at 12 to 14 picas should have about 1 pt. of leading.

9 pt. with 1 pt. leading

FranklinGothic
The amount of leading required depends upon the width of the line, x-height and design of the type. For newspaper purposes, 9-pt. type set at 12 to 14 picas should have about 1 pt. of leading.

Bookman
The amount of leading required depends upon the width of the line, x-height and design of the type. For newspaper purposes, 9-pt. type set at 12 to 14 picas should have about 1 pt. of leading.

9 pt. with 3 pt. leading

FranklinGothic
The amount of leading required depends upon the width of the line, x-height and design of the type. For newspaper purposes, 9-pt. type set at 12 to 14 picas should have about 1 pt. of leading.

Bookman
The amount of leading required depends upon the width of the line, x-height and design of the type. For newspaper purposes, 9-pt. type set at 12 to 14 picas should have about 1 pt. of leading.

9.4 Leading, the space between lines, is a function of the design of the type and the width of the line. For maximum legibility at newspaper line lengths, you should be around one point. Slightly more will make your page a little lighter. Too much, and you will slow reading speed.

FILLING BOWLS AND COUNTERS

eop

Times regular

eop

Times bold

eop

Helvetica regular

eop

Helvetica bold

9.5 The bolder the type, the less space there is inside the bowls and counters. The more open the letters, the faster we can read them. However, bold display type is not a legibility problem because of the type size and few words. A small amount of bold text, such as in a cutline, is also not a problem.

Type reversed slows reading speed 15 to 20 percent. The contrast is the same, so why the difference? It's because we read by shapes, not by individual letters. We don't recognize the shapes of type when it is reversed, so we have to slow down and look at the words and letters. Reverse type offers some dramatic possibilities for the designer, however. The fact that it is slower to read this copy doesn't mean you should never use it.

This paragraph is set in 11 pt. Times New Roman. You can compensate for most legibility problems by changing other variables. Even though this line length is a bit short for 11 pt. type, you can see that the copy is easier to read. That's because the type is larger. If you want to reverse type, do it in small amounts and increase the type size. Consider running 12-24 pt. type as a teaser.

9.6 Because reverse type takes nearly 20 percent longer to read, designers avoid it except for small amounts. The larger the type size, the easier it is to read in reverse.

that requires capitalization of all words. In addition, the more capitals used, the more space required. All-cap style in text headlines is not economical. An occasional headline or title in all caps, however, has no effect on legibility.

Another aspect of form that is increasingly coming into question is whether to justify the copy to produce an even right margin or to run it unjustified (ragged right). The research to date suggests that there is no significant difference in reading speed between justified and ragged right copy (Fabrizio et al. 1967). Hartley and Barnhill (1971) found no significant differences in reading speed when the line length was determined by grammatical constraints and hyphenation was avoided whenever possible, when about 33 percent of the lines were hyphenated, or when type was set ragged right over double column formats of varying widths.

Although there may be no difference in reading speed between justified and unjustified lines, there certainly is a difference in appearance. Justified type in narrow newspaper columns requires a great deal of hyphenation and causes variation in the space between words. Unjustified type permits the editor to standardize the word spacing and avoid illogical breaks in words. The choice of justified or ragged right type is reduced to a question of personality. The *Hartford Courant* claims it was the first American newspaper to use ragged right throughout the newspaper.

Justified type is formal, and the orderliness of the margins gives a feeling of precision and control, factors that may enhance a news product. Ragged right type is informal, more relaxed, less precise. Consequently, it may be more appropriate for feature and commentary sections. If ragged right is chosen, it is preferable to use a modified ragged right type, which permits hyphenation whenever a line is less than an established minimum length, such as 50 percent of the potential line. This eliminates unusually short lines, which are noticed for their length rather than their message.

Ragged left type should be avoided except in small amounts. If the reader doesn't have a fixed left hand margin, reading speed is seriously impaired. Ragged left should never be used in textual material of any significant length.

Contrast

The contrast in color between the type and its background is another important factor in legibility. Black on white offers great contrast and therefore is legible. (Black on yellow is even more legible, but who wants to recreate yellow journalism?) The reverse, however, is not true. White print on a black background slows reading speed significantly (Holmes 1931). The dramatic effect that can be achieved by reversing type must be balanced against the loss of legibility. Reversed type should be used only in small quantities, such as a paragraph or two, and in larger-than-normal text type, such as at least 14 points. When it is not, the copy often becomes unreadable (Fig. 9.6).

Be careful when color tints are used over text type. Screen the color back to 5 or 10 percent. If the story goes longer than 10 inches, consider increasing the type size. Black print on yellow paper and red print on white paper have scored well in legibility tests (Tinker 1963).

Newspapers are fighting an increasingly difficult battle to produce a legible product. As newsprint prices have increased, paper quality has decreased. In the mid-1970s, in an attempt to restrain increasing costs, newsprint mills dropped the basis weight of newsprint from 32 to 30. The lighter paper is cheaper, but according to an analysis by the Knight-Ridder group, it has caused expensive web breaks and reduced printing quality. Now some newspapers are using even thinner paper. Unless new inks are developed, the result for newspapers will be more show-through of ink from one side of the page to the other. This in turn will decrease legibility.

Reproduction quality

If the quality of newsprint continues to decrease, it will become even more difficult to control other variables, such as camera and press work, which affect the reproduction quality. Offset presses need good-quality paper. As the basis weight for newsprint decreases, the pressroom operators have to work even harder to control the amount of ink. Unfortunately, there is a limit to how much the operators can do to prevent show-through with lighter-weight paper. The introduction of color in newspapers has stemmed the trend toward a lighter weight of paper because good color quality demands a heavier paper. Although the texture of the paper does not directly affect legibility, it does affect the reader's attitude toward the product. It is almost impossible to read a newspaper these days without getting ink all over your hands and clothes.

SELECTING TEXT TYPE

Although x-height, set width and color are important in selecting a display typeface, many editors put a premium on aesthetics and trends. Text type, however, is less susceptible to trends. It is the workhorse of the newspaper—not much appreciated, but if readers start to notice it, the publication is in trouble.

Earlier in this chapter, we cited several text typefaces that will work well. All of them meet the basic criteria: uniform or nearly uniform stroke widths, good x-height and shorter-than-average set width. In addition, whichever typeface is selected, editors ought to use medium weight or slightly bolder than medium weight.

The problem for newspapers is that the faces with the best x-height usually have the widest set width or longest lowercase alphabet. For instance, Olympian and Corona have large x-heights but also produce fewer letters per line. Times New Roman and Utopia have slightly smaller x-heights but offer more letters per line. To compensate, some newspapers are altering the set width of the text type. That way the large x-height can be preserved while increasing the number of characters per line. Another compromise is to drop the leading from one point to approximately one-half point. Editors should be careful, though, not to damage legibility in order to jam more text onto the page.

Editors should avoid the temptation to change the size of type without considering the line width, leading and type design. Editors must eschew the dramatic at times to produce the legible. Nevertheless, every factor discussed here can be violated to a minimal extent. Type can be reversed if it is done in small quantities and in larger type. Screening type decreases contrast and thus legibility, but as a labeling device it can be effective. A 5 or 10 percent screen over type should be used only on short stories. If the story is longer and a screen is used, increase the type size. There is no doubt that all-caps type is more difficult to read than lowercase, but a two- or three-word headline in all caps is not going to affect reading speed. All these factors should be considered in relation to one another.

One application of these factors is in sports agate. (Agate is a metal-type term meaning 5 1/2 points; these days, agate simply refers to the small type used to list sports standings and results.) Most newspapers run the sports standings in 7 or 8 points. Much of the material is in tables—league standings, batting averages, and so on. You can use the space more efficiently by going to a seven- or eight-column grid. Readers who look at sports agate don't read it as they do text. They scan and select. That's why smaller type is acceptable, although it does rule out perhaps 10 percent of the readership. Beyond that, you can get more type in the same amount of space because the narrower column results in less space between tabular columns. Sans serif is the popular choice because the smaller the type, the less likely the serifs will reproduce well.

10.1 Our ability to communicate with type goes beyond the literal. By the selecting of the font, by the size and placement of the words, we can add meaning and richness to our messages, as the designer did when merging truth and rumor.

A message that we hear is soon forgotten, but the one that we see and read is more permanent because it penetrates memory on more than one level and can be referred to over and over again. This explains the growing significance of typography as a world-wide communication tool—a tool that we must improve steadily by studying it as we use it.

Will Burton
Typographer

10. Using Type

Just as the clothes we wear reveal our personality, the type used to dress our newspaper says a great deal about the publication. Type is an essential part of a newspaper's personality. Imagine reader reaction if the *New York Times*' nameplate was set in Helvetica:

The New York Times

Or if *USA Today* were set in a text letter font:

𝕌𝕊𝔸 𝕋𝕠𝕕𝕒𝕪

Those type choices would be as inappropriate as wearing a T-shirt to a formal dinner party. Researchers have shown that laypeople are able to attribute characteristics to type similar to those used by professionals (Tannenbaum et al. 1964) and that the selection of a correct typeface appears to make more difference with some types of content than with others (Haskins 1958). Benton (1979) found that the sans serif face Helvetica was not perceived as differing significantly from serif faces Garamond, Bodoni, Palatino and Times Roman, except that Helvetica was considered more modern. For years many newspapers used a lighter type in the women's section than elsewhere. Haskins and Flynne (1974) found that even though readers ascribed feminine characteristics to certain typefaces, the use of those faces in the section did not affect readership. Not enough research has been done to determine whether readership is enhanced by appropriate typefaces, but it is generally conceded that type does have a connotative effect. That is, type communicates an emotion, a feeling. The successful designer uses type with the understanding that the form is part of the message and not merely a decoration.

We discussed text type in Chapter 9. This chapter will look at selecting and using display type.

HEADLINE TYPE CHOICES

Headlines are the bridge between the reader and the story. Readers scan 70 to 80 percent of the headlines and decks and choose which they wish to cross. Considering that readers look at about 25 percent of the stories, it is obvious that headlines play an important role in attracting readership. That's why designers should be concerned not only with the selection of the display faces but also with the formats and wording of headlines.

The selection of a proper headline typeface rests on legibility considerations, the image the editors wish to project, the tradition that needs to be preserved and the mood and lifestyle of the community. After World War II, Americans were hungry to improve their lives. A home, two cars and vacations became possible for millions. Americans trashed the old and devoured the new. During a period like that, modern-looking typefaces such as Helvetica and Univers had a strong appeal. Moods change, however. When the oil embargo overturned the world economy in the late 1970s, Americans first elected a president who preached self-denial and then one who advocated a return to traditional values. Throughout the country, there was a strong yearning for the "good old days," and political conservatism enjoyed a revival.

The theme of the administration that took office in 1981 was "A New Beginning," but it was based on a return to classic American values. At that time, many American newspapers going through redesigns selected classic typefaces instead of the more modern ones. The *Dallas Times Herald* and the *Los Angeles Times* adopted Times New Roman. The *Kansas City Star* chose Goudy Bold. The *Milwaukee Journal* adopted Baker Argentine. All these are serif typefaces. Times change; tastes change. There is no "right" display face. Type should be chosen on the basis of its legibility, its connotative image, its credibility and the mood of the community in which the paper is published. Type is a large part of the newspaper's personality. To check the personality of your paper, draw up a list of opposite characteristics (traditional/modern, credible/not credible, old/young, aggressive/passive, cold/warm) and put them on a scale of 1 to 7. Compare the staff's perception with that of an audience sample. This kind of measurement is also a good way to field-test a proposed type change.

ASSURING CONTRAST

Contrast is as important to typography as harmony is to a choir. Publications with a single headline weight are as interesting as a one-note singer. Fortunately, you have several ways to provide contrast in the display face. The easiest—and safest—is to choose one typeface with two or more weights. Here, compliments of Shakespeare, is a line from *As You Like It* in Times Roman with bold in the main head and medium weight in the deck.

All the world is a stage

And all the men and women merely players

One font with two or more weights assures you of concord, the blending of typographic elements to give a uniform impression. Although it is possible to ensure concord by using the same serif font for your text—Times Roman would be one choice—most publications switch to another serif for text. That's because most fonts that work at display sizes do not work in text sizes. Whatever the choice, the bold-light interplay offers contrast. The basic headline face is usually in the medium-to-bold range. Many newspapers use a black or heavy version of the face for the lead story only. Different weights are used most effectively in subordinate type—the decks, readouts and blurbs. As an alternative, some newspapers alternate bold and light or medium weights in main heads throughout the page. This approach is more suited to a paper with a vertical format. The two weights help to solve the problem of tombstoning, the bumping of headlines in adjacent columns.

Now let's stay within Times Roman but add another layer of contrast by changing the form of the deck from roman to italic.

All the world is a stage

And all the men and women merely players

Italic is the most common form variation, but condensed is another popular choice. Condensed offers you a better count for headlines, too.

	Display	Avant Garde Gothic*	Bauhaus*	Bembo	Bodoni	Bookman*	Caslon*	Century*	Cheltenham*	Franklin Gothic*	Futura	Garamond*	Gill Sans	Helvetica	Kabel*	Korinna*	Optima	Palatino	Quorum*	Souvenir*	Times Roman	Univers	Zapf Book*
Text																							
Avant Garde Gothic*		1	1	1	1	1	1	1	3	1	1	2	3	1	1	1	2	1	1	1	3	1
Bauhaus*		3	1	1	1	1	1	1	1	2	2	1	2	2	2	1	2	1	2	1	1	3	1
Bembo		1	1	3	1	1	2	2	1	1	2	2	2	1	1	2	1	1	2	1	2	1	1
Bodoni		1	1	1	1	1	2	2	1	1	1	1	1	1	2	3	2	1	1	1	2	1	3
Bookman*		1	1	1	1	1	1	2	2	1	1	1	1	1	1	2	2	1	2	1	1	1	2
Caslon*		1	2	2	2	1	1	2	2	1	2	2	1	1	1	3	2	1	2	1	2	1	2
Century*		1	2	2	2	2	2	1	1	1	2	2	1	1	1	3	2	1	2	1	3	1	2
Cheltenham*		1	1	1	1	2	2	1	1	1	2	1	1	1	1	2	1	2	2	1	1	2
Franklin Gothic*		3	1	1	1	1	1	1	1	1	1	1	1	1	2	3	1	1	1	1	1	3	1
Futura		3	3	1	1	1	1	1	2	1	1	3	3	2	1	3	1	2	1	1	1	3	1
Garamond*		1	2	3	1	1	2	2	1	2	1	1	1	1	2	2	1	2	2	2	1	1
Gill Sans		2	2	1	1	1	1	1	1	2	1	1	1	2	1	1	2	2	1	1	3	1
Helvetica		3	1	1	1	1	1	1	1	3	1	1	1	1	1	1	1	1	1	1	3	1
Kabel*		2	3	1	1	1	1	1	3	3	1	3	3	2	1	2	1	2	1	1	3	1
Korinna*		1	1	1	2	2	1	1	3	1	1	1	1	1	1	1	2	1	2	1	1	2
Quorum*		2	2	1	1	1	1	1	1	1	2	1	1	3	1	1	2	1	2	1	2	1
Optima		2	1	1	1	1	1	1	1	1	1	2	1	1	1	1	1	1	1	1	1	2
Palatino		1	2	3	1	1	2	2	2	1	3	2	2	1	1	2	2	1	1	1	2	2	1
Souvenir*		1	1	1	1	2	1	1	2	1	1	2	1	1	1	1	1	1	1	1	1	2
Times Roman		1	2	2	2	1	2	3	1	1	2	2	1	1	1	2	2	1	2	1	1	1	2
Univers		3	3	1	1	1	1	1	1	3	3	1	3	3	3	1	2	1	2	1	1	1	1
Zapf Book*		1	1	1	3	2	2	2	2	1	1	1	1	1	2	1	2	1	2	1	2	2	1

Legend:
1 - Combine at will
2 - Not a conservative choice
3 - Think again

—ITC TYPEFACE

10.2 ITC offers this chart for mixing typefaces, but it must be applied carefully in newspapers, where several typefaces sit on the same page. In a magazine or brochure, where there would be few display heads on the page, some mixtures are more acceptable.

All the world is a stage
And all the men and women merely players

There are even more layers of contrast available. This time, let's go to the sans serif race to use Franklin Gothic as the deck head. That provides contrast of weight and race.

All the world is a stage
And all the men and women merely players

Many newspapers use typefaces from different races in their basic formats, and most are better for it. But if the proper types are not matched, the effect will be the same kind of clash that results from mixing a striped shirt with plaid slacks. The International Typeface Corporation has published a chart with suggestions for type interplay (Fig. 10.2). They are bold enough to suggest even mixing typefaces within the same race. Be careful, though. There is a difference between type use in an advertisement or a magazine spread and selecting typefaces for something as repetitive as newspaper headline formats. If you are going to mix typefaces in a headline schedule, *go outside the race*. The most common pairing of races is serif and sans serif. You can also mix square serif with sans serif. Text letter, cursive and ornamental are not logical choices for a headline schedule because they are harder to read. However, if you use any of them for a one-time feature title, you can always use sans serif, the neutral race, for contrast.

Traditionally, newspapers have relied on more than one size of type. Size variation not only breaks the page monotony but also communicates to readers your news judgment. The more important the story, the larger the headline. The *Wall Street Journal* lacks type hierarchy on its front page, but nearly every other newspaper in the United States starts with large headlines at the top and uses smaller as it progresses down the page. Most papers will use a large horizontal headline again at the bottom of the page. The size of headlines depends on the newspaper's personality, whether it is a street edition or home delivery and the weight of the font. Some metropolitan papers use headlines even exceeding 100 points for street editions; others never exceed 48 points for a lead story. Newspapers such as the *Sedalia Democrat*, which uses Franklin Gothic Heavy, do not need as much size to carry a page (Fig. 10.3). *The heavier the weight, the less size you need for impact.* The banner on the *Democrat* is 72

10.3 The heavier the weight, the less size you need to achieve the same level of impact. This banner headline is in Franklin Gothic Demi, just one step down from the boldest weight in the family, Franklin Gothic Heavy.

points. However, metropolitan papers often range above 80 points for street sales editions.

In the 15,000-circulation *Jacksonville* (Ill.) *Journal-Courier*, the lead headline on the Region page is 60-point Franklin Gothic Heavy, a sans serif (Fig. 10.4). The feature head, "A LITTLE MET-TLE," is approximately 80 points, but it is still not as loud as the smaller lead head because of the weight difference. Size is important, but you think about size in connection with the type weight. Together, they speak softly or loudly.

WORKING WITH DISPLAY TYPE

Once you have built contrast in your display schedule, turn your attention to the content. Content depends directly on the format. Headlines inform and entertain. They make history, incite emotion and cause people to laugh or cry. In most cases, however, they are dull.

Newspaper headline writers have been straitjacketed into some unusual formats. Once, it was fashionable to write headlines that exactly filled each line. At another time, headlines had one to two counts less in each succeeding line—the stepped-down format. Narrow columns and capitalization requirements further restrict the ability of headline writers to tell and sell stories. Developments in newspaper design that accompanied the introduction of cold type eased some of the restrictions but also took away an essential element of the headline—the deck. Functionalism was incorrectly interpreted to mean that decks were superfluous. When designers eliminated decks, they overlooked the fact that decks allow headline writers to tell the story more fully and accurately. The elimination of decks for design purposes was a case of form over content. Both form and content are served by the increased use of well-chosen display type. Regardless of size, headlines average six words. That's not much space to tell and sell the story. Bring on the subordinate type.

For the most part, the decks that are reappearing are decks only in the sense that they are subordinate to the main head. Traditionally, decks were one column wide and three or more lines deep and had to be written to fit a tyrannical count system. Now type that is subordinate to the main head appears in a variety of formats: traditional decks, summary decks, blurbs, quotes and summary boxes. The traditional deck still must be written to fit, although the format no longer is always vertical. Easier-to-write, horizontal decks are becoming common. Traditional decks usually are one-half the size of the main head and must conform to a strict count, just as the main heads do. Some of the subordinate head styles avoid the restrictions of count.

The *Tampa Tribune* may have been the first newspaper in the United

10.4 Franklin Gothic Heavy provides the designer with a font that identifies the lead story on the page. It is significantly bolder than any other headline on the page.

States to use summary decks, and now many papers are using them. In the early 1980s the *Tribune* introduced what it called nut graphs. By whatever name—they are also known as summary decks, key decks, lead-ins and WHATTAA graphs (What's This All About?)—they are an effective way of getting more display type into a small amount of space. The summary deck, usually written in 14- to 16-point type, can offer 10 to 20 words in less space. Many newspapers write them in complete sentences, not headlinese. Some introduce them with a word or two, usually in boldface:

County ponders real estate transfer tax revenue

Faced with a $2 million deficit, officials have not ruled any tax out, but they are focusing on transfer tax

Some papers use bold on the first couple of words without the label introduction. Bold is used initially to draw more attention to the deck. Some editors and designers are uncomfortable with the relatively light weight present in 16-point type. By putting the first couple of words or the first phrase in bold or even heavy type, the designer can draw the reader's eye to the deck without sacrificing all the contrast of weight:

Two killed, two injured in shooting near Denver

Police believe that the attack in a posh suburb was planned; police tell residents that killers have fled

Some newspapers set the entire summary deck in bold type. In doing so, they forgo the contrast of weight.

Unlike traditional decks, which are written to specific counts for each line, editors write summary decks without regard for count and often without regard for the number of lines. A designer can accommodate a difference of one or two lines in 16-point type.

The format has three strengths. First, it offers scanners more information than the traditional deck format. The *Albany Times Union, Akron Beacon Journal* and *Los Angeles Times* average about 12 words in summary decks.

The *Atlanta Journal Constitution* averages 14, and the *Des Moines Register*, 19. That means summary decks ought to be able to entice more people to read the story. Second, even if scanners read the headline and deck and still choose not to read the story, they have more information than they would with the traditional format. Third, the format is space efficient. A traditional 24-point, three-line deck takes slightly more than an inch of space. A three-line summary deck in 16-point type takes about three-quarters of an inch. When you multiply that difference by the dozens of headlines in the paper each day, you will have saved several valuable column inches while providing more information.

Many editors will tell you that the primary source of complaints from readers is headlines that are misleading, incomplete or unfair. It is possible to report an allegation in a headline, but putting the response in the headline is often impossible in the traditional headline-deck format. The summary deck allows the editor to do a better job of telling controversial stories in display type.

Blurbs, quotes and summary or highlight boxes serve a function similar to decks. Sometimes they appear along with decks; sometimes they appear in lieu of them. They represent layers of information: one layer for the hurried or less-interested reader; another layer for the reader with more interest. Look at the layered page from the *Virginian-Pilot* (Fig. 10.5). The designer summarizes the big events of the day by highlighting the four main actions over the top of the lead headline. All but two stories have decks. "THE PRINCIPAL MISSION" story offers a summary deck, a logo, a map and a "What it means to you" pullout. The teasers above the flag offer a detailed look at what is inside. The layering allows a scanner pinched for time to learn what happened between the United States and Iraq in some detail by using 95 words in display type. Those who have the time and interest can read the details in the stories. The gambling cruises layout shows an example of layering on a single story (Fig. 10.6). A reader in a focus group looking at the *St. Louis Post-Dispatch* offered all journalists a guideline for writing layers. She told the moderator that she wants to know "what, so what and what's next." She's not alone.

Summaries are especially useful when reporting on meetings at which several issues are discussed. The story lead will contain the issue the reporter believes affects the most readers. Even if the reporter is right, the most readers will still be a minority of readers. Because the headline reflects the lead, readers who are not affected by that particular issue may ignore the entire story. Readers are self-centered; they look for information that helps them. A summary pullout allows the designer to let more people know that the story contains information of interest to them.

10.5 Layering is the technique of creating information for everyone from scanners to loyal readers. On the Iraq bombing story, the designers created one layer of information with the summary of events above the banner headline, another in the banner and another in the deck. Scanners get the news in display type; readers can follow the text.

10.6 The layering speaks directly to the reader who may be rushed. Under "The Details" header, readers are told "Who," "What it would offer," "How it would work," and "What it means to you." A reader who didn't have time would have the essential details. Those with time and interest could read the story.

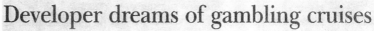

City councils, school, hospital and planning and zoning boards all take multiple actions. A summary pullout allows you to highlight many actions, not just one:

The council also:
- ☐ approved a recycling program
- ☐ rejected commercial rezoning on Broadway
- ☐ delayed Providence Road repair
- ☐ approved five bike paths

The average reader spends about 15 to 20 minutes with the daily newspaper. Even if scanners are not enticed to read the whole story, and some will be, they should be given as much usable information as possible. Readers who find their newspapers useful are likely to continue subscribing.

TYPE CAN TALK

Type screams. Type whispers. You can add inflection to type by using capitalization, changing the size or weight of type, or varying the form from regular to italics or condensed or expanded. Most of the time, newspapers and magazines speak in monotone. All the words in a headline or title are the same size and weight. In feature displays, however, you can add inflection that adds meaning. For instance, consider this title:

The joy of biking

As with all titles, you would add a deck, but let's first look at how we can add inflection to the main title:

The joy of BIKING
The *joy* of biking
The **JOY** of biking
The *JOY* of *BIKING*

Say each of those titles aloud with the inflection. For instance, in the first one, you would say "BIKING" louder than the rest of the words. In the second, you would say "joy" softer than the others. By varying the form, we are able to add inflection, which adds information. If someone were standing on your foot and didn't know it, you might first say, "Get off my foot." If they didn't hear you, you might say it again. "**GET OFF MY FOOT!**"

Once you have determined what you want to say, it's time to arrange the type. It's easier to stack type in vertical spaces. Type run horizontally echoes the news presentation.

The Joy
of biking

Let my people go

Now add inflection

Let my people **GO**

The inflection can be changed again:

Let **MY** people **GO**
or
LET MY PEOPLE GO

Now start arranging the type:

Let my **GO**
people

and changing the shape and form:

Let my **GO**
people

Let my *GO*
people

VUSE **V**ERTICAL SPACES **to stack titles**

DMAKING HATE **D**ISAPPEA**R**

Oriental
HARD
Soft
Love
ɑbnormal
PASSION
DIMINISH
S R ENS

10.7 By manipulating size, weight and form, the designer can add inflection and meaning to the messages in display type.

10.8 Type has a connotative message. That is, the design of the type comments on the message, as the serif italic does on *"Soft,"* and the sans serif heavy does on *"**Hard**."*

Stacking allows you to look for alignment, tighten the fit. Start with the title. Then look for repetition of letters. Remember that uppercase eliminates the extenders and allows you to set the words tight. A combination of uppercase and lowercase allows you to connect the letters or tuck smaller lines into bigger words (Fig. 10.7).

CONNOTATIVE MESSAGES

Connotative messages are those that are embedded in the design of the type. You read the literal message. You understand the connotative message if the typeface reflects the topic. Not every publication allows you to go outside your basic headline schedule to choose such a typeface. At those that do, you have more freedom to communicate clearly, but you also accept the responsibility that you might choose an inappropriate typeface. Study the words and the typefaces in Figure 10.8. The connotative message embedded in the type design adds a layer of meaning to the words. One way

10.9 Think of word pairings, such as love and marriage, and find typefaces that reflect the meanings of the words. Then play with ways to arrange the words.

10.10 Type can talk. The more creative and innovative you are, the more creative and innovative your designs will be.

to practice is to take common phrases and find typefaces that connote their meaning (Fig. 10.9).

Selecting a typeface that matches the subject matter is tricky business. Others may not see what you see. That's because your experiences and your culture determine what you see in the typeface design. The examples in Figure 10.9 are easy ones, yet not everyone will agree on them. What if the subject were hunting, sewing, vegetables or sexual abuse? Not every subject has a typeface suited especially to it. Some subjects work with three or four choices. Don't overreach. If it isn't obvious, not only to you but to others, use your regular typeface. But if others can see what you see, have fun.

Used to its potential, type attracts attention, tells what the story is about, converts scanners to readers, creates a focal point, adds inflection, entertains and pleases with its aesthetics. An excellent example of this is international designer Herb Lubalin's "Families" and "Marriage" (Fig. 10.10). He took something complex and made it simple. The TRUTHRUMOR pun in Figure 10.1 works because of its simplicity. It doesn't take a genius to improve the use of type in newspapers, but it does take knowledge of the alternatives and the willingness to try.

11.1   The palette is a sizzling yellow-orange for the tongue-in-cheek ride through the northwest theme park. Designers are paying more attention to color choices as they create pages that attract and communicate. Knowing how to select the colors, though, is the subject of this chapter.

Color is content. It imparts mood, message and meaning—the wrong meaning if used carelessly or inappropriately. . . . We must think about every color decision and explain its use and how it improves the communication process.

Design Sourcebook
The Times, Munster, Ind.

11. Communicating with Color

One of the enduring myths of color is that bulls get mad when they see red. In truth, bulls can't see color. They're attracted to the motion of the cape. Another myth is that lots of color attracts readers. Readers aren't attracted to color; they're attracted to color used well. Roy Peter Clark, synthesizing the Poynter Institute for Media Studies research, wrote: "It appears that color is just one of many tools that editors can use to present the news to readers in powerful ways. Color seems not to work independently, but synergistically" (Garcia and Stark 1991, p. vii).

Clearly, color sells. Media General researchers placed newspapers in boxes at seven locations. In one version, a photograph in the upper right hand corner was black and white. In the other, the photo was in color, and two blue lines ran across the page above the photo. The rest of the paper was identical. Color outsold the black-and-white version four to one (Mauro 1986). In a similar study reported by the *Orange County Register,* the color version outsold the black-and-white version two to one. The Poynter Institute color study found that readers like color even when it doesn't always translate into higher readership. But there were some caveats: "Color can guide the reader's eye from top to bottom on the page. . . . Readers prefer color over black and white when presented with a choice. . . . Color tints over text do make the information stand out more prominently. . . . The size and placement of a photograph appear to have greater importance than the question of color versus black and white" (Garcia and Stark 1991, p. 2).

Color in newspaper advertising gets results at a higher rate than black-and-white advertising. The results vary, but all the tests show at least a 30 percent increase in readership. Color not only sells papers and affects how readers investigate a page, it also can help journalists communicate information better. Some pictures are more easily read in color; some graphs are more understandable with color used to distinguish the lines or bars; some relationships can be established more clearly with color. Color has become a design basic, and it is up to the generation now entering the profession to learn how to use it to communicate effectively.

RESPONSES TO COLOR

Colors, like type, carry connotative messages. That is why, when we look at red, we think "red." We also may think hot. Scientists at the Institute of Biosocial Research in Tacoma, Wash., found that pink reduces anger, aggression and physical strength. As a result, holding cells in the U.S. Naval Correctional Center in Seattle were painted pink. Red is a favorite color at restaurants because it's supposed to make you hungry. Red is also associated with anger and love. Even without research, we know instinctively that we associate certain colors with certain emotions. Research shows us that many of us react to colors in the same ways. Researcher Bernard Aaronson asked 33 women and 33 men to rate certain hues and black and white according to a list of adjectives. Both red and orange were rated as assertive; yellow was active but did not draw a negative response; yellow-green was regarded as aggressive; blue-green was adventurous but calm; blue was the calmest; purple was regarded as antisocial; white was associated with obedience, gray with depression and black with official or somber moods (Aaronson 1970).

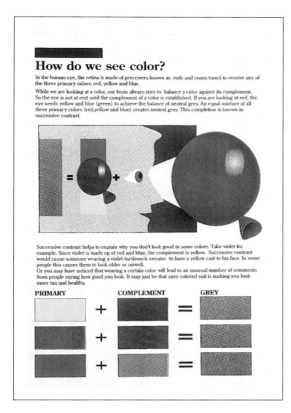

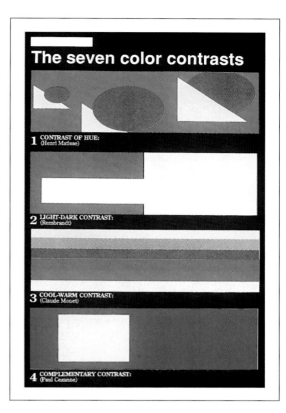

11.2 The fact that our brain always tries to balance a color by adding its complement has an impact on how we match colors and how colors look next to each other.

11.3 The seven color contrasts are a way of understanding how to mix and match colors.

Red is hot; blue is not. Yellow is active; tan is passive. Designers must think of the effect of the package, not just one element. A reader looking at a page full of active colors would be bouncing all over. Every color would be screaming for attention. Yellow is so active that a small patch of it detracts from a large picture or the headline on the lead story. Red and orange are also aggressive. Green is a calming influence on yellow; yellow-green and green tend to sit on the page. Green is static. Blue is calm because it has a tendency to recede. Blue-green attracts you. Gray is neutral, a rest stop. It is a good buffer between other colors or between colors and the white of the newsprint. Designers should try to match these qualities with the content of the article.

UNDERSTANDING COLOR

When we see color, our brain adds the complement to create a neutral gray. Equal parts of the three primary colors create a neutral gray. The way our eye sees color and the way our brain creates the neutral gray lead to four general principles in presenting color (Figs. 11.2-11.4):

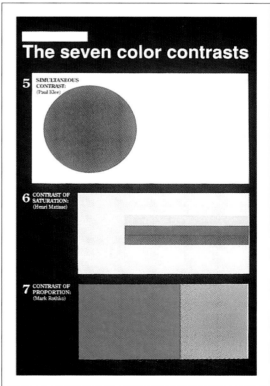

11.4 Designers who deal with color use the contrast of proportion daily.

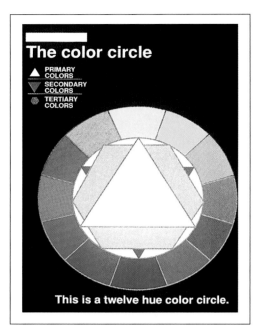

11.5 Every designer should have a color circle available to help guide color choices.

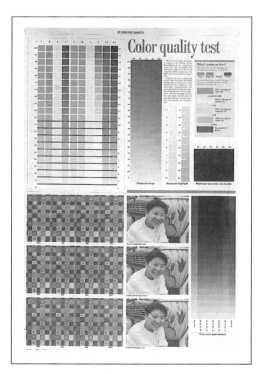

11.6 Every newspaper should run color tests on its presses with color choices and screens selected on its own computers. The color is dependent on everything from the kind of light you have at your computer to the acidity of the water on the press.

1. Color put against another color seems to absorb the complementary value of the background color.
2. A color looks lighter against a darker color and vice versa.
3. Complementary colors seem to emphasize each other when placed next to each other. They will not change each other's hue.
4. Color, as an element that creates contrast on the page, adds depth. It can make elements recede or come forward.

Of the many theories of color harmony, the two most applicable to the journalist are analogous and complementary harmonies.

Colors are next to each other on the analogous color wheel. The wheel shows that yellow-orange and yellow-green would go with yellow; that red-violet or blue-violet would go with violet; that is, the colors on either side of a color match each other. Working with that philosophy, a designer who had a color picture with a dominant color of blue could pick blue-violet or blue-green as a color for a title or other accessories in the package. One advantage of adjacent colors, Birren (1961) points out, is that they define a precise mood—"active where the arrangement is warm, passive where it is cool."

However, the harmony of complementary colors is based on contrasting colors. Designers more commonly use it to guide color choices. As we see on the complementary color wheel, red and green complement each other. So do red-orange and blue-green, orange and blue, yellow-orange and blue-violet, yellow and violet, and yellow-green and red-violet. Colors opposite each other on this wheel are complementary (Fig. 11.5). In addition to getting guidance from a color wheel, designers can consult books that suggest two, three and more color combinations.

Designers who are choosing colors should remember not only the emotional values of colors but also the mix on the page. Birren (1961) recommends using warm colors as the feature color because they are aggressive. Cool hues are useful as background colors because they are passive. Tints, shades and tones are also retiring. The stronger the color, the less is needed.

With active colors, the designer can use pastels—soft, pale shades of colors such as tan. The *Orange County Register* has used peach so effectively as an accent that it has become known informally in the industry as "Orange County peach." The *Register*'s peach is 10 percent magenta and 10 percent yellow. That would be shown as 10R, 10Y. That means the color is produced by using a 10 percent screen of each color, the same effect you get by calling for a 10 percent gray screen. Another way of saying this is that you want 90 percent of the color withheld. Thus, a 10 percent gray screen means you block 90 percent of the black. A 100 percent gray screen, if there were such a thing, would produce white.

Every newspaper that runs color regularly should produce a color sample chart showing exactly what the color combinations will look like on your press (Fig. 11.6). That's because what you see on the screen is not what will be produced on your presses, and the combinations used to produce a certain color at the *Orange County Register* will be different to produce the same color in St. Louis or New York. Color must be calibrated at each newspaper. It is affected by whether you use negatives or transparencies, the method of scanning, the press, paper and the chemicals. Some programs, such as FreeHand and Illustrator, allow you to recalibrate your computer so that the colors on the screen much more closely approximate the colors that will appear on the press. You run a test with 100 percent cyan, yellow, magenta and black. With the newsprint in hand, you return to the computer and adjust the color programming to the sample. It will never be exact. The type and amount of light in the room and the ability of the person at the computer to "see" color accurately ensures that the match will not be perfect. That's why a press test of the color combinations you build into a palette is preferable.

If the designer is making an effort to harmonize colors, it's important to be able to get as close as possible to the actual color that will be produced. To give you some idea of the complexity of trying to specify colors, consider this: Your color monitor can create 16.7 million combinations. You can produce fewer than 5,000 of them on newsprint, and most of us can't distinguish among many of them.

PRODUCING COLOR

While newspapers have printed color since the late 1800s, few used it daily until the 1980s. Before May 1980, the *Detroit Free Press* had never published color photography in its news section. Since then, the newspaper has published it nearly every day. *USA Today*'s debut in 1983 demonstrated that newspapers could print quality color on a daily basis. It was a watershed moment. The *Chicago Tribune* ran spot color often, but it wasn't until the 1980s when it built a new printing plant that it started reporting the news in color. At the *Tribune,* the installation of offset presses preceded the frequent use of color photographs. The industry's gradual acceptance of color photography was due less to a lack of enthusiasm than to the mechanical requirements needed to produce it. The *Tribune,* for instance, invested several million dollars in a new plant with new presses and new prepress systems to print color. The *New York Times* took its time getting to color. The company spent $450 million on a new printing plant in Edison, N.J. It began operating in 1993. Color appeared in advertising, then the feature sections and finally, in 1997, on page 1.

Smaller newspapers began printing color earlier than most metros. That's because most of them were already offset, which produces better color than letterpress presses. When scanners became affordable for small papers and when desktop publishing systems allowed them to make separations on a computer, color became common in newspapers.

Rapidly developing technology has cut the time needed to produce color, and that is a critical reason why more newspapers are running color photography on page 1. The same technology is also allowing newspapers to produce good-quality color. That technology begins with the film and extends through the presses.

Here is how color is produced: The print or transparency must be separated into the three primary colors and black. This is done in a program such as Photoshop or on scanners.

Scanners can produce the four separations in 15 minutes to an hour, depending on the model of scanner and the size of the image. Scanners and desktop publishing systems have cut the time required to make separations and increased their quality. After the photograph is separated into the four versions of the same picture, each representing a process color and black

11.7   The cyan or blue separation.

11.8   The magenta or red separation.

11.10   The black separation.

11.9   The yellow separation.

11.11   When you put all the separations together, you produce a color photograph.

(Figs. 11.7-11.11), a plate is made to place on the press. A plate must be made for each process color and black. That's why printing color requires so much press capacity. Instead of the entire page requiring one plate position on the press, a page with process color requires four plate positions.

Producing quality color on newsprint requires the combined talents of everyone from the photographer to the people operating the press. Many newspapers expect the printers to make up for any inadequacies in preparation, but papers with the most experience in producing color place the least amount of responsibility in the pressroom. Of all the people involved in color production, the press operators are the least able to adjust for poor-quality transparencies or separations. Color can be adjusted on the press, but any adjustment affects the entire picture or page, not just an area of the picture. Press operators should be primarily concerned about getting the press in register once the color is adjusted. Because a page with process color is printed four times, the page must be "in

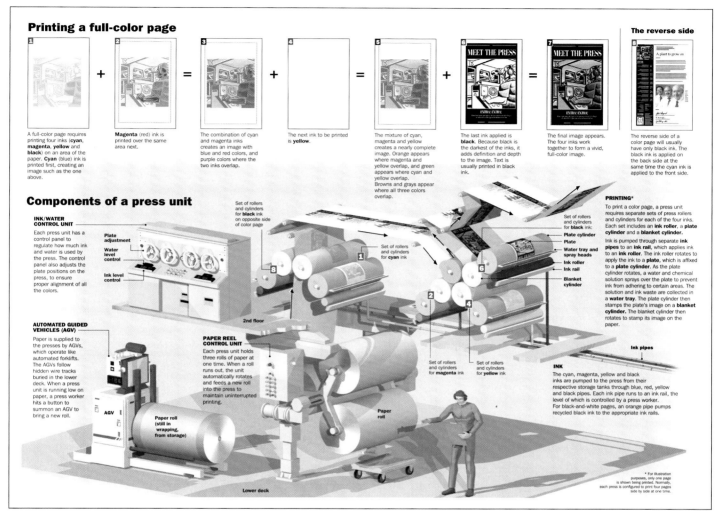

Printing a full-color page

1 A full-color page requires printing four inks (**cyan**, **magenta**, **yellow** and **black**) on an area of the paper. **Cyan** (blue) ink is printed first, creating an image such as the one above.

2 **Magenta** (red) ink is printed over the same area next.

3 The combination of cyan and magenta inks creates an image with blue and red colors, and purple colors where the two inks overlap.

4 The next ink to be printed is **yellow**.

5 The mixture of cyan, magenta and yellow creates a nearly complete image. Orange appears where magenta and yellow overlap, and green appears where cyan and yellow overlap. Browns and grays appear where all three colors overlap.

6 The last ink applied is **black**. Because black is the darkest of the inks, it adds definition and depth to the image. Text is usually printed in black ink.

7 The final image appears. The four inks work together to form a vivid, full-color image.

The reverse side

8 The reverse side of a color page will usually have only black ink. The black ink is applied on the back side at the same time the cyan ink is applied to the front side.

Components of a press unit

INK/WATER CONTROL UNIT
Each press unit has a control panel to regulate how much ink and water is used by the press. The control panel also adjusts the plate positions on the press, to ensure proper alignment of all the colors.

Plate adjustment

Water level control

Ink level control

Set of rollers and cylinders for **black** ink on opposite side of color page

Set of rollers and cylinders for **cyan** ink

2nd floor

AUTOMATED GUIDED VEHICLES (AGV)
Paper is supplied to the presses by AGVs, which operate like automated forklifts. The AGVs follow hidden wire tracks buried in the lower deck. When a press unit is running low on paper, a press worker hits a button to summon an AGV to bring a new roll.

AGV

Paper roll (still in wrapping, from storage)

PAPER REEL CONTROL UNIT
Each press unit holds three rolls of paper at one time. When a roll runs out, the unit automatically rotates and feeds a new roll into the press to maintain uninterrupted printing.

Set of rollers and cylinders for **magenta** ink

Set of rollers and cylinders for **yellow** ink

Paper roll

Lower deck

Set of rollers and cylinders for **black** ink:

Plate cylinder

Plate

Water tray and spray heads

Ink roller

Ink rail

Blanket cylinder

PRINTING*
To print a color page, a press unit requires separate sets of press rollers and cylinders for each of the four inks. Each set includes an **ink roller**, a **plate cylinder** and a **blanket cylinder**.

Ink is pumped through separate **ink pipes** to an **ink rail**, which applies ink to an **ink roller**. The ink roller rotates to apply the ink to a **plate**, which is affixed to a **plate cylinder**. As the plate cylinder rotates, a water and chemical solution sprays over the plate to prevent ink from adhering to certain areas. The solution and ink waste are collected in a **water tray**. The plate cylinder then stamps the plate's image on a **blanket cylinder**. The blanket cylinder then rotates to stamp its image on the paper.

Ink pipes

INK
The cyan, magenta, yellow and black inks are pumped to the press from their respective storage tanks through blue, red, yellow and black pipes. Each ink pipe runs to an ink rail, the level of which is controlled by a press worker. For black-and-white pages, an orange pipe pumps recycled black ink to the appropriate ink rails.

* For illustration purposes, only one page is shown being printed. Normally, each press is configured to print four pages side by side at one time.

11.12   Ed Gabel, then of the *Asbury Park Press*, explained to readers in this graphic how color is produced. The process is typical of any newspaper.

register." That is, each time the page is printed, the image must be laid on the page in exactly the same place. If it is not, the photos will look as if you are viewing them in 3-D without the proper glasses (Fig. 11.12).

At the *St. Petersburg Times* and other newspapers that have taken the time to study the process, the responsibility starts with the photographers. Because the *Times* uses transparencies, photographers know they must fill in shadow areas, which usually means using flash and flash fill. *Times* staff photographer Ricardo Ferro says that the original quality of the photograph is the most important determinant: "If you start your color reproduction with an inferior product . . . and process it through the world's best production system, the end result will be a perfectly reproduced poor-quality photo." The scanner operators there know that the press gains, or produces a darker color, on blue and loses on red, and they make the separations accordingly. The platemakers must reproduce the separations dot for dot and place the material in exactly the right position on the plate to reduce registration problems.

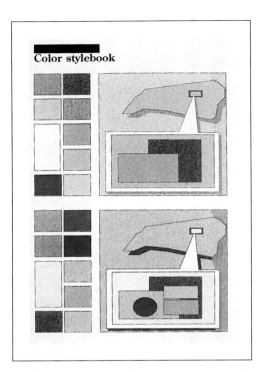

11.13 This sample stylebook shows two palettes from which to construct maps. Every newspaper should consider creating a color stylebook to achieve consistency and improve quality of color usage.

11.14 *Die Woche* uses lots of color, but it operates from a palette that ensures the colors are going to be complementary and that the text will show through the tints.

CREATING A COLOR STYLEBOOK

Color is just as important in creating a personality for a newspaper as is typography. The philosophy that guides color usage should be well thought out in each market. The audience and the geography both can help guide your choices. If you are producing a publication on music for children or teenagers, you probably would use hotter colors and more of them. If you are producing a newspaper for a general circulation daily in the United States, you probably would tone it down. However, the color palette in northeast Maine will probably be different from one in southwest California because of the difference of the environmental colors in those two areas.

Color choices create a personality for the publication. Those newspapers that do not operate off a palette—a color stylebook—risk creating a different and unintended personality each day. One reason it is important to have a color stylebook is because many of the people making the day-to-day decisions have had little or no color training. There is another good reason for specifying color use: Some of the people who decide which colors to use are color-blind. Eight percent of North American white males are color-blind compared with only 1 percent of North American white females. The inability to distinguish between red and green is even more prevalent among men; some estimates are as high as 25 percent. Color blindness shows up in about 4 percent of black males and in only 2 percent of Hispanic males. Few females in any category are color-blind (Sharpe 1974). These statistics lead to the first rule of newspaper color usage: Test for color blindness those staff members who are making color decisions.

A color stylebook, like an editing stylebook, prescribes consistency based on intelligent use of the colors. Such a stylebook might prescribe one or more palettes for such standing elements as graphics and teasers (Fig. 11.13). It might specify how to pick up a color from a photograph to use with a related story by matching or using a complementary color. It might specify the color mix of screens over copy or blurbs. It might specify how to create the memory colors, those of familiar objects such as water, trees and fire trucks. The *Chicago Tribune*, for example, specifies that water is 15 cyan and 3 magenta. A second water tone would be 15 cyan. The *Tribune's* color philosophy can be summed up in these six directives from its stylebook:

1. Avoid straight process colors.
2. Use warm colors to highlight areas.
3. Use cool colors for backgrounds.
4. Use memory colors in graphics.
5. Use color sparingly.
6. Avoid color rules around photographs.

Other newspapers, including *Die Woche*, have different philosophies, but the important thing is to adopt one and be consistent (Fig. 11.14).

One thing that all newspapers should have in common is the idea that color is used to communicate, not decorate. This means not simply applying a paintbrush to a page but building color into the page. When selecting color for the standing elements on the page, your goal is to highlight them without spotlighting them. Allow your fresh daily content to star. Designers selecting color on standing elements, such as teasers and bars, may choose to dull or dilute their choices. To dull a color, you mix it with black or the color's complement. Note that the *Chicago Tribune* dulls its blue by adding magenta. Its second blue is created by diluting it. Designers screen out 85 percent of the color to leave a 15 percent cyan. To dilute a color, you add white or screen it. If you use the pure color, you probably would use it in small amounts to keep it from competing for attention with the color in your news or feature packages.

For better or worse, color is a powerful tool. It helps create a personality for the publication. It attracts attention. Along with size, weights and shapes, it creates a hierarchy on the page. It helps readers decipher photographs and graphics. Color helps define the beginning and end of a package and shows relationships among related items. One researcher found that given a mixed set of triangles, circles and squares, most people will arrange them by shape. That is, they will put all the triangles together. However, if you color one triangle, one circle and one square the same color, most people will arrange them by color. Designers should use that knowledge in using colors to show relationships on the page.

One way to show relationships is to pick either the dominant color from the lead photograph or its complement for the feature title or drop caps. Another way to show relationships with color is to start and end a package with the same color, often used on a bar or quote marks, and so on.

The flip side of the fact that color shows connections is that you must be careful when you are using color on other unrelated elements on the page. For instance, if blue, or its varying shades, is your key color in a package, do not use blue elsewhere on the page on standing elements.

Some designers frame photographs with color. Remember the general principle of color cited earlier in this chapter. Color around color photos changes the look of the color in the photos. When two colors are complements, they will strengthen each other's intensity. Place gray next to red and the gray will appear to have a green tint. That's because our eye constantly seeks the three primary colors to form a neutral. Some publications will use a complementary color when framing; others build a buffer of white space between the photo and the color; still others prohibit placing color around photographs.

Many publications use color screens at least on blurbs if not also over text. Color screens influence a reader's perception of the publication. *USA Today* uses color tints to create an active publication. The tints are consistent with its short stories, graphics and bold typography. Many other newspapers use color screens in all sections. Some restrict them to feature sections, and some outlaw them altogether. The *Times* of Munster, Ind., discourages color screens on stories with this directive in its stylebook: "If your page is lifeless and gray, look at the page's structure and redesign. Screening stories imparts a dated look and may hinder readability." Screens apparently do attract attention to the stories, but they don't necessarily translate into readership at any greater rates than unscreened stories (Garcia and Stark 1991). They can also cause legibility problems if the color is too dark and the type is too small (Fig. 11.15). It is important to dilute the color when it is placed over text.

Color choices for the information graphics palette are critical. Most designers attempt to select a palette that will be subordinate to color pictures while allowing the graphic artist to use memory colors and differentiate elements in charts and diagrams. The Swiss paper *Tages-Anzeiger* has 16 colors in its map palette and 14 for charts and graphs. The *Philadelphia*

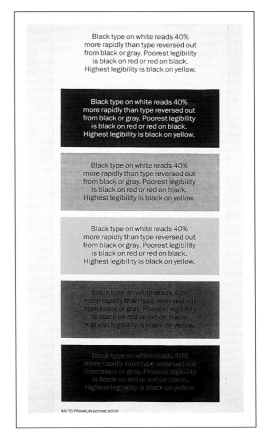

11.15 Legibility is determined, in part, by the contrast between the type and the printing background. Black on yellow, as you can see here, is easy to read. Black on red isn't. Screen colors to about 10 percent if you are running them over text type.

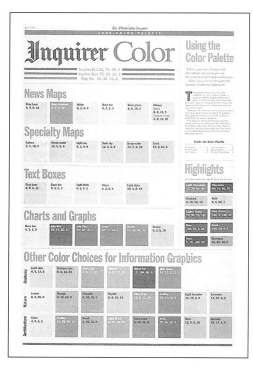

11.16 The *Philadelphia Inquirer*'s broadsheet style sheet specifies the exact percentages of the colors for everything from text boxes to the colors used to produce the local professional team logos.

Inquirer's color palette shows the recipe for colors in everything from text boxes to diagrams (Fig. 11.16). In the style sheet, the editors state that artists should use the colors shown for news maps, text boxes, charts and graphs. However, they allow artists to use other colors for special graphics. It's a living document. "The palette will be updated periodically to include newly developed colors," the editors say.

Newspapers would do well to remember what a circulation director of a Dallas paper said when asked about the value of color. We should consider, he suggested, which attracts more attention, the red bird or the sparrow. The corollary is also true: In a flock of red birds, the sparrow stands out (Fig. 11.17).

VOCABULARY OF COLOR

1. Four-color process printing: color reproduction achieved by separating each color on individual pieces of film and burning them on separate printing plates. The process colors are cyan (process blue), magenta (process red), yellow and black. They are known by the abbreviations C, M, Y and K. Black is K so that it doesn't get confused with B for blue.

2. Color separation: the product of a method of separating a color print or transparency by camera, scanner or computer into its three primary colors and black.

3. Duotone: one color plus black, achieved by shooting two halftone negatives of a picture and producing two plates for the page. A duotone look can be produced by using a color screen tint behind the black halftone. This merely tints the reproduction.

4. Transparency: a positive photographic image produced on slide film. A transparency is viewed by passing light through it.

5. Color print: a color photograph produced from negative film and commonly referred to as reflection copy because it is viewed by reflected light.

6. Spot color: a single color other than black on paper.

7. Key plate: the printing plate that prints the most detail. All of the other plates must be in register with the key plate to prevent printing what looks like two or more images.

8. Scanner: electronic device that transfers visuals into impulses. Scanners separate the four process colors of a photograph or illustration and transfer the image to a negative called a separation. Scanners are either electronic or laser.

9. Hues: a specific color. Red hues include burgundy and crimson.

10. Tints: white with a hue.

11. Shades: black with a hue.

12. Tones: white and black with a hue.

13. Value: the degree of lightness or darkness of a color.

14. Chroma: the strength of a color as compared with how close it seems to gray. Also called intensity or saturation.

15. Secondary colors: mixture of two primary colors.

16. Tertiary colors: mixture of one primary and one secondary color.

17. Cool colors: all of the hues except yellow on the left side of the color wheel.

18. Warm colors: all of the hues except violet on the right side of the color wheel.

19. Analogous colors: colors adjacent to each other on the color wheel; from the same color family.

20. Complementary colors: colors opposite each other on the color wheel.

A COLOR PHILOSOPHY

1. Link related elements by using the same color.

2. Limit color selection to colors from the style sheet or the color press test.

3. Color screens on stories and packages are discouraged.

4. Small breakout boxes are appropriate candidates for tints, but colors should be subdued and complement story content.

5. Colors off our press do not necessarily match those on your monitor. Consult the press test.

6. Story and photo borders should always be 100 percent black on news pages. Putting a color border around a story only calls attention to the border.

—Design Sourcebook, The Times, Munster, Ind.

USING COLOR IN GRAPHICS

1. Use the strongest color to show the most important information. This color should not exceed more than 50 percent of the overall area, or the impact will be lost.

2. Use on the secondary information a tint of the color used on the primary information, to create a link between the two.

3. When there are two or more equally important facts to highlight, choose a set of strong colors, such as yellow, red, blue-green, brown or purple, and edit them so they appear to sit on the same plane. All strong colors appear to come forward from a lighter background but to differing extents.

4. On a background that is 60 percent or more black, most colors will appear to recede unless they are used as tints.

5. When in doubt, use fewer colors rather than more.

—Peter Sullivan

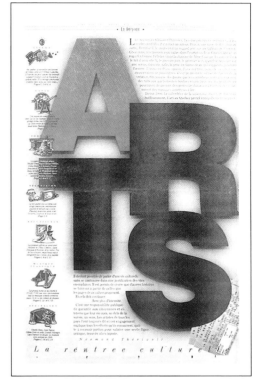

11.17 In a flock of blackbirds, a red bird stands out. The corollary is also true.

Part III

The Team Effort

It's **amazing** that the amount of n e w s that *happens* in the world every day **always just exactly fits** The Newspaper.

Jerry Seinfeld

12.1

We have created a common purpose and flattened the hierarchy of newsroom decision-making. Whenever possible, we look for team solutions and decisions, rather than individual decisions.

Dan Blom
Newspaper editor

12. Management by Design

When Henry Ford introduced the assembly line to produce his automobiles quickly and cheaply, he started a revolution in mass production. He proved he could manufacture a car in 93 minutes; others adapted the technique to include manufacturing everything from cans to toothpaste.

As Ford was tinkering in Detroit with his new concept, newsrooms were already operating on the assembly line principle: Reporters reported, writers rewrote, copy editors edited and wrote headlines, and layout editors placed it all in the paper. As the copy moved along the symbolic conveyor belt from reporter to layout editor, each desk applied its expertise. Journalists seldom talked to one another.

Now fast-forward to the year 2000. At the modern newspaper, an editor calls a "huddle"–a brief gathering of a reporter, city editor and photographer–to discuss how they are going to report a story. At another newspaper, a maestro, or team coordinator, calls a meeting of a section editor, reporter, photographer, copy editor, graphic artist and designer. They are brainstorming an idea. The maestro listens to the reporter's idea. "Why should I care?" she asks. "So what?" someone else asks. As the meeting continues, the questions change. "What else does the reader need to know?" "What's the best way to tell that part of the story?" This is a team, and it will carry this story through to production.

Variations of alternatives to the assembly line process are sprouting up in newsrooms everywhere. These variations appear under such names as "maestro," "newsroom without walls," "News 2000" and "clusters." All of them are designed to produce a newspaper that is more useful to readers. These innovations haven't reached every newsroom, nor will they ever. Most newspapers still operate under the traditional hierarchical system. We'll look at that system and then look more closely at how newspapers are reorganizing.

TRADITIONAL ORGANIZATION

Newspapers today carry more pictures and information graphics, and many use color, but their format is not unlike those in Ford's day. This is not surprising because newsroom organization hasn't changed substantially in most newspapers since that time. However, readers and the ways they spend their working and leisure time have changed. Radio, television, special-interest magazines and electronic delivery systems have captured some of the readers' time and interest. Although technological developments permit newspapers to publish a better product faster with fewer people, the organization of most newsrooms tends to fragment the work of highly trained, highly specialized journalists.

Traditional newsroom organization is a barrier to successful communication with the reader. Ever since photography became a part of the newspaper, the disadvantages of the assembly line process have outweighed the advantages, but few editors recognize the problem. The result is a product that fails to convert data to understanding for the reader. Too often, the system fails to take advantage of the synergy of the reporters, editors, photographers, artists and designers.

The traditional newsroom is organized vertically to move the raw materials horizontally. As Figure 12.2 illustrates, the decision-making authority flows downward from the editor to the departments. Each department produces its own product: stories from the city desk, photographs from the photography department, graphics from the art department, headlines from the copy desk and layouts from the news or design desk. This structure creates unnecessary barriers. Photographers often are not involved in the story early enough. Reporters often are not consulted about editing changes, and photographers are seldom asked about selection, cropping or display. Artists too often are told to produce illustrations, charts and maps on short notice and with incomplete information. Furthermore, the designer who puts all these efforts together often doesn't know what is coming until it arrives. The managing editor often specifies what should be on page 1 with little regard for the effect on photo size, white space or the number of jumps.

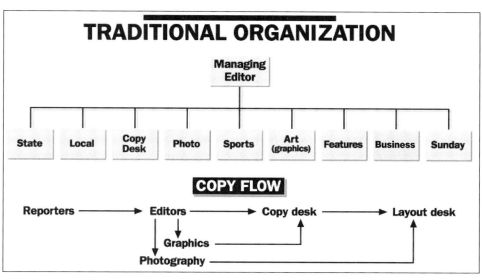

12.2   In the traditional newsroom organization, authority and direction flows downward, and the newspaper production process is organized much like an assembly line.

It doesn't have to be this way, even in the traditional newsroom structure, and at some newspapers, it isn't. Copydesks consult with reporters; reporters suggest headlines; a photo editor trained in photography works at the copydesk; planning sessions are held in anticipation of big projects or disasters; the person who writes the cutline is the same person who has edited the story and written the headline. Talented people can and do make any system work. But it can work better and more easily if we tap the creative power of minds working together.

Newsroom specialization is the classic good-news/bad-news joke. It's good news when reporters know more about a particular field, such as medicine or the environment, or photographers know how to operate a variety of equipment, gather facts on film, crop for maximum effect and display to attract attention. But it's bad news when the division of labor inside the newsroom becomes so severe that journalists don't talk to each other.

In the 1970s some farsighted publishers, such as those in St. Petersburg, Fla., and Allentown, Pa., began to tinker with newsroom organization because of their growing awareness of the newspaper as a visual medium. Oddly enough, at most newspapers it wasn't the management experts who started this newsroom evolution but first the photographers, then the designers.

Photographers argued loudly and often eloquently that the photo department needed to be more than a service agency that took orders but had no say about the assignment or display. These photographers saw themselves as photojournalists who were able to report with a camera, often more dramatically than reporters. They needed a voice in the planning and execution of the product.

It was only natural that journalists trained to deal with words were reluctant to invite photographers, much less designers, into the councils where news judgments were being made. There was, and still is, little appreciation for the total product in those councils. The efforts of Professors

Cliff Edom and Angus MacDougall, through the University of Missouri Pictures-of-the-Year competition, had a profound effect on the industry. The contest—and the ideas that flowed out of it—emboldened photographers to argue forcefully for the merits of photojournalism.

At many newspapers, photographers still have little voice in planning. A University of Georgia Journalism School survey in 1983 found that only 17 percent of photographers are usually involved in the early planning, 24 percent are involved midway in the project, 39 percent after planning is complete and 20 percent after the story is done. Photography is gradually moving from a service department to equal footing with other departments.

Now art departments need to travel the same route. Designers, who put the package together, started showing how their involvement could attract attention and explain the content. As early as 1960, the *St. Petersburg Times* recognized that the presentation of information was part of the message. In the 1970s at the *Allentown* (Pa.) *Morning Call,* art director Robert Lockwood and executive editor Edward Miller revolutionized the newsroom process. The design director became an equal to the assistant managing editor in making news judgments and coordinating the paper's content. Miller and Lockwood also experimented with "villages," teams that worked together and included everyone from reporters and photographers to paste-up employees. In each case the newsroom organization was changed to make the newspaper a better product for readers and advertisers.

REORGANIZING THE NEWSROOM

Any reorganization of the newsroom must be based on the goal of the organization. The most successful publications are those that recognize they are selling understanding, not just newspapers.

Newsrooms are not organized to produce stories, type, charts and photographs that work together. Many stories have no pictures or graphs, and the traditional system facilitates the need to meet daily deadlines. If stories do or should have pictures, maps or graphs, the system depends on the whims of a reporter and city editor, who may or may not think of photos and graphics early in the process. There are plenty of disaster stories.

At one newspaper, a five-member reporting and photography team worked for three weeks on a special fashion section. The two employees responsible for laying out the section found only the pictures and cutlines when they came to work on a holiday. They put together the entire section without any of the stories. The layout editors weren't involved in the planning, and the section was a disaster.

At another newspaper, a reporter worked for days on an exclusive story about a local judge who was a client of the prostitutes who were being brought before him in court. The story contained a vivid description of the judge meeting the pimp in a seedy bar, walking across the dark street to a three-story house and going up the carpeted stairs to the third floor to visit a prostitute. Although nearly two pages were devoted to the story, it didn't have a single picture or illustration. Why not? The reporter and his city editor failed to tell other departments they were working on the story until it was too late to make photographs or illustrations without delaying the publication date. The story was written, passed on for editing and a headline, and placed in the paper in classic assembly line fashion.

Those examples both involved enterprise stories, but it also could have happened with spot news. Contrary to what most journalists believe, little news is unexpected. A fire breaks out. Someone is shot. Two cars collide. You never know when these things are going to happen. Still, most of the stories in the news section can be anticipated. A study of three large dailies for three days revealed that 75 to 85 percent of the stories in the news section can be anticipated (Moen 1992). In the sports section, this percentage is even higher. You know when the high school basketball team will play. You can plan your coverage. You know when the city council and school board will meet and what is on the agenda. You can plan your coverage. You know ahead of time candidates' schedules and, often, what they are going to say. You can plan your coverage. You know the court docket. You can plan your coverage. Add your enterprise stories, and you have accounted for more than three out of four news and sports stories.

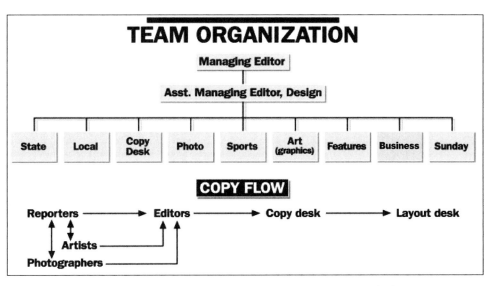

12.3   When the newsroom is organized in teams, ideas can flow from the bottom up or top down, and everyone responsible for part of the production is involved from the beginning.

A newsroom that treats each day as a surprise is a newsroom that is always two cycles behind the readers. Fortunately, this sort of thing is happening less frequently. That's because two changes are occurring: Design editors, who have an interdisciplinary concept of how stories can be told, are being integrated into the management structure; and teams, including the people who traditionally originate stories and those who traditionally present stories, are working together. Some papers tap the expertise scattered throughout the newsroom only in the planning of major stories and projects. Others are building it into the daily process.

A key player is the graphics or design editor, a relatively new position. So new, in fact, that Hilliard (1990) found substantial confusion among executive and managing editors about the role of the design editor. Of 67 large-circulation newspapers responding to his survey, 35 senior editors compared the position of design editor to that of a city editor, 29 compared it to the features editor and 14 compared it to an assistant managing editor. (They could select more than one.) The survey showed that design editors are being integrated into the newsroom management structure slowly but surely. Thirty percent of the respondents said that the decision on how to tell the story was shared by the graphics and news editors; 26 percent said it was shared by the graphics and city editors; 16 percent said the managing editor decided; and 10 percent indicated that the news editor decided.

Figure 12.3 shows that a new position has appeared on the newsroom chart: Assistant Managing Editor—Design. This position is at the hub of the newspaper. The design editor or a designee must be involved in both the daily production cycle and special projects and also have the authority to make news judgments in consultation with others.

Design editors, whether they are called art directors, graphics editors or assistant managing editors, come from a variety of backgrounds. They may have been photographers, designers, artists or former copy editors who did layout. Because of the standards being established by these pioneers, those who follow will need to be even better qualified. For the design editors of the future, there are at least seven requisites:

1. *They should be journalists.* Design editors must understand news values, know how news and features are gathered and be aware of readers' expectations.
2. *They should be photo editors, though not necessarily photographers.* They must be able to differentiate between situations that have potential for pictures and those that do not. In addition, they must know how to select, crop, group and display pictures.
3. *They should be artistic, though not necessarily artists.*
4. *They should be typographers, knowing how to work with type and use type legibly.*
5. *They should know publication reproduction processes.* Design editors need to know everything from programming the computer for proper type spacing to color production methods.
6. *They should be able to work with others.* Design editors must be able to persuade others by earning their respect. In turn, they must respect others.
7. *They should have the vision to think the unthinkable, the courage to experiment and the wisdom to remember always that the reader must be served.*

It is not necessary for the design editor to have firsthand knowledge of all the functions of the job. The designer needs to know the best spacing between letters in headlines and text, but a computer programmer can achieve the desired results. The designer needs to know how to use photographs, but a photo editor can make most of the day-to-day decisions. The designer needs to understand how color is reproduced, but the artist can make overlays. Ironically, the smaller the publication, the more important it is for the design editor to have a broad base because it is less likely there will be computer programmers, photo editors, artists or lab technicians to do the actual work.

Because of the nature of the job specifications, photojournalists who have a background in typography are likely candidates for design editor positions. In fact, more than half of the first design editors were former photographers (Gentry and Zang 1989). Regardless of whether the design editor is a former photographer, the photography and art departments must be elevated from service agencies to departments on equal footing with other newsroom divisions. This will allow the photo editor to initiate assignments, make suggestions on photo orders from other departments and even reject inappropriate requests. Such an action would be subject to an override only by the design editor or managing editor.

It is important that the authority of the design editor, photo editor and chief artist be built into the newsroom structure (Fig. 12.3). If it is left to the preferences of the editor or managing editor, it can change overnight as editors move from one position to another. If authority rests on the shoulders of only one person, it also leaves with that one person. This is particularly true at small and medium-size newspapers that, like a campfire, glow brightly with the work of a single person but die quickly when the editor leaves. Once the structure exists, management must provide the means for the appropriate departments to work together. The assembly line system requires cooperation but doesn't provide for the interchange of ideas or offer the benefits of collaborative efforts. The team system does.

Newsrooms are being restructured to bring specialists onto a team. When it works, no managing editor or design director has to issue decrees. The team will have made the decisions as the story progresses. More important, the right questions will have been asked early enough in the process for answers to be found. The readers' questions will be answered in a story format that makes sense. Text, pictures, illustrations and a range of information graphics will be used to tell appropriate parts of the story.

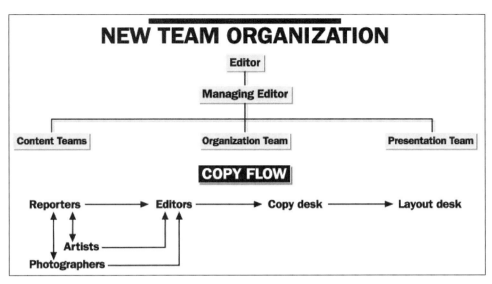

12.4   When one newsroom decided to reorganize, it decentralized, redefined beats and created teams of reporters and editors.

THE TEAM SYSTEM

The team approach, which involves more people earlier in the process, ensures adequate planning. One version of the team approach is the maestro concept, popularized by Leland Ryan of the University of Kentucky. The approach requires one person to orchestrate brainstorming story sessions. If the reporter can justify the story from the readers' standpoint, then the group turns its attention to defining the best ways to tell the story. Main story? Sidebar? Pictures? Graphics? Illustrations? How much space? What's the headline? What will it look like on the page? The maestro leads the team to the crescendo. One Midwest paper flattened its structure and created teams to create and present stories (Fig. 12.4).

At other newspapers, the composition of the team is determined by the project. If it is a sports feature, the sports editor, reporter and design editor are included. At the initial conference, which may take only a few minutes for some stories, the team determines the subject, focus and deadline. The design editor might have suggestions about angles or tie-ins with other departments and may also assign a photographer to work with the reporter from the beginning. The reporter-photographer team might make decisions in the field that will change the focus. Even so, the words and visuals will still work together because of the team effort.

Planning sessions for other projects may need to include more people and be more formal. For instance, an investigative project might include the reporters and their project editor, design editor, copy editor, photo editor, artist, and managing editor or assistant managing editor. The wide variety of perspectives strengthens the fact-gathering process. By involving all the people who will be working on the package at some stage, management is making the most use of available talent, ego and pride. Because everyone is involved and has a stake in the success of the project, they will work harder and understand what they are doing. Participating in idea and planning sessions is always stimulating to creative people. Ideas subjected to challenge and scrutiny become more clearly focused. The process is enriching for the participants, fruitful for the newspaper and beneficial to the readers.

Teams offer many advantages. The copy editor who is reading the daily memos along with the project editor is less likely to delete essential information, insert errors or write a bad headline. Involving the design editor at the beginning of the project ensures that the photographers will have access to the reporters, people, places and events as well as sufficient time to complete their work. Planning also permits artists and photographers to go into the field with the reporters, not two weeks later when conditions have changed. In addition, the design editor can have a series logo prepared ahead of time rather than one hour before deadline. Finally, the package can be designed for maximum effect in the appropriate space.

Some newspapers have a backout schedule, which shows every deadline until publication. It indicates deadlines for reporters, photographers and artists, and it also shows when the copy and management editors must complete their work. Such a schedule helps organize the team members and assigns responsibility to each.

EXPECTING THE UNEXPECTED

Every newspaper that has survived a major disaster—a hurricane, earthquake, major fire—becomes a convert to planning. After Hurricane Hugo, the *Charlotte Observer* put together a list of recommendations so they could be prepared for the next big event. Many of the recommendations will work for any newspaper. Here's what they suggest for the photo department:

1. Keep the photographers' communication network—scanners, radios, cellular phones—working.
2. Photographers should have a set of maps in their cars.
3. Keep at least a week of lab supplies on hand. In a disaster, there won't be any deliveries.
4. Make sure local police, firefighters and paramedics recognize you. In a disaster, it might be the difference between access and no access.
5. Know your legal rights.
6. Carry protective gear in your cars.
7. Develop access to the local ham radio system.
8. Establish charge accounts with helicopter and airplane rental companies.

And for the graphics department:

1. Back up files on disks weekly.
2. Be sure your map files are organized and accessible, even after a crash.
3. Keep an additional master file of regional cities.
4. Keep a comprehensive set of street maps on hand.
5. Keep your newspaper's headline and body copy fonts loaded on a PC. The mainframe may go down.

Design is a process of planning. Is your newspaper ready for a major flood, fire, earthquake, hurricane or tornado?

13.1 In math, one plus one equals two. In design, it equals three. First, you have great pictures (1), then you add the right words (2) and you create packages (3) that are greater than the sum of the parts. The ultimate goal of the designer is to make the words and the visuals work in harmony as the *Lexington Herald-Leader* did on its snow package.

No matter how great the author's wisdom or how vital the message or how remarkable the printer's skill, unread print is merely a lot of paper and a little ink. The true economics of printing must be measured by how much is read and understood and not by how much is produced.

Herbert Spencer
Philosopher

13. Words and Visuals in Tandem

Advertising agencies form creative teams to work on a client's campaign. The team is composed of specialists who work together with other team members. Their product is the best that the team can produce. Most newsrooms operate, for the most part, on the Lone Ranger principle, which holds that each individual applies his or her expertise to the problem, then passes it on to the next person. The product is the best that a group of individuals working alone can produce.

But this product isn't as good as can be. In Chapter 12, we discussed the advantages of the team approach. When it comes to integrating the words and visuals in the display, newsrooms either have to adopt a team approach to the design, make certain someone coordinates the work or provide for one person to cross the specialty lines. Fragmented work produces fragmented or redundant information.

This chapter supposes that the package that moves to the copy or design desk has been conceived and produced by a team. Now it remains for the designer and copy editors to make the words and visuals supplement each other. Elements that work in tandem show a dependence on each other. Photographs, cutlines, headlines, decks, pullouts and graphics depend on each other to tell the story. Even thorough readers make decisions based on headlines, photographs and secondary display type. Each of these points is a visual stop sign for scanners. Only when scanners pause and read do designers have an opportunity to tell and sell. The goal, then, is to get people to stop and listen to the sales pitch. Each of the stops—the headline, photograph, cutline, decks and pullouts—should add new information to the sales pitch.

The picture and headline are the heavyweights; more than any other element, they attract attention. The picture should feed to the cutline, which should explain the photograph and foreshadow the story. The headline bridges what the reader sees in the photograph and will find in the story. The deck continues with enticing details. The pullouts and blurbs sell a quote or tidbit that piques interest. Look at Figure 13.1. Editors of the *Lexington Herald-Leader* created a fun package in which the headlines, pictures and cutlines work as a team, not as individual parts.

Big news events and special reports are more likely to produce interdependent packages than the daily flow. That's because of fragmentation of efforts at the copy and design desks. A designer draws the page. A copy editor edits the story and writes the headline and decks, often without seeing the design. A photographer writes a cutline without seeing the story. A copy editor, sometimes not even the same one who edited the story, may rewrite the cutline. The chart arrives from the art department; someone has written the chart's headline and copy block without seeing the headline and story. Yet another person may pull a quote or blurb, and even if it's the same copy editor who has edited the story, the choice often is not made in the context of the total package.

Fortunately, it doesn't happen this way at every newspaper, but even a casual observer of today's newspapers can see that everyone involved in the package isn't working toward the same goal. As a test, let's check the execution for the straightforward package of two pictures and one story in Figure 13.2.

The first thing you notice is the wonderful headline that plays off the picture. It could not have been written if the copy editor had not been looking at the picture as well as reading the story. The title bridges the picture and the deck, which gives scanners enough additional information to under-

stand the pun in the ti-
tle. The deck also plays
off the secondary pho-
tograph: "Local Dixie-
land band has Colum-
bians kicking up their
feet." So far, so good.

Now let's look at the
cutline under the domi-
nant picture: "Susan
Currier of Columbia
places head in hands
and laughs as sousa-
phone player Lloyd
Shatto gives her an ear-
ful of music." This
wouldn't be an effective
cutline even if it didn't
repeat the information
in the headline. As you
know from Chapter 5,
cutlines shouldn't state
the obvious. We can see
she has her head on her
hand (not hands). The
cutline identifies the
people, but it doesn't tell
us why Lloyd is blowing
his horn at her or why
they are outdoors. Are
they both members of
the band? Are they hav-
ing fun during a break

13.2   The picture and headline share the humorous tone.
This package will grab readers by the ear to read on.

13.3   The headline and deck uses *molds* and
shape to tie the picture and story together.
The designer created a package, but could do
nothing about the fact that the writer and
photographer didn't work together. The story
focuses on a parent and child not pictured.

in practice? And what could be extracted from the story to entice us to read?

Now let's look at the second picture. We've been attracted to the package with a large picture of a close-up; now we're given a context shot. They
complement one another. The cutline tells us, "John Rhein and Vivian
Barner of Columbia cut loose at Katy Station to the music of the Storeyville
Stompers before a Missouri home football game." This cutline does a better job of telling us what we can't see: the names of the people and the band,
the location and the occasion. Like the first, though, it doesn't tease the
reader into the story. If the cutline writer had dipped into the story, he or
she could have told us the connection between the band's name and its New
Orleans origin, or that the band makes the rounds of six restaurants before
each home football game and the date of the next outing.

Another headline bridges the picture and the story about activities at the
Children's Museum. "Class molds young artists" sits under a picture of a
couple working with clay (Fig. 13.3). The use of the word "molds" isn't an
accident. The same theme extends into the deck with the use of "shape." The
cutline introduces us to Sue Sumpter and her son. However, the story starts
with another parent-child couple at work on a pottery sculpture. The desk
did the best it could with what it had to work with, but what it had to work

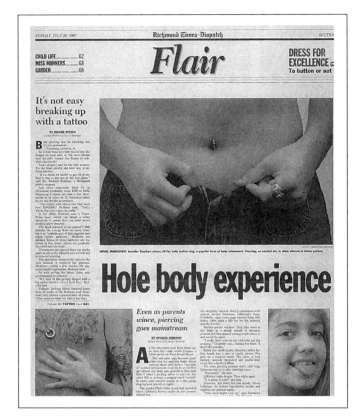

13.4   The tight cropping on the dominant picture ensures scanners will stop and look, but the words beneath that picture tie the story to the picture.

13.5   *Dog-Ma* is a nice play on words. The woman who is the "mother" to the dogs has a well-defined philosophy about raising pets.

with was the output of a reporter and photographer who didn't work together. The story has been edited with the pullout in mind; the information is not repeated in the story.

The "Hole body experience" title (Fig. 13.4) pulls together two stories and three pictures. The packaging is so tight that it looks as if the designer had read the story, laid the pictures on a desk and then composed the title. Look at the deck under the main headline: "Even as parents wince, piercing goes mainstream." Then look at the picture in the lower left. The cutline informs readers, "For some teens, tattoos and nipple piercing are expressions of rebellion. Unfortunately, tattoos are hard to remove." The picture shows the extent to which some teens will go. The sidebar, "It's not easy breaking up with a tattoo," focuses on the difficulty of getting rid of tattoos and ties in with the picture and cutline. This is an integrated effort that can only result from a designer and editor looking at the parts as a whole.

Dogs apparently bring out the best in some designers. The "Dog-Ma" story (Fig. 13.5) is about a woman who has eight dogs. The title plays off the large photo right above it. The deck tells us more: "Being a mom to eight springer spaniels can be a tough job. Carol Sommers believes the key to raising dogs is getting them used to people at an early age." The cutlines tell part of the story and invite readers to the text. For instance, one of the cutlines says, "Sommers holds Samantha, 10, in her kitchen as Misty, 2, dines with her four-week old puppies in their whelping box. She raises springers because she enjoys them, and they bring her a sense of pride. `It's fun and comical to watch them play,' she said." Quotes in cutlines are a good way to tease readers into the story.

In keeping with the animal theme, the *Daily Times-Call* in Longmont, Co., wasn't sheepish about the puns (Fig. 13.6). "Mutton but Trouble" is followed by this deck: "Kids bust their chops on wild and woolly rides."

The dominant picture supports the main head, and the secondary picture plays off the deck.

Many editors think the pressure of producing pages against a deadline prevents them from creating packages. That may be true in extreme deadline situations, but for all those occasions when the picture or pictures are available when the headlines or titles are written, editors can create packages. Making elements work together requires that the duties are not split among two or more people. If they are split, the people must work together. To write cutlines, an editor must know not only what is in the headline and deck but also what, if anything, is being used as a pullout. To write headlines and titles that tie the dominant image and the story together requires the editor to look at the picture and read the story. Too often, headlines and titles are written without the photo in mind. Here are four guidelines for producing packages rather than assembling parts:

1. Write the main headline or title only after you have read the story and seen the picture.
2. In the deck or dropout, enlarge upon the theme and give story details.
3. When you are writing the cutlines, don't stop at telling us what we can't see or know from looking at the picture, but also pull something from the text, such as a quote, that would make readers interested in the story. The cutline is a point of sale.
4. Don't repeat information in the headline, deck, cutlines and pullouts unless absolutely necessary. Understandably, a person named in the deck may also have to be named in the cutline.

Twins will make you see double; so will the photo and the headline on the feature on twins (Fig. 13.7). The deck narrows the focus of the story: "Parenting twins full of hidden surprises, unique challenges."

What all these examples have in common is teamwork. If the headline or title writer isn't looking at the story and photo or illustration, there's little chance the words will bridge the visual and verbal. Visuals,

13.6 The designer/title writer isn't trying to pull the wool over your eyes. These kids really are riding lambs. It's a light-hearted photo and title, which is consistent with the tone of the story.

13.7 The creative use of the screen to echo the "Double Duty" title plays off the picture and story on twins. The designer/headline writer created a package.

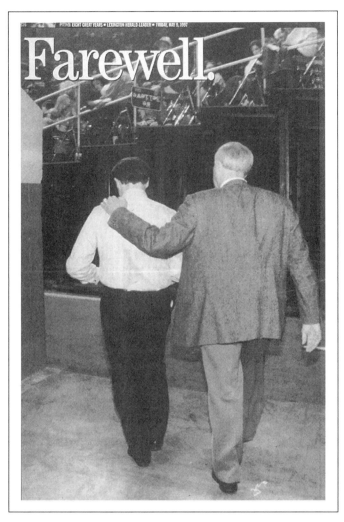

PITINO: EIGHT GREAT YEARS • LEXINGTON HERALD-LEADER • FRIDAY, MAY 9, 1997

Farewell.

cutlines, headlines and pullouts have a symbiotic relationship. The sum is greater than the parts. A system that encourages communication among the people working on the packages gives them a chance to produce this kind of journalism. The people executing the package also have to know that the goal is to make the elements work together.

When the *Lexington Herald-Leader* produced a special section on the resignation of basketball coach Rick Pitino, they chose precisely the right word to play off the cover photo (Fig. 13.8). As you design packages, you, too, will have many opportunities to choose precisely the right words. When you do, you will increase readership and offer readers many pleasurable moments. When you do that, you will be following Herbert Spencer's dictum not simply to produce pages but to concentrate on making people read and understand what they read.

13.8   When the beloved coach leaves, what else is there to say?

Part IV

Applying the Lessons: Specialized Applications

14.1 Using photography, an information graphic and large type, the *Missourian* designers were successful because the editors first were willing to focus on the main events rather than try to jam too many events on the page. It illustrates an important principle: When displaying big events, simplify.

A lot of these college designers have a better shot at landing a job right out of college than five years ago.

Brett Benson
St. Paul Pioneer Press

College newspapers are a breed apart, though you often wouldn't know it. For all the differences in audience, many of you merely echo what you see in general-circulation daily newspapers. That's okay as a learning tool, of course, but it may not serve the market of the college paper. If 20-year-olds can create computer software and build solar cars that outdo those from General Motors, surely college designers can create pages that will attract college students.

That's not easy work, but who better to do it for than fellow students? You know their interests. You know how to reach them. And now you have the tools. Pagemaker and QuarkXpress put the tools of invention in the palm of your hand. If you're able to turn college students on to newspapers, the profession will be indebted to you.

The audience defines the content and design of college papers, and that audience is college students. Primarily 18- to 22-years-old, primarily single. Interested in relationships, entertainment, and the price of tuition, books, room and board. Graduation requirements. Who the good profs are. Sports. Campus safety. Sure, they're also interested in history and physics, but they don't look to the newspaper for that. Ask a random sample of college students to rank their interests and then compare the results with the space devoted to those subjects in the campus newspapers. Would you find a good correlation?

Would you find a good correlation between the presentation of the information and the graphic world in which this audience lives? Look at the posters on the students' dorm and apartment walls. Look at *Rolling Stone,* the *Village Voice* and the alternative press. Then look at your newspaper. Does your newspaper have more in common with your local *Hometown News* than *ray gun*? Most of your audience sits somewhere between those extremes.

One-quarter of the college audience turns over annually. Change is a constant on campus. So it should be a constant in the newspaper. That means that redesigns could occur almost annually. New people have new ideas. Your *Hometown News* has essentially the same audience year after year. It has subscribers who are still mad about the last time the crossword puzzle was moved.

Play to the strengths of your staff this year. Do you have strong photographers? Feature photographs in your coverage. Do you have illustrators? Invite them to illustrate stories and do information graphics. Use diagrams and maps. Do you have someone with expertise in type? Free them. At some schools, you always have good photographers or good illustrations because of a good photo or art program on campus. At other schools, those strengths come and go with the students. Instead of forcing each year's staff to work to last year's template, create a format and a philosophy that reflect the strengths of the people now on your staff. The staff at the *Harvard Crimson* (Figs. 14.2-3) and Miami University (Figs. 14.4-5) introduced new designs that are much more appealing than the old.

Look at the winners in college and professional design contests. The winners in the SND College News Design Contest are posted on the web at www.missouri.edu/~jourdrm. The College Media Advisers also conduct a design contest, and SND publishes a book of winners each year. To join, consult the SND web site at www.snd.org.

Most college students wouldn't even remember what the paper looked like last year. The professionals are looking to you for ideas. They're find-

14.2 Before the redesign, the *Crimson* looked old and presented the news quietly.

14.3 The redesign put more elements on the front page and also added white space. The result is a pleasing presentation that provides more emphasis to the stories and pictures.

14.4 Before the redesign, the *Miami Student* page was cluttered and lacked focus.

ing them in some corners. In the examples on the following pages (Figs. 14.6-22), you'll find the familiar and the unfamiliar, the classic and the outlandish. All of them have lessons to offer. Probably the most important lesson, though, is to stretch. Do you have to break the rules to be innovative? The answer is summed up in this exchange quoted by Dale Peskin in the Society of News Design's magazine:

There was Bob Shema, the innovator from Dallas, touting the twisted typography of the avant-garde publication *ray gun.*

And there was Tony Sutton, the classicist from Toronto, stroking his beard trying to read the letterforms.

"We need to mimic this, to be inspired by this," Shema implored. "What do you think, Tony?"

"This sucks . . . BIG TIME," responded Sutton.

Shema wasn't necessarily advocating type chaos, and Sutton wasn't saying that all innovation is bad. Just as professionals are trying to find the limits, so should you. Here are some examples from college papers to guide your search.

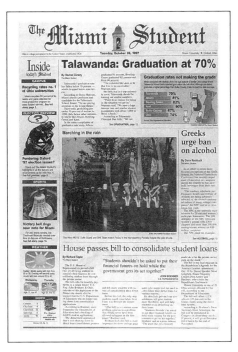

14.5 The redesigned paper is cleaner and more forceful. The new typography offers a pleasing color contrast that allows the designer to emphasize the important story.

14.6 The condensed type and ample white space creates a classic look for the *Daily Orange* of Syracuse. There are only three stories, but there are eight elements on the page.

14.7 The *Sagamore* plays off vertical and horizontal elements on a magazine-style front page.

14.8 No photo? No problem. The type design solves the problem.

14.9 *El Don* of Santa Ana College uses a great illustration and strong arrangement of type to create a showstopper on its front page. In the original, the illustration is in color.

14.10 *f newsmagazine* is produced by graphic arts students. They take advantage of their talents to produce a newspaper that has a look appropriate to their audience at an arts school.

14.11 When sports is the big news, it should be on the front page. The designers made the visuals and the words work together.

14.12 The designer frames an outstanding illustration with white space to create a powerful feature page. In design, less is more.

14.13 The designer is working with facing pages, not a double truck. Setting the text in larger type in a wide column offers a counterpoint to the powerful graphic photo.

14.14 Strong photography and an inventive grid shows off the content. This is another example of a designer letting the content tell the story, rather than decorating.

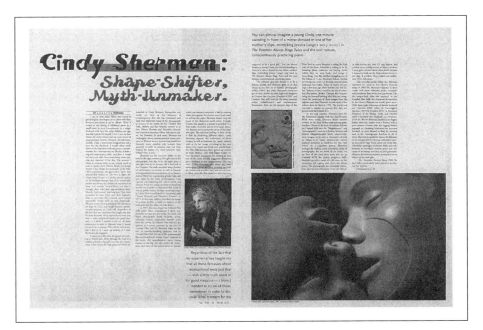

14.15 The white space at the top left margin and on the left side of the double truck balances the large photo at the right side.

14.16   The unusual treatment of the photo at the left with the margins fading into the story and the person looking into the title puts the emphasis in the right places. This layout leads the reader around the page.

14.17   There's a lot of activity here that the designer expertly handled. By playing off the vertical column, the designer organized the page and created an interesting feature package.

14.18   The designer recognized that the excellent photograph told the story and created a page with impact.

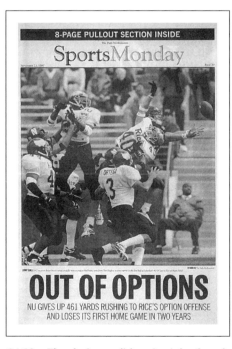

14.19   The designer did a nice job of wedding the photograph with the words and teasing the reader inside the section.

14.20   Design doesn't stop at the editorial page. The page is nicely organized in modules. The white space and illustration provide relief to a text-heavy page.

14.21 The main story is set ragged right, which introduces needed white space. The illustration provides an excellent focal point.

14.22 The editorial page format features a vertical-horizontal contrast. The two gray boxes add needed graphic weight.

15.1   The tabloid format offers designers many options for front page display. They range from the billboard approach taken by the *American,* a publication for Americans living and traveling abroad, to a standard newspaper front page. The Society of News Design (SND) selected the *American* one of the world's best-designed newspapers in 1997.

If young readers spend time reading tabloids and magazines, why do we continue to feed them large, unwieldy, old-fashioned broadsheets? Would tabs help capture a lost generation?

Tony Sutton
Design Consultant

15. Designing for Tabloids

The idea for an American tabloid newspaper came out of a visit between a son of a publisher of the *Chicago Tribune* and an English press baron. Joseph Medill Patterson told his cousin, Robert McCormick, of his meeting with Lord Northcliffe, and in 1919 they started publishing the *Illustrated Daily News* in New York. They hoped to emulate Lord Northcliffe's success with the tabloid *Daily Mirror*, which had a circulation of 1 million in England. Before achieving that kind of success, however, they had to slog through the yellow journalism sensationalism of the 1920s and 1930s and battle upstart competitors.

The excesses committed in the name of circulation peaked in 1928 when the *News* brought in Tom Howard, a *Chicago Tribune* staff member, to surreptitiously take a picture of the execution of Ruth Synder, who had been convicted of murder. Public reaction to such sensationalism finally forced this type of newspaper to change or shut down. The *News* changed and went on to become the largest general-circulation newspaper in the United States at one time. Unfortunately, the stigma associated with yellow journalism lingered long after the worst practices had been corrected, and it slowed the acceptance of tabloids.

In 1940 Alicia Patterson, Joseph Patterson's daughter, started a tabloid on Long Island. *Newsday* has since become one of the most successful newspapers in America. Now owned by the Times Mirror Company, *Newsday* grew up with Long Island and, in content and looks, redefined the image of the tabloid. *Newsday* made the tabloid so respectable, in fact, that by 1979 even the conservative *Our Sunday Visitor,* the largest Catholic weekly in the country, had changed from broadsheet to tabloid and reported that reader reaction to the restyled paper was "overwhelmingly positive." On the other hand, the *Tempe* (Ariz.) *News* switched to tabloid but returned to broadsheet two years later because of reader complaints. The *Middletown* (N.Y.) *Daily Record* went from tabloid to broadsheet and then back to tabloid.

The attitude toward tabloids in Europe is much different. Most Spanish newspapers are tabloids. In Britain, all but a few of the papers are tabloids. In Austria, most of the papers are even smaller at 12 inches by 9.5 inches. In the United States, while only 33 mainstream newspapers are tabloid, the format is popular among the alternative city papers, city and regional business press, religious and ethnic press and on college campuses. However, even designers at broadsheet newspapers will design for special sections in tabloid format.

These days tradition and the fear that a smaller format will bring less advertising revenue, not the negative image of tabloids, keep publishers from switching to the smaller size, which is widely acknowledged to be more convenient for readers. In tabloids, advertisers can buy smaller ads, usually at higher rates, and still dominate the page. Even a full page in a tabloid is only a half page in a broadsheet paper. Most national advertising is designed for broadsheet newspapers; tabloids often must reduce the ads to make them fit.

MAKING THE DECISION

Every successful business organization tries to maximize the strengths and minimize the weaknesses of its product. Publishers who are trying to decide whether to publish a broadsheet or tabloid must first know the advantages and disadvantages of tabloids.

Advantages of tabloids

1. *Tabloids are more convenient for the reader to handle.* At the breakfast table, the open broadsheet is big enough to cover three cereal bowls and the coffee; the tabloid is less intrusive. On the bus or subway, the reader doesn't have to fold the tab to read it. The four most successful daily tabloid newspapers, the *New York Daily News, Newsday,* the *Chicago Sun-Times* and the *New York Post,* try to maximize the advantages of their size. All are published in cities where mass transportation is available, yet all sell thousands of copies to homes also. If mass transportation were better developed in other large cities, the tabloid might be more popular because of ease of reading while riding. San Francisco and, to a lesser degree, Washington, D.C., have decent mass transportation systems. In those two cities, the second newspapers, the *Examiner* and the *Times,* might be candidates for tabloids, but both are established as broadsheets, and the disadvantages of a change in size probably outweigh the advantages.

2. *Editors usually have more open pages.* At *Newsday* the first four pages are considered to be equivalent to the front page of a broadsheet. It's more economical for small papers with less advertising to set aside a full page for departments. An open page in a broadsheet represents twice the investment in the editorial product than in the tabloid.

3. *Content, even within a section, is easier to divide in a tabloid than in a broadsheet, where many stories on various subjects appear on a single page.*

4. *The format permits smaller papers to look and feel hefty with only half the content of the broadsheet.*

5. *Tabloids offer publishers more flexibility in the number of pages that can be added or subtracted.* Depending on the press, broadsheet papers must go up or down in increments of two, four or eight pages. The number of pages in a tabloid can be changed in increments of four on most presses.

6. *Because of the preponderance of broadsheets, the tabloid offers publishers an opportunity to differentiate their product from others in the market.* This is particularly advantageous to new publications in competitive markets.

7. *The advertiser benefits by spending less money to dominate a page.*

Disadvantages of tabloids

1. *What advertisers gain, publishers lose.* Although large advertisers may buy multiple pages of advertising, smaller merchants often settle for less than they would in a broadsheet. Rates can be increased to make up some of the difference but only if the tab is operating in a noncompetitive market.

2. *Advertising and circulation success breeds problems. Newsday* and the *Rocky Mountain News* are often too bulky. Successful broadsheets have problems with heft on Sundays, but tabs often face this problem several days of the week.

3. *A smaller front page limits the number of elements tabloid editors can use to attract the same variety of readers obtained by the broadsheet.* And when the big news event occurs, the broadsheet can use multiple pictures and stories on the front page. The tabloid can't do this without sacrificing impact.

4. *The tabloid can't be sectionalized as easily as a broadsheet.* The tab has only one section, even though it may have pullout. The broadsheet, however, can be divided into numerous sections, depending on press facilities.

15.2 *Diario de Noticias,* a tabloid in Paomplona, Spain, teases four major stories with its billboard front page and refers to several others.

15.3 The *Stars and Stripes,* published for service personnel throughout Europe, offers a traditional front page but adds reefers to six inside stories.

5. *Tabloids still suffer from a lingering image problem.* Present generations aren't as influenced by memories of yellow journalism, but some people still associate tabloids with sensational papers.

DIFFERENTIATING THE TABLOID

Beyond recognizing the advantages and disadvantages, editors must also identify the unique problems and possibilities that a tabloid presents, or it will be treated merely as a small-size newspaper. The tabloid is different from a broadsheet in six areas: page 1 philosophy, sectionalizing, spreads, sizing, typography and jumps.

Developing a page 1 philosophy

Editors of broadsheets must decide whether they want a high or low story count, but tabloid editors must decide whether they want a low story count or no stories at all. On page 1, tabloids have more in common with newsmagazines than with broadsheets. Both must concentrate on one or two elements because of size restrictions. Like the news weeklies, tabloids must retain immediacy while providing focus. That means stripping away the clutter. Some concentrate on type, some on pictures, some on art. Some look like a smaller version of a broadsheet.

There are five ways to present the tabloid cover:

1. Use it as a poster to sell several stories inside. Both display type and illustrations can be used, but even one decently sized illustration will substantially restrict the number of items that can be teased (Fig. 15.2). Look to the competitive magazine market to learn how to use sell lines.
2. Use it as a small newspaper page (Fig. 15.3). The *Stars and Stripes,* a newspaper for military personnel in Europe, uses a traditional front page in a small format.
3. Emphasize illustrations. Instead of display type, use one, two or even three photographs to sell the paper. The image would be more visual than that of a traditional newspaper.
4. Use a single-cover illustration in the tradition of newsmagazines. Overprinting permits giving the illustration a title and promoting other stories inside. The *Wheaton* (Ill.) *Sun* (Fig. 15.4) and the *Delaware County* (Pa.) *Daily Times* (Fig. 15.5) use this approach with distinctly different results.
5. All of the above. An editor may believe that the flexibility to choose any of the approaches on consecutive days is more important than being consistent. Any publication will discard a standard format to handle the big event; extraordinary news requires extraordinary handling. *Die Woche,* once selected as one of the world's best-designed newspapers by the Society of News Design, shows a willingness to match its cover presentation to the news of the day (Figs. 15.6 and 15.7).

It does not matter whether the cover contains news, display type or illustrations, because readers don't spend much time on page 1 of a tabloid. That's why it's even more important for tabloid editors to lure the reader inside and provide a wealth of material there. Most of the successful tabloids

15.4 The *Sun*, a newspaper tightly focused on suburban community coverage in Wheaton, Ill., features one large photograph on its front, an approach reminiscent of a magazine.

15.5 The *Daily Times,* a 52,000-circulation tabloid in Primos, Pa., uses the same approach as the Sun, but the noise level is higher because of the bold type.

15.6 *Die Woche,* published in Hamburg, Germany, and judged one of SND's best-designed newspapers in 1997, is willing to change its front-page approach. Here it has created a magazine cover.

open the first few pages to editorial content. Whatever items are located up front, the first few pages are essential for creating reader traffic throughout the publication.

Sectionalizing

None of the successful tabs can adequately overcome the problem of size. *Newsday* usually publishes more than 200 pages an issue. To create internal departments, some large tabs start sectionalized interest areas on the right hand page so that readers can pull out the entire section. Unfortunately, unless readers work from the middle out, they will probably pull out several other sections too. *Newsday* once developed a thumb index punch on the side of the paper to help readers find sections but dropped the idea. Many tabloids start the sports section on the back page and work in. Some run a broadsheet food section tucked sideways into the tab. That section, which takes advantage of the full-page grocery advertisements, can easily be pulled out. After widespread criticism, the *St. Louis Post-Dispatch* found a way to create a pullout sports section for its Saturday edition, which is a tabloid.

Design is an important element in identifying sections. The move from news to a section can be signaled not only by the traditional labeling but also by a different grid, different use of white space, altering the horizontal-vertical emphasis and typography. Because it isn't easy to separate sections physically, it's more important that tabloid sections have different personalities. The *Jackson Hole News* signifies the opening of its style section with

15.7 In contrast to the magazine cover, here *Die Woche* creates a front page that is text heavy. Content drives the decision daily.

15.8 When readers of the *Jackson Hole News* arrive at the life section, they immediately see a contrast. The designer has used the large page label, white space and a different grid to signal that the subject matter has changed. Broadsheet publications have the luxury of pullout sections for different subjects.

a large-type page header and a grid that contrasts with the news section (Fig. 15.8).

In the softer feature or lifestyle sections, ragged right type can be used to signify a less formal approach. In entertainment, it might be appropriate to use heavy rules freely, but in a fashion section, thin rules would give a more dignified aura. Headline formats, if not the typeface, can also be changed according to section. The news can be presented in a traditional style, whereas features rely on titles, labels and readouts.

It's important to create different personalities for each section, but the publication should be unified. One way this is done is by standardizing section headers. Standardized identifiers can be designed by using the same headline face throughout, even if the format is different; using the same basic format for teasers on the section fronts throughout; or stipulating that all section fronts have summaries or standard indexes. The effort to unify sections becomes more important as differentiation between sections increases. The points are not contradictory. Publications that don't choose to create separate personalities for sections have less need for standardized promotional approaches and indexes. On the other hand, publications that do create different personalities must show the reader that the sections are part of the same family even though they are different in content and approach.

Inside, the tabloid has an opportunity to adopt a newspaper or magazine format. A newspaper format has headlines running over all the legs of the story, and the heads usually are large. A magazine format is more vertical, has smaller heads and wraps type out from beneath heads (Fig. 15.9).

Spreads

The manageable size of an open tabloid permits the design editor to treat facing pages as a single unit. Even when stories or pictures don't use the gutter between facing pages, the designer should treat the pages or spread as one unit for the purposes of balance and flow. In the tabloid, it's often possible to continue stories and pictures from the left hand to the right hand page, and even the gutter can be used on the spread in the middle of a section (called a double truck). Using the gutter elsewhere is risky because a continuous sheet of paper is not always available, and headlines and photographs may not align properly.

When a double truck is done properly (Fig. 15.10), it takes advantage of the extra inch or so in the gutter and brings two vertical pages together into one horizontal unit. To apply the principles of focus and proportion, the image in a spread usually extends across the gutter; often the space is divided one-third type to two-thirds image.

Sizing

The most important design principle for tabloid editors to remember is that sizing is relative to the dimension of the publication. A one-column picture in a broadside newspaper would look large in *Reader's Digest* or *TV Guide.* A three-column picture in a broadsheet would look large in a tabloid. The fact that *National Geographic,* with its 33-by-52½–pica page size, has been able to establish itself as a quality photographic magazine is a testament to the principle of proportion.

Certainly a tabloid can never match the broadsheet newspaper's ability to run a picture 78 picas wide on page 1. A photograph run as wide as the

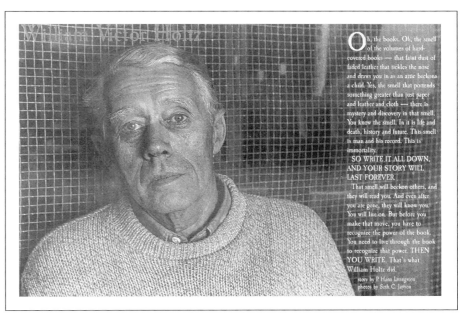

15.9 The inside page layout of *Diario de Noticias* looks more like *Time* magazine than a newspaper. The five stories and three pictures are arranged in modules and distributed to spread the weight around the page.

15.10 A double truck gives the designer the extra space in the gutter and allows the designer to create a single unit rather than facing pages. The one-third, two-thirds apportionment of space is critical to the success of the layout.

tabloid page will look large in relation to the size of the newspaper. Consequently, it's important for editors to use photographs properly in tandem to emphasize large and small shapes.

Typography

Display type selection is also different for tabloids because there are fewer headlines and choices of size. Consequently, weight becomes an effective way to show contrast. A headline schedule built around a bold or extra-bold face would permit the editors to downsize heads, an appropriate measure for a tabloid. Smaller heads save space and preserve the proportions on a tab page. A lighter face should be available for decks and blurbs.

Jumps

Jumps are a problem in any publication but, properly handled, are less so for tabloids than broadsheets. In a tabloid, however, the writing must be tighter to avoid the necessity of jumping a large number of stories. A medium-size story in a broadsheet might jump past several pages and, in the process, lose the reader. The tabloid can capitalize on its magazinelike format and continue to the next page, which is less annoying to the reader and is a pattern familiar to magazine readers. When tabs jump stories several pages away, they lose their advantage over the broadsheets. Tabloids can also jump from one page to a facing page without using continued lines if ads don't intervene. A blurb or pullout quotes would be good devices to replace the jump head.

16.1   The best-designed advertisements focus on a minimum number of sale points and combine words and visuals to create an immediate message. Page designers should learn to work quietly around ads that have large type and visuals. The contrast attracts more attention than trying to yell louder.

In selecting and arranging elements, the advertising designer tries to achieve both order and beauty. The order which the designer creates out of a chaos of pictures, copy blocks, headlines, and white space makes it easy for the reader to read and understand the ad. The beauty makes the reader glad to be there.

Roy Paul Nelson
Textbook author

16.2   When the ads are squared off, the editorial and advertising matter coexist peacefully. There is no research to support the idea that advertising gets better readership if it touches editorial matter, which is the basis for the pyramid advertising stack.

Few newspaper managers look carefully at the newspaper as an integrated whole. The advertising and editorial departments are as separate as church and state. That's necessary to ensure editorial integrity, but editorial and advertising messages share space on most pages. They shouldn't both just show up there; the interplay between the two affects readership of both. The arrangement of the advertisements, the spacing and rules between editorial and advertising, the typography in the ads, all contribute to—or detract from—the overall presentation of the page and thus the readership. Conversely, editorial has understandably guarded traditional open pages on front, editorial, op-ed and section fronts. The concept of such open pages is more common in the United States than in other parts of the world. It is possible that at least some papers should examine the design relationships between editorial and advertising.

THE SYMBIOTIC RELATIONSHIP

The arrangement of advertisements on the page is the major factor affecting presentation on inside pages. Perhaps one of the strongest myths in advertising is that readership of ads is increased if editorial copy touches the ad. That sales pitch, designed to counter competition from shoppers, which don't carry editorial, justifies advertising wells and pyramided stacks. Although few newspapers use the wells—with the ads stacking both right and left on a page—most use a pyramid stack either right or left. The alternative is a modular stack, in which the ads are squared off. Editorial and advertising coexist more peacefully in modular stacks (Fig. 16.2). Researchers have found no significant difference in the readership of advertisements that don't touch editorial copy from those that do. In addition, readers said they found the pages with modular advertising stacks more attractive (Lewis 1989). Ironically, more than 70 percent of daily newspapers now also offer shoppers as part of a total market coverage strategy.

Modular ad stacks require that the newspaper restrict ad sizes to quarter, half and full pages and any ad that runs the width of the page. A compromise is to sell any size and square the ads off as much as possible. Three two-column by 5-inch ads, for instance, square off as a six-column by 5-inch ad. Regardless of the arrangement of the advertisements, newspapers should consider leaving at least 2 picas between advertising and editorial and specifying that all advertisements have a cutoff rule.

The typeface used in headlines should also be off limits to the advertising departments. If English Times is used in headlines, it can be confusing to see it also as the lead headline in an advertisement. Although it is impossible to control the typography of agency ads, most newspaper ads are designed in-house. Such a rule would have a beneficial effect on the overall look of the page.

Similarly, editorial departments should reexamine the traditional open pages. Newspapers in many countries offer advertising on page

16.3   Although few U.S. newspapers run ads on the front page, it is common practice in many other countries. The *Globe and Mail*, a national paper in Canada, runs a strip ad across the bottom of its page 1. This didn't prevent SND from designating it as one of the world's best-designed newspapers in 1997.

1 without confusing readers or unduly interfering with the news presentation. The *Globe and Mail,* a Toronto, Ontario, paper, runs a strip advertisement at the bottom of page 1 (Fig. 16.3). Whether they appear on page 1 or section fronts, such ads in dedicated spaces that span the width of the page can be accommodated into the design of a page and increase newspaper revenues. Section fronts usually are advance pages; that is, they are done a day or two before publication. To make this workable, the advertising department also has to have an early deadline or sell the space only on a long-term contract basis. If the dedicated space were 3 to 5 inches deep and six columns wide, the page designers would have no trouble accommodating them. *USA Today* has introduced an advertisement at the top of page 1; the *New York Times* has run a quarter page on its op-ed page for years.

Another approach that has appeared in magazines is the flex form ad, which breaks out of the traditional rectangle or square. Such an ad may run not only across the bottom but also extend one or two columns wide the length of the page. Such approaches are guaranteed to attract readers' attention to the ad but are not calculated to create an integrated display of editorial and advertising.

Still, it's a subject worth researchers' time. Whether it's flex form ads or placement of ads less obtrusively on traditional open pages, newspapers should know not only how ads affect the ways in which the reader views the elements on the page, but also how the reader perceives the newspaper.

16.4 In an advertisement intended to reach the younger generation, designers used a typeface that reflects a young child's printing. The style of the illustration is consistent with the light-hearted feel of the ad.

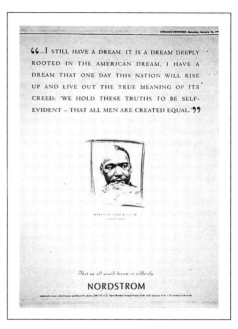

16.5 In contrast to the personality created in Fig. 16.4, this advertisement from an upscale merchandiser uses classic typography, ample white space and an understated illustration to create a dignified personality. The two ads are on the same subject, but the selection and use of type, illustration and white space produce two different personalities.

TYPOGRAPHY

Typography is to advertising what style is to an automobile. The type not only communicates what the advertiser wants said but carries the message in the proper body. The connotative message of type—the message that derives from the design of the typeface—is part of the overall message. The designer selects the proper typefaces, some to communicate the feel or atmosphere or subject matter, and some to carry the load of communicating the details. The different atmospheres typefaces can create are illustrated in two advertisements commemorating Martin Luther King Day (Figs. 16.4 and 16.5). The typeface in Figure 16.4 reflects children's handwriting; the typeface in Figure 16.5 reflects chiseled Greek inscriptions. One is playful; one is formal. Look again at the company signatures. Pepsi is young, modern, forward looking. Nordstrom, a top-of-the-line department store, is quiet and dignified. The typefaces reflect the messages and the advertisers.

Typeface weights and forms offer the designer opportunities to use contrast to avoid typographic monotony and to emphasize some parts of the message. The principles explained in Chapters 8 through 10 apply here. Designers use bold to speak loudly, light to speak softly; they use large type to yell, small type to tell. When you walk down a carnival midway, everyone is yelling at you. Most of the messages are lost. But if you spot one barker nodding, speaking softly, you would be attracted. We pick out a whisper in a cacophony of voices, a shout among whispers. Contrast is a powerful typographic tool. The designer uses large sizes and bold weights to emphasize, smaller sizes and medium weights to provide details.

The designer protects the legibility of type by making certain that if type is reversed, it's run large; if a gray screen or color tint is used, the type size is increased to compensate. Stylized typefaces that are fine for signatures and large headlines may not be for advertising text.

WORKING WITH VISUALS

Designers work with photographs and illustrations. With the availability of software that manipulates photographs, it's easier and less expensive to create photographs designed to sell products. A warning, however. It's illegal to use photographs intended for noncommercial use in an advertisement without the consent of the people pictured. To be safe, you should use only photographs with models or those for which you have the written permission of the people involved.

As discussed in Chapter 5, photographs are the single highest readership item in the editorial section of a newspaper. It's safe to say that they attract high levels of attention in advertisements, too. Photographs normally have more impact than illustrations. They usually are heavier graphically and are more credible. Photographs without any special treatment are the strongest, but in some situations, special screens may produce an appropriate image. Illustrations sometimes are easier to tailor to the specific advertising message. Advertisements with illustrations also attract more advertising readership than those without illustrations, and the bigger the illustration, the higher the readership.

Both photographs and illustrations can help direct the reader's eye. If someone in the visual is pointing, the copy or headline ought to be at the end of the finger. If the people are looking down, put the headline underneath.

USING COLOR

Color sells. And color in newspapers is probably even more effective than color in magazines. One reason is contrast. In the newspaper's black-and-white world, editorial and advertising color stand out. How much varies widely with the study. Some have shown readership almost twice as high; others at 40 to 50 percent higher. Either way, it's significant. Although the specific numbers are debatable (though not to the advertiser, who's trying to decide whether the premium price is worth it), the trend is consistent. Readers will buy newspapers with color on the front more consistently than the same paper in black and white. Advertiser returns, as measured by such things as coupon redemption, always increase with color.

Color also affects eye flow. Readers move from color to black and white. Designers should use color to influence the sequence of readership. When color appears in an advertisement, either the signature should be in color, or color should appear close to it to complete the sale.

Designers should also be conscious of the colors chosen. Different colors have different messages (see Chapter 11). In one study, 200 people were asked to comment on coffee. The respondents didn't know it, but different-colored coffeepots were used to serve different groups the same coffee. Of those served from a brown pot, 73 percent said the coffee was too strong. Of those served from a red pot, 84 percent said it was rich and full-bodied. This illustrates the power of color to influence perceptions, and that's why color choices in advertising are important. Because darker colors recede and brighter colors come to the front, colors can be used to emphasize some points over others.

Sometimes a dab of color may be more effective

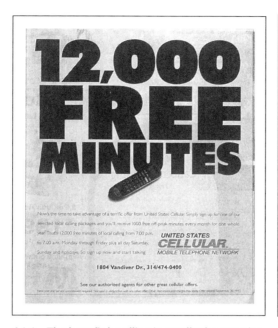

16.6 The benefit headline is usually the most important element in the advertisement. No word has more pulling power than *free*. The headline must immediately show the readers what the benefit is for them.

16.7 "Good Deals on Your New Wheels" is a benefit headline that also rhymes, a device that increases the chances that readers will recall it. The illustration makes it clear that the "wheels" are a vehicle, not tires.

than the whole paint can. When television was mostly black and white, color drew attention to advertisements in color. Soon, all commercials were in color. The networks wouldn't even permit black-and-white commercials. However, when competitive pressures finally forced them to rescind the rule, Dr Pepper jumped at the chance. Its black-and-white ads drew a disproportionate amount of attention because they appeared in a sea of color. Soon, other advertisers began using black and white in all or parts of commercials. Contrast is a powerful weapon in video and print.

PUTTING IT ALL TOGETHER

Effective advertisements have strong headlines and, usually, strong visuals. There are several categories of headlines, but four of the most common are:

1. The benefit headline. Sell the sizzle, not the steak. Sell the free time, not the lawnmower. Sell acceptability, not deodorant. Sell safety, not tires. If it's free, say so (Fig. 16.6).
2. The news headline. The advertiser has a new product. Timeliness makes it news, and the news becomes a sales tool.
3. The how-to headline. The advertiser hooks on to the service journalism trend by promising the customer the solution to a problem. It may be a home-repair problem or a sex-appeal problem. The headline concentrates on the how-to aspect.
4. The testimonial headline. Other customers or celebrities testify on behalf of the product.

The headline combined with the illustration attracts the eye because of size and placement, and the content should focus the reader on the benefits of the product or products. The headline on car loans (Fig. 16.7) is a rhyme

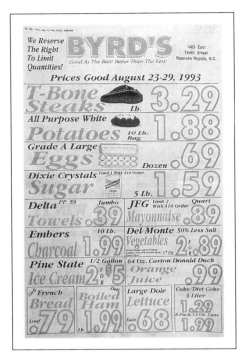

16.8 This multiple-element ad organizes the items but does not emphasize any of them. Ads benefit from having one dominant element.

16.9 By contrast with the ad in Fig 16.8, this grocery ad offers one element that's larger, and therefore more important, than the others. It likely will attract more scanners. With a dominant element, the page also looks more organized.

that, if reinforced, may echo in customers' minds. The typeface is playful; the illustration is playful; and the white space buffers both from the adjoining advertisements or editorial copy.

The headline and illustration together create the focus or lead for the ad. The most successful are those that have a dominant element. The four items that lead the Byrd's grocery ad (Fig. 16.8) are larger than the others, but because there are four, they compete with each other. Nothing has dominance. Compare that with the Schnucks grocery ad (Fig. 16.9). One module is dominant, and so is the type. The ad has a focus. It also has unity. Each element is presented with the same graded screen. In the original, the name of each item appears in red.

The Schnucks design also illustrates another important principle: organization. On multiple-element ads, designers should create grids and work in modules to organize. Large modules are devoted to the most important product or products; smaller modules sell other items. The grid helps organize elements and show the relationship among them. But the grid alone doesn't remove clutter. Even ads with clearly defined grids can suffocate the content with too many bells and whistles (Fig. 16.10).

The reader's eye moves from left to right, top to bottom, big to small, dark to light, and color to black and white. Designers should take advantage of these natural patterns. For instance, the lead headline will be big. The gradation in type size and weight will lead readers to the punch line, product or price, which should be larger and bolder than the copy. The reader moves from large and dark to small and light to medium and bold.

Every advertisement should give the customers the information they need to take action. That information usually includes address, phone and fax numbers, store hours, whether customers can order by phone, which credit cards are accepted, whether the store takes checks, date the sale ends, and so on. It doesn't do any good to create an advertisement that falls short of critical information.

GENERAL PRINCIPLES

Here are some other things to keep in mind in advertisement design:

1. Rules and borders should define the advertisement, not draw attention to themselves. Heavy rules may emphasize a small ad on a broadsheet page, but they also can obscure the content. Decorative borders

16.10   A grid alone won't organize an ad if too many rules, borders and decorative elements are added. They distract readers from the advertising message.

16.11   On a page with bold type, white space offers the loudest message. Contrast is the most important element for the designer.

occasionally help create the proper environment, but more often, they simply clutter the ad. Use restraint.

2. Used correctly, white space isn't wasted space. It's used to its greatest effect when it is to the outside of the type and illustrations. It buffers the ad against other advertisements or editorial copy. Surround a 2-by-5 ad with other ads, build white space into it, and it will stick out of the crowd. Don't trap white space inside the elements, however, or you'll draw attention to the white space instead of to the content. Let the signature breathe by building in white space around it (Fig.16.11).

3. Align elements in the ad with other elements. This is easier to do if you have a grid. For instance, once you locate your lead headline and illustration, the copy block might align vertically with the headline or illustration.

4. Create a "look" for an advertiser. There should be aspects of the design—the typeface, the signature, the use of white space, the grid— that identify the frequent advertiser.

17.1 The birth of a redesign is occasion to celebrate with—and to sell to—customers. In a move typical of newspapers introducing a redesign, the *Kansas City Star* promoted and explained the changes the readers would encounter. Such efforts diffuse the normal resistance to change.

A redesign can be completed, but it is never completely finished. Design, like matter, is in a constant state of motion. Everyday decisions must be made about layout. New thoughts are generated.

Rolf Rehe
Design consultant

17. The Process of Redesign

"We are in a liberated age where technology permits newspaper people to produce newspapers we could once only dream about. The only constraints are those concerned with knowing what to do and how to do it; not with who is to do it."

Bob James
Newspaper Consultant, England

Matt Mansfield, former deputy managing editor of the *Times* in Munster, Ind., tells this story of showing prototypes of a redesign at a management meeting:

> Advertising loved it.
> Circulation had no problems.
> Editorial thought it was the holy grail.
> Robert Blaszkiewicz, the newspaper's night editor for design and my comrade through the whole process, looked over at me as we both basked in the glow of all the adoration. We thought we were home free.
> Then we heard from the publisher. . . . He wasn't sold on the front page.
> Boy, we were hurt. Hadn't he seen everyone else loving it? Didn't he know it was great?
> The truth was, though, that the front page flag was the one area of the changed newspaper where we were sure we had more work to do. We knew it needed more, but we weren't sure what. We wanted to float the prototype for reactions.
> "It doesn't have enough presence," Bill (Howard, publisher) said succinctly.
> Sure, it's vague and leaves you wondering. But the worst part was our publisher was absolutely right.
> Robert and I went back to the drawing board.

Eighteen versions later, they took the prototypes to reader focus groups. The readers endorsed the changes (Mansfield 1997).

The process of redesign starts with a set of goals and ends with the introduction of the new product. For many newspapers, it takes about a year and a lot of toil and turmoil. Nearly everyone who has been involved in a redesign will admit to missteps and mistakes. They know that if they had it to do over, they would do some things differently.

This chapter should help you avoid some of the missteps. Although each redesign is different, depending upon everything from the size of the newspaper to whether a consultant is involved, the steps are similar. Regardless of size or wealth or expertise, every newspaper staff involved in a redesign will learn one thing: Many people, internally and externally, are uncomfortable with change.

Habit is a powerful force when dealing with consumers. Just ask the Canadian marmalade company that produced three flavors. The labels were color-coded to the flavors. In a redesign of the labels, the color-coding system was eliminated. Sales dropped dramatically. The field marketing staff identified the problem, the colors were put back on the labels and sales were restored.

Change makes people uncomfortable, but it can be anticipated and managed. At the *Waco* (Texas) *Tribune-Herald*, the management, which had set a goal of attracting younger readers without alienating the older, loyal readers, was uncomfortable with changing the newspaper's traditional Old English flag. But when the older, loyal readers in a focus group enthusiastically supported the change, management accepted it, too.

Change is also uncomfortable to many people in the newsroom. When a redesign is properly defined as an examination of process and content as well as organization and appearance, it strikes at the heart of everyone's work. A redesign takes time and commitment. It requires the involvement of readers and staff members throughout the newspaper. When it is done right, it can be one of the most rewarding experiences in your career.

GETTING OTHERS INVOLVED

Just as tapping the creative resources of people in the newsroom results in a better product, so will tapping the resources of a wide variety of the newspaper's employees. Depending upon the size of the newspaper, the editor or publisher may be on the redesign committee. In addition, the committee should include the staff member primarily responsible for graphics; departmental editors and representatives of the copydesk; reporters; and personnel from the production, advertising and circulation or marketing departments.

Why should non-news people be on the committee? The news or editorial department may be responsible for content and form, but the marketing or circulation department has to sell it. Unfortunate as it may be, the people in marketing often talk to more customers than editors do. And no design is going to be successful unless the production department has the opportunity to point out mechanical possibilities and limitations.

Advertising representatives are equally important. Column widths can't be changed in any publication without involving advertising and management. Other changes that may result from the redesign, such as restrictions on small editorial holes at the top of inside pages or dedicated space for news, also require involvement of the advertising department.

There is yet another important reason to include all these people: It's good management. A broadly based committee offers a variety of perspectives and experiences, and because the members are responsible for the formulation of the plan, they will be more enthusiastic about implementing it. A committee can't design a paper, but it can establish the goals and provide feedback. The designer translates those goals to paper.

PREDESIGN QUESTIONS

Design, as we have seen, involves process, content and form. The process is how the newsroom is organized and how its members interact to generate ideas and stories and how they determine the means to tell those stories (see Chapter 12). Here is a set of questions to help guide a redesign:

1. *What are the goals?* Says designer Daniel Will-Harris, "If you start with 'why' as in 'Why am I doing this; what is it meant to accomplish?' you will already be about 100 times ahead of designers who are just wondering 'how should it look?'" One of the goals in the *Hartford Courant* redesign was to accommodate the greater variety of stories and photos already being published and to give the paper a fresher, more distinctive look. The Swiss newspaper, *Tages-Anzeiger*, boiled down a nine-point program to two statements: A. Content before form. B. A serious newspaper has to look like a serious newspaper.

2. *What content changes will you make?* Readers can help make decisions about content changes, and newspapers can determine relatively cheaply what readers think. Some newspapers use focus-group sessions. The newspaper invites groups of readers and nonreaders, sometimes at separate sessions, to a roundtable discussion. If possible, the editors watch through one-way windows. Otherwise, they can listen to a tape recording

"I'm positively thrilled! Don't let any belly-bitchers tell you otherwise. This is something worth getting up for!"
Reader
Jackson Sun

or watch a videotape. I have conducted several focus group sessions with the editors sitting in the back of the room. Another approach, sometimes used in addition to focus groups, is to survey a scientifically selected group of subscribers and possibly nonsubscribers. What you ask depends on what you have identified as potential problem areas. A semantic differential scale such as that used by Click and Stempel (1974) to test readers' reactions to the front pages is useful to check their perceptions of personality and credibility factors. Respondents are asked to rate the newspaper on a scale of 1 to 10 with word pairs at either end. You can see from the following categories and word choices that the scale is also useful for testing design prototypes and the redesign after it is published:

> "The redesign is interesting and attractive but you're breaking my heart—where's Tank McNamara? We need Tank. He's the funniest thing about sports."
> Reader
> *Kansas City Star*

Evaluative: pleasant/unpleasant, valuable/worthless, important/unimportant, interesting/boring.
Ethical: fair/unfair, truthful/untruthful, accurate/inaccurate, unbiased/biased, responsible/irresponsible.
Stylistic: exciting/dull, fresh/stale, easy/difficult, neat/messy, colorful/colorless.
Potency: bold/timid, powerful/weak, loud/soft.
Activity: tense/relaxed, active/passive, modern/old-fashioned.

It is enlightening to have readers, editors and staff rank the present paper on these factors. The staff often has a perception quite different from management, and readers may respond differently from either the staff or management. However, the scale provides only guidelines, not answers. Important questions about content and organization can't be answered with this kind of scale.

Another important method of examining content is by gathering staff members from all departments and posing this question: What do your readers and nonreaders do with their time and money? The question will produce hundreds of answers. The next step is to ask which beats cover these activities. The exercise illustrates the gap between what newspapers cover and where people's interests lie. From there, the staff can select the most important of the uncovered items and find ways to include them in the beat system.

Related questions are "What's in the paper that shouldn't be?" and "What's not in the paper that should be?" The first question forces the staff to look critically at what's there. Like a ship picking up barnacles, a newspaper adds content that may have been important 10 or 20 years earlier but may not meet readers' needs now. The second question is another way of asking what readers want.

3. *What are your marketing goals?* How many editions do you have, and who are the audiences of each? Are you trying to increase single-copy sales? Who subscribes to your paper and why? Who doesn't and why not?

4. *What are the characteristics of your market?* Is it highly competitive? Does the competition come from other newspapers, shoppers and broadcast or home-delivery information systems? What is the white collar/blue collar mix? What time do people go to work and get home? What kind of a mass transportation system exists? Are you near lakes, mountains or forests where people spend hours in recreation? Are you in an urban area where movie rentals, theater, dining out and sports are important recreational activities? Is there a mix of religions or does one denomination dominate?

5. *How will the paper be organized?* In survey after survey, market after market, readers repeat that their primary design concern is with the organi-

zation of the paper. When the *Kansas City Star* introduced a redesign in late 1998, one of the key features was anchoring state, national and international news. Readers want regularly appearing content, ranging from national news to comics, in the same place every issue. Beyond the basic divisions for news, what additional sections do you have for your particular audience? For instance, Dallas is a fashion center, so the *Morning News* has a big fashion section (Fig. 17.2). The *New York Times* has an outstanding books section. The *Monroe* (Wis.) *Evening News* has a weekly outdoors page. Each market has its own peculiarities, and each newspaper ought to reflect them. When answering questions about organization before a redesign, some newspaper managers, especially if they are consulting with the advertising and marketing departments, may find potential sections that will broaden the newspaper's appeal.

6. *What personality do you want to project?* Type used in combination with other devices creates a personality. Ask key management personnel to describe the personality they want the paper to have and compare the responses. If they agree, the management team has a common goal. However, there probably will be differences of opinion. Agreement must be reached on the personality desired before the designer can select the elements to achieve that personality. Although readers get their first impression from the typography of a newspaper, the content must be consistent with the rest of the message. That's why *Tages-Anzeiger* edited one of its goals from "A newspaper must look like a newspaper," to "A serious newspaper must look like a serious newspaper" (Black and Jones, 1998).

7. *What are your personnel limitations?* Is the staff large enough to have a design editor? How many staff members will be responsible for the daily implementation of the design? Who are they? Will someone watch for variation in the design and make the necessary adjustments as problems arise? Does the staff have artists to create illustrations, maps and charts? If the staff is limited, should you consider a formatted design? If the editorial management doesn't include a strong graphics voice, the design can't be executed no matter how well intentioned the editor may be. The format can change, but lack of visual thinking will not produce good word and picture combinations or a paper that explains with graphs, maps and charts. On the other hand, if the staff has talented designers and artists, provide a design framework that will allow those talents to emerge daily.

8. *What are the limitations of the production system?* If color is to be used daily, is there a photo staff capable of producing it, a production staff capable of processing it and enough press capacity to print it? What limitations does the production process impose on the design?

The content and organization of the newspaper can be determined largely by the answers to these questions. That is important because design is the proper organization of the content in an artistically pleasing and technically legible package. The way to design is through long-term planning to establish the newspaper's goals and short-term planning to produce the stories and illustrations that appear in the newspaper daily.

IMPLEMENTATION

Using the responses to these eight questions and others that arise in the process, the designer can begin to organize and label the content of the newspaper and select the elements to achieve the personality desired. The choice of type is a key component in creating a personality, let alone legibility.

17.2 Reflecting the local market, the *Dallas Morning News* offers a fashion section because Dallas is a regional fashion center. Prior to a redesign, newspapers should re-examine their content to ensure that it meets the needs of its readers.

"I can give you nothing but praise for the new styling of the *Post-Dispatch*. It definitely has a more beautiful presentation and makes for easier reading. I congratulate you for making this progress. But the print on the New York stock market is very faint and difficult to read. I realize that space is limited, but it seems that the old type was somewhat larger and the print was darker."
Reader
St. Louis Post-Dispatch

17.3 *Word & Way* used one weight of Goudy for headlines before its redesign.

17.4 Now *Word & Way* uses Franklin Gothic, a sans serif, and Garamond condensed. The combination gives the designers contrast of form and weight.

Christian Potter Drury, art director of the *Hartford Courant,* took a month to choose new type. "That's the armature you build a sculpture on; that's the outline of your novel," she said (Anonymous 1997). Designers usually choose a headline font from either the serif or sans serif races. Until the 1960s, most U.S. newspapers used Bodoni, a serif font. As a reaction, when newspapers redesigned, many of them chose the sans serif Helvetica. In the next round of redesigns, many newspapers returned to serif faces. *Hartford* uses Minion, a serif font. In Boulder, Co., the *Daily Camera* chose both Century 725 bold and Helvetica Neue condensed. *Word & Way,* the state Baptist paper in Missouri, chose Garamond Condensed and Franklin Gothic (Figs. 17.3-17.4). Each of those choices creates a different personality.

If the newspaper wants to build a reputation for local coverage, the second section, clearly labeled, could lead off with local news. However, the front-page story selection is also vital to that image. Decisions about the packaging, placement and location of columnists must be determined by how hard the editors want to sell them. If the paper has large amounts of record copy (real estate transactions, court news and police blotter material), material must be gathered efficiently and presented coherently.

As the designer tries to solve each of these problems, the redesign committee, or a smaller group representing it, needs to see and respond to proposed changes. Incorporating some of the committee suggestions into the redesign will be helpful in getting the committee's support and will save the designer a great deal of time. Problems or disagreements that surface early in the process can be solved much more easily than those that surface at the last minute. A designer who is deeply involved in the project may find it difficult to compromise or to separate ego from practicality. If the committee members have seen the various parts of the redesign, they are more likely to approve the whole.

Once the committee approves the project, it must be sold to both staff and readers. If the staff has been kept informed during the course of the project, the results will not be a surprise. However, the committee and the designer must have enough flexibility to adjust the plan when the staff members find weaknesses.

One of the first questions editors ask is whether to phase in the redesign or to introduce it entirely in one issue. The answer lies in the local market conditions. Introducing all or most of it at once allows the newspaper to use the redesign in a circulation promotion campaign. Many newspapers introduce it to advertisers a few days before readers see it. A phase-in takes away much of the impact of the changes, but depending on your readership, that might be necessary. Both the *New York Times* and the *Wall Street Journal* phased in changes by sections. Any dramatic change in format or content could have been disastrous because of their special niche roles. Most other papers introduce the redesign at one time. It allows them to gain the biggest promotional advantage. When the *Telegraph Herald* in Dubuque, Iowa, decided to switch from afternoon to morning publication, it also redesigned so it could promote a new time and new product (Fig. 17.5).

PROTOTYPE PHASE

The designer translates ideas into concrete examples in the prototype phase. Designers should be willing to produce several formats for each page and to listen closely to reactions. Prototypes first are directed to an in-house group. When general agreement is reached on one or two approaches, it's time to take the prototypes to a reader focus group. When the pages are taken to readers, they should be printed on the newspaper's press to make it look as realistic as possible and to see how your design elements reproduce on newsprint. In Waco three groups of readers were convened to represent three demographic segments: older, loyal readers; young, frequent readers; and, finally, young residents who didn't read the paper.

In Munster, Ind., focus group participants approved the changes. "This still feels like my newspaper," one said. "It's just easier to get through now." Another said, "I liked the way you give us a menu of what's in the paper. Sometimes it's tough to find things now."

In St. Louis the designers showed the first set of prototypes to a management committee. The editor, Cole Campbell, didn't like what he saw. "I want a blue collar *New York Times*," he told Bob Rose, assistant managing editor for graphics.

Rose and consultant Alan Jacobson constructed a second set of prototypes. This time, the readers in the focus group didn't like them. "We got hammered," Rose said. "Not by everyone, but by too many."

They went back to the drawing board. They reworked the design. They changed text type, introduced more pictures and concentrated on news. "Readers and carriers in 14 focus groups loved it," Rose said. "They wanted to take copies of the prototype home. They thought the paper was being printed on brighter stock. They said they didn't need glasses to read it any more" (Rose 1998).

The feedback from the readers influenced the results at the *Post-Dispatch*, as they should. In Figures 17.6–17.8, you see the progression

17.5   When the *Telegraph Herald* in Dubuque, Iowa, switched to morning publication, it introduced a redesign. The promotions teased the redesign change by using what would be the new flag.

17.6   This is how the *Post-Dispatch* looked before the redesign.

17.7   The designers took two prototypes to readers before they found acceptance. This was the second of the set.

17.8   The new *Post-Dispatch* emphasizes a vertical layout to get more elements above the fold. Managers hope this will help them increase single-copy sales.

17.9   The prototype edition of the nation and world page featured several short stories.

17.10   In the end, the world and nation pages were separated. The editors decided they would run a combination of briefs and then concentrate on explaining one story in depth.

from the existing *Post-Dispatch*, to a prototype version, to the final version. The examples in Figures 17.9 and 17.10 demonstrate the changes on a key inside page that occurred after the focus group feedback.

With proper guidance from the moderator, focus group participants will respond both to big picture questions and minutiae. Here are some comments from a redesign focus group session for the *Telegraph Herald* in Dubuque:

Reader: This shadow box, where they pull out a quote in the article and shadow box like that, that's cool.
Moderator: How are those quotes useful? How do you use them?
Reader 1: I think it really draws you into the whole article . . .
Reader 2: I look for it to be repeated in the article and to see if my take on it is what the rest of the article shows.
Reader 3: It's almost like a secondary headline for me. I'm a headline reader first. I look at all the headlines and pick up what I want to read. I always read what the pictures are, the subscripts under the pictures, I always look at that. The pullout thing, I like that.
Reader 4: Letters to the editor looks kind of small and condensed. I think the letters to the editor ought to be more prominent.
Reader 5: I'd put Gary Trudeau on the comics page.

By the time the session is over, you will have collected reader reaction to everything from how easy—or difficult—it is to read the text type to your use of color. If you can't videotape the session, capture it on audiotape. Then review the comments to see what changes, if any, you need to make. Just because a couple of participants criticize something doesn't mean you need to change it. Use common sense.

THE RESULTS

Rollout is the most exciting—and sometimes the most frustrating—day in the process. It is exciting because the work of dozens of people is coming to fruition. They all hope not only that their community of readers will accept the redesign, but that it will attract even more readers. It is frustrating in that no matter how many dry runs you've made, staff members will have trouble remembering all the style changes, some of the new computer programs will not work right, and, most important, some readers will object. Oddly enough, the most loyal readers are the ones most likely to object, particularly when you change the location of their favorite features. The *St. Louis Post-Dispatch* received typical comments. One reader wrote, "I feel like a lost soul. For the first time in 40 years I am without a morning *Post-Dispatch*. I can't decipher the new style of print. I have only seen this type of fancy print on greeting cards or stationery, never before on magazines, books or newspapers. The letters are dark, curving and close together. I shall miss my *Post-Dispatch*." Another wrote, "As a long-time subscriber, I find the new format the most innovative and ambitious project ever undertaken by the *Post-Dispatch*. I wish the paper success in this bold venture. . . ."

At the *Kansas City Star*, reader representative Miriam Pepper shared the reaction with her readers in a column:

The change in design drew more compliments than daggers, and numerous suggestions for improvements.

The highlights:

"It's a smashing success! It looks very elegant, sophisticated and credible."

"It has a gray drab feel now. It's just not readable for us."

She added, "By the end of week one, compliments were ahead, especially from many older readers who remarked that the new type was easier to read" (Pepper 1998).

And so it goes. While some redesigns meet universal applause, it is not uncommon for the first wave of reaction to include many criticisms as readers get used to the changes. By the end of a week or two, more compliments roll in.

As redesigns go, the *Star*'s was modest. The paper changed typefaces and, most important, reorganized the paper to anchor standing inside pages, such as nation and world news. Editors also changed the color palette and cut down on the use of tints (Figs. 17.11-17.16).

THE STYLEBOOK

Like the editing stylebook, the purpose of the design stylebook is to enforce consistency and arbitrate disputes. It doesn't restrict creativity; it's a framework. Stylebooks should concentrate on what is or should be. The length and detail of a stylebook vary according to the size of the newspaper and the staff. Small newspapers, which don't have many sections, may get

17.11 Before the redesign, the *Kansas City Star* used tints frequently. Its color palette was not coordinated.

17.12 The redesigned *Star* cut down on the tints, corralled the color and restricted the display typography. The result is a calmer, classier look.

17.13 The *Star* published an extended table of contents and wire news on page 2 before the redesign. However, the subject matter of the stories would change from day to day.

17.14 Now page 2 literally is a second front page. It contains the most important stories that didn't make page 1.

17.15   The header on the top of the sports cover is consistent with all the other sections in the paper except . . .

17.16   . . . the Arts section. The paper decided to forgo consistency to give the arts a personality appropriate to its content. The name of the newspaper is printed in small type below the page header.

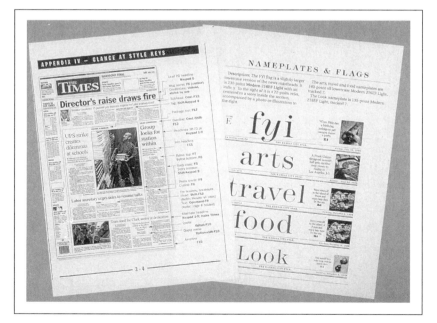

17.17   The design stylebook is an important element of any redesign. At left is a page from the *Times* of Munster, Ind., and at right is a page from the *Kansas City Star*. A printed version is important to speed access to some information, but the formats and templates should all be in your computer system.

by with a few pages; papers with several sections and a huge staff need a stylebook that will probably run 50 or more pages. Formats alone often take another 10 to 20 pages.

Typically, stylebooks include information on how the paper is to be organized, the grid, typography, spacing, rules, photography, color, and design accessories such as logos, cutlines and jump lines (Fig. 17.17). By the time the staff receives the stylebook, members should be well briefed on the contents.

Besides receiving the new stylebook and getting to know it, staff members need enough training with the new formats to become familiar with them, to work out the bugs and clear up ambiguities. The training schedule must account for advance sections.

EDUCATION AND PROMOTION

A good newspaper belongs to the readers, not to the staff or publisher. That's why it's important to talk to the readers when you're ready to introduce the redesign and again after it is introduced. You're changing their newspaper; they deserve the courtesy of knowing ahead of time what is coming and why. Besides, telling readers what is coming and how to use the new product will help head off criticism.

The newspaper can communicate through stories and advertisements. Like most newspapers introducing a redesign, the *St. Louis Post-Dispatch* ran advertisements promoting the redesign and explaining the elements in the new product (Fig. 17.18). Every newspaper that introduces a redesign should talk to its readers, and then let the readers talk back. Some have staff members take phone calls. Others ask readers to fill out comment sheets. Some invite faxes. All of the methods involve engaging the community in a conversation. *Kansas City Star* reader representative Miriam Pepper assured her readers, "Editors are listening to readers (even you doubters who begin your notes by saying you don't think you can have any impact), and we welcome more ideas. That part really *hasn't* changed."

Her point—that readers' views are welcomed—is an important one. Continue the conversation with your community.

17.18 The *St. Louis Post-Dispatch* ran a series of ads promoting and explaining the redesign. These ads usually run the week before the introduction of the redesign and on the day of the launch.

18.1 One of the more innovative newspapers in the country, the *Virginian-Pilot* lets the news of the day determine its front-page display. To cover revelations about the president's sex life, the editors blew out the top of the front page to give local reaction to the news.

The design of a daily newspaper is a difficult undertaking. Compromise on the niceties of typography is inevitable, control of layout minimal, and perfection unobtainable.

Alan Fletcher
Design consultant

18.2   On average, *USA Today* has about 30 elements on its front page. An element is a place that a reader may stop to read. For instance, each brief, when it is designated by a bold headline or lead-in, is an element. By comparison, The *Wall Street Journal* has about 50 elements on its front page.

18.3   In contrast with *USA Today*, the *Register* in Orange County, Calif., offers longer stories, larger photos and fewer elements. Even with the quieter approach, the *Register*'s frequent use of decks and pullouts creates ample entry points on the page.

"Sometimes I feel that they [the local paper] are out to hassle me," a participant in a readership study said. "You can't find things, you're always turning pages, and the whole paper begins to fall apart."

Defined sections are the beams that keep the newspaper from falling apart. Like members of a family from the same gene pool, each should look like the parent but retain its individuality.

Some readers toss aside the news and go directly to a favorite section. Many others flip through the folded paper, especially the large Sunday issues, and look at the top half of the section covers. That has encouraged some editors to demand more elements at the top of section fronts. Each section presents special challenges. In business, it may be how to illustrate stories. In sports, it may be how to present the sports statistics. In features, it may be how to design the calendar or the weddings and engagements. In Chapter 17, I laid the foundation for redesign of any section. In this chapter, I will look at the techniques that successful designers use to highlight the strengths and how they solve the unique problems of each section.

THE NEWS SECTION

More than any other, the front page *is* the paper. It's the first thing the reader sees. It sets the tone; it announces what's important; it's the gate to the rest of the publication. Through its structure, typography, visuals and element count, it proclaims the newspaper's personality.

Element count

As much as any other factor, the number of elements defines a newspaper's page 1 personality. That doesn't mean that all papers will look alike. Few readers would confuse the *Wall Street Journal* and *USA Today,* but the two papers have among the highest element counts on page 1 of any newspapers. Some editors count stories, but a more important factor is the number of elements for the window-shopper. Readers scan visuals and display type. Each headline, each visual, each promo, each brief is also an element. By that definition, the *Wall Street Journal* averages about 50 elements on page 1; *USA Today* averages about 30. Even the *New York Times* often has as many as 15 elements on the front page. Despite the high element count, the *Journal* doesn't look cluttered because the elements consist of understated briefs, some of which stand alone and some of which refer to inside stories. *USA Today,* like most newspapers today, uses color, photographs and bolder type to create an appearance of more activity (Fig. 18.2). Other newspapers, such as the *Register* in Orange County, Calif., choose to use fewer, larger elements (Fig. 18.3).

The *Register*'s layout usually is horizontal. *USA Today*'s is vertical. It sells nearly 70 percent of its copies on newsstands. A vertical format allows the designer to use more elements and to put more of them above the fold, but its bolder typography, pictures and color give it a different feel. Because a vertical format offers the opportunity to run more stories than a horizontal format, many newspapers have become more vertical in the last few years. When the *St. Louis Post-Dispatch* redesigned in late 1997, it presented a vertical format that permits the display of three or four stories, plus visuals, above the fold. The evidence that this helps sales is mixed. Mauro (1986) found that readers knew which paper they were going to buy before they approached vending boxes. On the other hand, metro papers report some success with efforts to increase single-copy sales by putting strong stories above the fold. The *Pittsburgh Post-Gazette* even experimented with a Sunday billboard front page—no stories, just teasers constructed of large text and visuals for newsstand sales. They reported enough success to expand the program (Collins 1997). The *Reporter,* a 20,000-circulation newspaper in Fond du Lac, Wis., reported modest increases in sales when it created a billboard on the top half of the paper (Fig. 18.4). Zachary Stalberg, editor of the *Philadelphia Daily News,* once ran the circulation department. "Regardless of whether you're a broadsheet or tab, home-delivery or single copy, you still have to create a face that people like and want to relate to," he says. "You have to be appealing, whether it's over the breakfast table or out on the street. I frankly wish other papers would forget that they have this home-delivery component, or at least de-emphasize it, as they try to decide what to put on the front of the paper" (Gyles 1998).

Element count is also a function of the grid. The more columns there are, the more elements usually appear. The *Portland Oregonian* has an 11-column grid. It permits the paper to introduce white space and put more elements on the page. *USA Today* has seven columns.

Teasers

Teasers, the items that promote inside content, increase the element count. Most newspapers have teasers stripped above the flag; some have them below the flag. Some, like the *Times* of Munster, Ind., surround the flag with them. The *Sunday Oregonian* devoted the top six inches of the page to teasers (Figs. 18.5-6). Readers look at teasers. In the Poynter Institute for Media Studies' "Eyes on the News" study, participants read the teasers in the Minneapolis and Orange County papers even more than in the St. Petersburg paper, where the teaser format is more modest. No study has yet been published to show whether readership of the teasers translates into higher readership of the stories they promote. Nonetheless, people who have the papers look at promotional items. That's another point of sale, and it also means newspapers can consider running them vertically or across the bottom to open up the top of the page again. Regardless of where they run, designers should change the format of the teasers often. Papers with small staffs usually create two or three formats for teasers. Larger papers often assign the teaser package to a graphic artist each day.

18.4   In an experiment to see if it could increase single-copy sales, the *Reporter,* a Wisconsin newspaper, used the top half of page 1 as a billboard.

18.6   On Sundays the *Oregonian* often devotes up to six inches at the top of its page to promote inside stories. This is a modified billboard approach.

18.5   With a short title, the *Times* of Munster, Ind., is free to use the rest of the space to promote inside stories.

Photographs

The trade-off for higher element counts often is less space to display pictures. The familiar battle in newsrooms across the country is between the news and photo editors. The news editor often argues for two or three stories above the fold. The photo editor argues that a large picture or pictures will attract more readership. Compromises often are made. The picture is run a column smaller; the picture is pushed down and disappears under the fold. Given the high readership of photographs, it's surprising how often they are misused. Good design starts with the photograph. However, selecting and sizing photographs is an art, not a science.

Digests

Many papers publish digests on the front. Digests are the easiest way to increase the element count and are at the heart of the page 1 presentation in the *Wall Street Journal* and *USA Today*. Digests are a reaction to people who say they don't have time to read the paper. A front page with a digest offers a more extensive menu of important information.

Framing

Often, the higher the element count, the more framing there is. The frame defines the built-in features. Some newspapers frame only across the top, where they promote inside content. Others add a vertical column of briefs. Still others add a horizontal strip at the bottom to run indexes, weather and other information. There are trade-offs. As framing increases, element count increases and flexibility decreases. Severe framing impinges on good photographic display. For that matter, even a vertical column of briefs restricts photo display.

Jumps

Also affecting the front-page look is the policy on jumps. Readers hate jumps, but most newspapers continue to use them. A paper that jumps stories generally will have more stories on the front page than a paper that has a no-jump or low-jump policy. Pioneered by the *News* in Boca Raton, Fla., the "Boca jump" is a story that stops on page 1 and refers to a related story inside, which can be a sidebar or even the main story. *USA Today* uses the same device. If stories are jumped, consider using "please," as in "Please see KEYWORD, p. X." One researcher found that readers appreciated the simple courtesy (Pipps 1985).

Continued stories should also be located on the same page and in the same place in each issue if possible. Some newspapers, including the *New York Times,* jump stories from one section to another, a practice that is inconvenient if not maddening to a reader who might not be able to find the section. From the readers' standpoint, jumps from page 1 or a section front should be located on the back page of the section. However, that is a highly coveted advertising page and often is not available to editorial. Page 2 is a questionable location for jumps because it is sometimes difficult to clip stories that appear on both sides of a page. Wherever continued stories are located, they should be there consistently so subscribers learn where to look.

What they see when they arrive is often a one-word label over the jumped story. That's not enough. The advantage of a label jump head is that readers easily recognize it. However, few readers go directly to a continued story. Most of them continue scanning the cover and may even read through the section before picking up a continued story. Others will not have seen the original story when they encounter the jump. A headline will attract more readers than a label. However, a headline that reflects the new material in the jump may not be recognized immediately as the same story. A combination of headline styles emphasizes the strengths of the two approaches.

One solution is a combination of a label and a new headline. There are several typographic ways of handling this combination. One is a small hammer head that serves as a keyword in identifying the story.

KEYWORD
The headline
offers new information

Another approach is to isolate the keyword typographically:

Keyword: The rest of the headline tells the story
Keyword: *The rest of the headline tells the story*

Headline choices

When selecting headline fonts, designers look for legibility, personality and contrast. If you are selecting fonts from the serif, sans serif or square serif races, at display sizes, only a few fonts create legibility problems. Selecting a typeface to match a personality is more difficult. Do you want traditional or modern? Understated or in-your-face? Serif fonts offer you more ways of creating a personality than the more neutral sans serif fonts. For example, compare Univers with Garamond:

This is Univers regular aghbr
This is Garamond regular aghbr

The strokes in Univers are even. Like a pencil, it is functional. With its serifs and slight differentiation in stroke widths, Garamond offers more details that create a personality. Because of its strong, even stroke widths, Univers offers a better black than Garamond. To the typographer, the sans serifs have notable differences, which lay readers may not detect. Compare the following:

Helvetica; Gill Sans; Futura; Univers

Chances are that more readers would notice the differences among the serif races:

Garamond; Century Schoolbook; Stone

Whatever the choice, designers look for ways to build contrast in their headline formats. Color contrast is the most basic. Main heads in bold and deck heads in medium are the most common way to provide color contrast. Some designers elect to create more levels of contrast by using fonts from different races or using italic.

Many newspapers use a blacker head, sometimes even a different typeface, on the lead story. Metros routinely use blacker, large headlines

18.7 With the advertisement at the right, the designer correctly located the pictures at the left of the package. Try to keep your photos and art from touching ads, because the ads can overpower them.

for early street sales editions. Many of those same papers tone down for home delivery.

Color

Readers love color. The designer's job is to create a palette that ensures that the colors are complementary and appropriate to the newspaper's personality (see Chapter 11.) If color is designed into the format, designers don't have to invent a new way to use it each day. You design color into the format by locating it in standing elements, such as teasers and digests. If you don't have process color photography, it becomes more important to locate spot color at the top and bottom of the page for page balance. If you have color pictures, the secondary photo usually takes care of the balance problem.

Consistency or innovation?

Should your front page be consistent from day to day, or should designers have a blank slate to present each day's news? The *New York Times* and *USA Today* vary little on the front from day to day. The *Virginian Ledger-Pilot* varies a great deal. Most newspapers tend to look the same each day. It takes a system of planning and teamwork to produce pages that reflect the day's news.

Inside news

Just as the front should reflect the unpredictability of the flow and intensity of the news, the inside pages should be organized to provide stability. News should be organized by categories and labeled. Readers want to know where to find everything from the weather to the national news. The best way to help the readers find content is to put it in the paper in the same order each day. The order of the departments in *Time* magazine is the same each week; the space devoted to the departments expands and contracts to reflect the content. The cover story appears in the logical department. The consistency helps the subscriber; the excitement is created by the surprises found within the departments.

On the inside news pages, here are some guidelines:

1. Work off the edge of ads to create modular spaces.
2. Try to keep photos and graphics as far away from the ads as you can. If the ads pyramid right, place the photo at the left (Fig. 18.7).
3. Don't box a story on top of an ad. It looks too much like advertising.
4. Run briefs vertically if possible (Fig. 18.8). On short stories, the fewer breaks to the next column, the better.
5. Vary the rhythm on a page containing two or more stories by using a wider setting on one.

6. Pages 2 and 3 are important for establishing readership. Keep these pages as open as possible.
7. Consider creating a table of contents. Magazine editors have discovered that a table of contents attracts high readership and that people who see a story listed in a table of contents are more likely to read the full story than those who do not. Newspapers have many more articles each day than a magazine, yet few make an effort beyond an index to help the reader find anything, let alone encourage them to read it. The *Wheaton Sun*, a tabloid, devotes most of page 3 to a table of contents (Fig. 18.9).

Page 2

One of the more interesting innovations in the last few years is the development of a newspaper within a newspaper. Reacting to readers who say they don't have time to read the entire newspaper, editors have created summaries of the paper, which serve as both a quick read and a promotion of inside stories. The *Virginian-Pilot* runs a vertical digest the length of the page called the "1minnews" (Fig. 18.10). The *Wichita Eagle* uses page 2 as a table of contents and a summary of the week's news in its Sunday editions (Fig. 18.11). Page 2 also is a favorite location for celebrity briefs and weather. Regardless of the size of the paper, there will always be a page 2, so it's a logical place to anchor standing features. Some newspapers place the summary on the back of the news section.

Briefs packages

Compared with the typical story, packages of briefs get good readership. Packaging is the key, however. Some newspapers even run maps and keys to locate each story (Fig. 18.12). A more typical digest combines pictures and copy. Designers should build in weight contrast and carefully control the white space to make the packages more pleasing. Some newspapers run digests in sans serif to differentiate them from the serif type in the longer stories.

Records pages

In smaller communities, a records page is a familiar sight. It is the heart of the newspaper. On it, you find everything from fire calls to birth announcements to real estate transactions. If the advertising stack permits, this is a good place for a seven-column format because you can get more listings into the same amount of space. It's important to provide typographic contrast and white space on these text-intensive pages. Bold or black headlines, sometimes even in a different but complementary typeface, permit a smaller size without sacrificing effect. Extra white space between the end of a listing and the next headline airs out the digest. If you have extensive records copy, consider building a window on the page in which you can run a standing feature or a stand-alone photograph or graphic. The weather map serves the same purpose at many newspapers.

Obituaries

Present obituaries in vertical formats, like any item you expect some readers to clip and save. This minimizes the number of wraps from one column to the next and makes it easier for readers to clip. Other items in the same category: school lunch menus, weddings, engagements and recipes.

18.8 When you gather several short stories into one package, you help yourself organize the page. Running them vertically gives you the necessary vertical element on the page and keeps the short stories from splitting in awkward places.

18.9 Some newspapers are content with running an index, but the *Wheaton Sun*, a tabloid, publishes a table of contents on page 2. Magazines have discovered that readership of tables of contents is high.

18.10 To attempt to satisfy those readers who say they don't have enough time to read a newspaper daily, many newspapers, including the *Virginian-Pilot,* publish a condensed version of the day's issue on page 2.

18.11 On Sunday the *Wichita Eagle* devotes page 2 to look back at the week's news as well as to run a digest of the top news of that day. Many people read newspapers only on Sunday.

18.12 The *Wheaton Sun* helps its readers locate where crimes occurred by running a map with the summary of incidents reported to police.

FEATURE SECTIONS

Lifestyle, Food, Entertainment, Arts and Travel often have separate staffs and separate sections. However, they share the same problems.

The poster or billboard (one-subject pages) was popular in lifestyle sections until the mid-1980s. Then the move to create more active pages reached many feature sections. The impact is illustrated at the *Times* of Munster, Ind. Its Lifestyles page offers nine elements above the section flag, then goes to a page devoted to a single subject. However, even the one-subject story is broken into several segments (Fig. 18.13). Fortunately, poster pages have not disappeared. The *Oregonian*'s food section cover offers an attractive layout on a Dickens Christmas (Fig. 18.14).

Here are some suggestions for section fronts:

1. There is still room for one-subject pages, but segment the package to make it look less daunting.
2. If you want to increase the element count, establish a frame. Designers tire of the formats long before readers do. Nonetheless, the frame shouldn't be a straitjacket. That might sometimes mean making a vertical digest into a horizontal element. Or even moving it inside.

3. You have more opportunity because of time and subject matter to use the range of story-telling devices available. Make the best of them. Your pages should use maps and charts, illustrations and photography.

4. Design with type. Manipulate the letters and stack the words. Use type appropriate to the content if your stylebook permits. The Dickens Christmas page uses a script with a swash letter to establish an appropriate environment for the story.

5. Even if you don't design with type, make use of alternate headline formats. A banner news headline on a feature page is as out of place as shorts at a formal wedding. Consider using titles, labels, readouts and blurbs.

6. Let the grid reflect your content. Use wider settings for your feature stories and narrower settings for your quick reads and listings.

18.13   Rather than creating one large text block, the *Times'* reporter broke the Viagra story into smaller bites. This enables the designer to segment the presentation. Inside of a single entry point, there are several on this one-subject page.

18.14   The poster, or single-subject page, is not common these days, but it is not dead. The *Portland Oregonian* uses the space to match photograph, display type and grid to the subject.

7. Use white space in inventive ways. The *Boston Globe*, for instance, uses more white space between elements in its Living Arts section than in its news section. That helps establish a section personality (Fig. 18.15).

8. Tease stories that are inside. Be aggressive. Sell.

9. Surprise the reader. Make it readable but make it different.

10. Offer the service-journalism angle. Tell readers what they need to know and tell them how to act on it. Pull out phone and fax numbers and addresses (Fig. 18.16). Show them how to make something with illustrations.

11. Think about how readers are supposed to use the information and present it accordingly. If you want them to clip it, don't wrap the information from one column to the top of the next. Put it in clipable modules.

12. If you don't have process color, think twice about food pictures. Instead of concentrating on the food, you might have to concentrate on the people making the food in black and white.

18.15   Newspapers normally run 1-pica gutters. In its Living Arts section, the *Boston Globe* creates a more relaxed atmosphere by separating the stories horizontally with several picas of space.

Inside feature sections

Many feature-section editors have to deal with calendars, columnists, weddings and engagements. Each presents special challenges. Probably what they have most in common, however, is that journalists dislike dealing

18.16 Service journalism is an approach that says you should provide readers with information and tell them how to act on it. Sometimes a telephone number will be sufficient. In this package, the reporters and photographers don't just talk about making something, they *show* how to make it. Readers can act on this information.

with these items and readers enjoy reading them. They're too important to be overlooked.

Just as creating a records page is important in the news section, creating a good calendar is important in many feature sections. The calendar should appear in the same place and at the same time. The typography should be legible and offer type contrast in weight, form or both. The *Register-Guard* in Eugene, Ore., has created a grid for its music calendar that is easy to access (Fig. 18.17) and a map to locate places where people go for entertainment. The *Bremerton* (Wash.) *Sun* offers an extensive page that includes events, roadwork schedules and information on where to seek help (Fig. 18.18).

Space or lack of it is the arbiter of whether or not advice columns are packaged. If possible, do it. If advice columnists can't be printed on the same page, they at least should appear in the same place every issue. Like calendars, they should appear in the same place at a regular time.

Numerous short stories cause one problem common to feature sections. Grouping them under common subject headings creates a larger graphic element, which is easier to handle, rather than running them as small stand-alone stories.

Weddings and engagements present another challenge to designers. To make these items useful to readers, keep the copy with the photograph. Readers should be able to cut them out in one piece (Fig. 18.19). Another solution is to create clusters of photographs and run copy beneath the related photograph. If the copy runs short, leave the white space.

SPORTS

A hybrid, sports offers the timeliness of news, the interest of features and compelling photographs. The section design should reflect that integration of content. Most do. Sports pages can be quiet and reflective or loud and excited, but they should always be planned. Probably less than 2 percent of the content in sports sections cannot be anticipated. Editors know when

18.17 The Eugene *Register-Guard* has created an innovative grid to present the music events in its community. The far-left vertical column contains the names of the establishments; the columns to the right are the days of the week. Within each rectangle is the name of the entertainer or group, the time and the price. Every other line is screened to help readers move horizontally.

18.18 The Yourtown page in the *Bremerton* (Wash.) *Sun* is the infrastructure of the newspaper. It includes an extensive calendar of events, scheduled road work and a rotating feature telling residents where to get help for a variety of problems, such as substance abuse and physical disabilities.

and where the events are. They plan features and columns. The only time they don't know when something is going to happen is if a league settles a strike, a team signs a player or a sports personality dies. Even then, they know it will happen, they just don't know when. As a result, sports editors and designers have the opportunity to be the strongest section visually in the paper. They can take the time to design feature packages (Fig. 18.20) or plan special displays for historic events (Figs. 18.21-22).

Regardless of the pacing, all sports sections have available to them action pictures, reams of statistics waiting for a chart to happen and good quotes. The section should reflect that content by bold photo editing, generous sizing and frequent use of pullout quotes, charts, tables and diagrams.

A special design challenge is the sports agate page. Designers must present a huge body of statistical data with the least amount of space and the highest amount of legibility the paper can afford. Many newspapers are using type in the 7- to 9-point range. At those sizes, and considering the kind of information in the scoreboards, designers save space and increase legibility by going to a seven- or eight-column format with gutters of about 6 points. The narrow format holds the word count per line at a reasonable level and leaves fewer unfilled lines. Six column grids waste space.

Designers of sports agate could also consider:

1. Build in a variety of medium and bold type. Readers need the visual relief, and the weights and size differentiation helps you categorize the information. Editors

18.19 You can be sure that several people will want to clip the wedding and engagement announcements from the paper. That's one reason to keep the copy and photos in a modular unit. Another reason is to help organize the page. Cluster the photos; seek common alignment.

18.21 Regardless of what section they are in, big events deserve big display. When Mark McGwire was setting the homerun record, the *St. Louis Post-Dispatch* sold thousands of extra copies each day by devoting its coverage to the story both on page 1 and in sports.

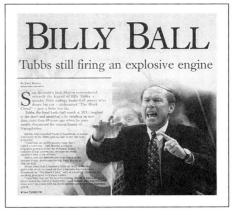

18.20 Sports designers have opportunities to create interesting packages. Those at the *San Antonio Express-News* didn't pass up the opportunity in this feature on basketball coach Billy Tubbs. The innovative photo and typographic display is an eye-catcher.

18.22 When McGwire broke Babe Ruth's record and again when he hit his 70th homerun, residents of the area bought thousands of copies of the extra that the *Post-Dispatch* printed. Crowds also lined up outside the newspaper building to buy copies of the paper.

18.23 To provide visual relief to the sports statistics page, many newspapers are creating a window on the page. The *Centre* (Pa.) *Daily Times* screens the professional football standings. Other papers run sports newsmaker features in a box on the page.

18.24 The *Detroit News* summoned several forms of story telling to report on Nissan. Notice how several entry points beckon readers: two information graphics, a picture, a story and a sidebar. Segmenting makes stories more accessible.

first need to categorize the levels of information so the designer can designate the headers. For instance, you could start with the largest division, Class I, as the name of the sport; Class II as the name of the item within the sport; Class III as a subhead if needed and Class IV as the listing. Class I is the largest and/or boldest. You can also use capitals to distinguish the categories:

PRO FOOTBALL
NFL standings
AMERICAN CONFERENCE
Denver ...

2. Use sans serif type. It is more legible in small sizes than type with serifs, which often disappear. A slightly condensed face will save significant amounts of space. Little or no leading is needed.
3. Use column rules. Narrow columns with narrow gutters need column rules to separate the type.
4. Use a window on the agate page for relief. A window is a space, usually carved into the top middle of the page, which contains anything from briefs to television listings (Fig. 18.23).

BUSINESS

Unlike sports, business sections have to create most of their visuals because most of what they cover doesn't lend itself to action photography. In addition, because most people take money seriously, the tone of the business section is also less flippant than sports. But that doesn't mean the presentation needs to be dull. Some people think information graphics were invented with business editors in mind. That's not true, but business editors certainly benefit from them. So do readers. The daily grist of the business section is numbers. Charts and tables are not only useful but also essential. Diagrams help explain, better than do long blocks of text, how the economy works. The *Detroit News* supplemented its text with a photograph, bar chart and a dateline to help explain its story on Nissan (Fig. 18.24).

Just because information graphics are so obvious doesn't mean that other forms of story telling aren't available. Editors can use illustrators to draw the people they are writing about, or they can do photographic portraiture. Good portraiture photography goes far beyond the usual newspaper head-and-shoulders shot. Crain's *Chicago Business* frequently uses environmental portraits to illustrate its stories about managers (Fig. 18.25). By contrast, the *Seattle Times* photograph is a candid documentary photograph (Fig. 18.26). Although editors should use all these forms of story telling, if one comes to dominate the pages, the section will take on an identifiable personality.

One problem business and sports sections have in common is dealing with stock market listings. Like sports agate, stock listings should be in sans serif type in narrower columns to save space and increase legibility. A few fonts were designed for small-type publishing, among them Bell Centennial and Poynter Gothic Text.

Column widths for stock listings depend on the amount of data your newspaper includes. Those that publish only the name of the stock and

18.25 Some publications create a style by adopting a type of photography. Crain's *Chicago Business* runs a lot of environmental photographs of the business people it writes about.

18.26 The *Seattle Times* builds its section around documentary photographs. Compare the photographic styles of Crain's (Fig. 18.25) and *Seattle*.

highs and lows can use a 10-column grid. Those that run the stock name and several classes of data can use an eight- or nine-column grid. Hairline rules should separate the columns. Stock listing pages don't need to be pretty; they need to be functional. The designer must find a way with type size and boldness to make it easy for readers to find at least the right letter of the alphabet when they are looking for their stock.

To relieve the intensity of the text, the designer can build a window on the stock page. Such a window usually is a collection of market statistics; its placement with the stocks airs out an otherwise dense page. Advertisements also create windows—and bring in revenue. Advertisements floating on stock pages don't intrude on the readership flow because readers pick out stocks; they don't read columns of listings as they do text. Some newspapers, including the *Chicago Tribune*, offer a useful graphic on how to read the listings (Fig. 18.27).

EDITORIAL

The editorial or opinion pages are the last of the great untouched pages in most newspapers. Editorial pages haven't changed much in 40 years, even at many papers that have redesigned. The editorial page content generally consists of opinions from the newspaper editors, columnists, cartoonists and readers. A few newspapers use photographs to support an ed-

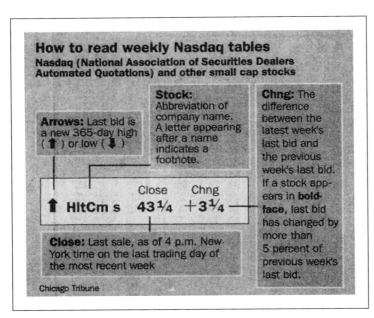

18.27   As a service to readers, many papers are now running a daily graphic explaining how to read the stock tables.

18.28   Although there are three lengthy articles on the page, the *San Jose Mercury-News'* Opinion page is accessible. The designer opens up the page by using white space and line illustrations. The ragged right setting on the type also permits more white space in the columns.

itorial point; some use photos or drawings to illustrate the concerns in readers' letters. These are admirable improvements. Photographs and illustrations increase readership and add impact. Another area that tradition rather than logic dominates is the signature on a letter. Readers will look to see who the writer is before reading; why not put the writer's name at the beginning of the letter?

In most newspapers, the editorial page's format is the same each day by tradition. Most newspapers prefer to create an environment in which issues are discussed rationally. Credibility could be damaged by flashy display, but that doesn't mean the pages have to be dull. The appropriate use of photographs, illustrations and charts and innovative use of typography can help here as well as anywhere else in the paper. The *San Jose Mercury News* uses grid, typography and illustration to attract its readers to its Opinion page (Fig. 18.28). The narrow column at the left adds visual relief in addition to serving as a location for the names of the editorial board members. Each of the top two articles are editorials, and they are identified by an insert. The story at the bottom is a column.

While the standard position for editorials is a vertical strip down the left side of the page, the *Journal-Courier* in Jacksonville, Ill., stripes its editorial across the top. The two right hand columns create the vertical element. One reason this page works is the combination of horizontal and vertical. Notice that the division of space in the middle module is 2/5-3/5. The contrast in widths makes the page more interesting (Fig. 18.29).

Although columns on editorial and commentary pages usually are wider, that doesn't preclude using a narrow column to introduce white space, to place column logos or to locate service journalism information.

18.29 Although most newspapers run the editorials vertically, the Jacksonville, Ill., paper runs its editorials horizontally. The designer creates the necessary vertical element with a columnist. The page is open because of the white space. The 3:2 apportionment of columns sets up the proper proportions in the body of the page.

19.1   To test different versions of the flag they were considering in their redesign, the managers of the *Telegraph Herald* in Dubuque, Iowa, ran a test page. Each version had a different color combination and a different engraved background for the letters.

Readers are getting a well-planned, guided tour through a potentially awesome wilderness of information, building great reader involvement, the one most important ingredient in product renewal.

Belden Associates
Research firm

19. Designing Accessories

Accessories are, by definition, secondary. In a newspaper, the design accessories include the nameplate, teasers, labels, bylines, logos and icons. Readers don't buy a newspaper to look at accessories, but these accessories help readers find their way through the publication. Like a king's aide, accessories should be seen and not heard. They do their job when they direct readers' attention to the content, not to the accessories themselves.

FLAGS

The flag, or more properly, nameplate, sets the tone for the newspaper. Its design is important because it is usually the first thing the reader sees. In designing the flag, designers consider everything from the publication's history to the number of words in the name. Cost is another factor. The flag is the brand. When you change it, the publication needs to change everything from vending boxes to business cards.

Many designers first look back to view the evolution of the flag. Sometimes, they will even use the base of a previous flag to create a new version. The nameplate can say to the reader, "This is an old-fashioned newspaper" or "This is an up-to-date newspaper." The difference between traditional and old-fashioned is a thin line. The type chosen to convey the name can be old without being old-fashioned. Compare the *Des Moines Register, Detroit Free Press* and *Seattle Times* (Fig. 19.2). The *Register* uses the traditional Old English typeface; the *Free Press* has altered it slightly to eliminate some of the flourishes; the *Times* has used it as a starting point but created a modern version. Other newspapers have completely severed ties with the traditional nameplate. The *Muscatine* (Iowa) *Journal* sports a delicate, classy flag (Fig. 19.3). Waco looked at several possibilities—and asked for responses from focus groups—before selecting the last flag pictured here (Fig. 19.4).

The *Dubuque* (Iowa) *Telegraph Herald* (Fig. 19.5) has a long name, a designer's nightmare, but when I arrived at the newspaper's building, I noticed the large "TH" on the side of the building. I later discovered that the paper

19.2   All three of these newspapers use Old English typefaces, but each has been modified to create a unique personality.

19.3   The *Muscatine* (Iowa) *Journal,* a 9,000-circulation daily, sports a classy flag design that results from using a typeface with extreme thicks and thins. Note the pages to the bottom of this flag. They are labeled "Saturday" and "Sunday" and denote that this is the weekend issue.

19.4   Readers in focus groups looked at several versions of proposed flags. Even older readers preferred a newer looking flag to the Old English version the paper had been running. The one selected is at the bottom of the list.

19.5   The long name restricts the designer's options, but the newspaper had called itself the "TH" in its columns for years.

19.6   The managers elected to use TH in the flag with the full name of the newspaper in smaller type. The letters are silver, chiseled against a blue background.

19.7   If *College Heights Herald* were given equal size, the type would have to be smaller. By subordinating *College Heights,* the designer was able to emphasize *Herald* and add a pleasing contrast of color and form to the flag.

had been referring to itself as the "TH" for decades. I created unconventional variations of a chiseled TH against a color background, and several versions were tested on the press (Fig. 19.1). The newspaper management selected one with the TH in silver against a blue background (Fig. 19.6).

Because all the words in a newspaper's name are not of equal importance, the designer can subordinate some words to others by changing the size and boldness of type. This gives the designer a chance to use larger type for the main part of the name (Fig. 19.7). It also gives the designer the option of creating a horizontal flag or stacking the words and creating a vertical flag.

It's easy to clutter a nameplate, but a simple insignia can help establish the identity of the paper. The insignia can reflect the area or a major landmark, or it can be a trademark for the newspaper. Whatever the insignia, it should be simple and fit neatly into the nameplate. The *News* in Kingstree, S.C., uses the pine so familiar to the state to shade its letters (Fig. 19.8).

Letter spacing is a critical issue. The designer may want to consider kerning and even ligatures. On the other hand, the designer may wish to build in more space between letters to customize the flag. Just don't get caught in between: too loose to be tight and too tight to be loose. When you are stacking words, tight is better than loose.

The design of the flag includes the name of the paper and all those elements that surround it: insignia, folio lines, cutoff rules, even weather blurbs. The weight of cutoff rules should be selected carefully so there is a clear delineation to show where the nameplate ends and the news begins. When this isn't clear, the lead headline often sits uncomfortably close to the type in the flag. If the flag is ever dropped to permit promotional boxes or a story to run above it, at least a 1-point rule should be placed between the flag and the material above. Generally, the weight of type in the flag dictates the weight of the cutoff rule: bold type, bold rule. Many designers have successfully put extra white space under the cutoff rule, as much as four picas, to buffer the news from the flag.

LABELS

Page labels tell readers where they are in the paper. They are read differently than headlines and text. Like the sign on a rest-room door, they merit only a glance. Large page labels, such as the ones used by the *San Antonio*

Express-News, can overwhelm the page if the designer does not take steps to tone down the weight. The "S.A. life" section head is large—the A is three inches tall—but the letters are light. The titles on the rest of the sections, such as sports, are scaled back by use of screens. With no screen, the page title would be the dominant element on the page daily (Fig. 19.9).

Designers establish classes of page headers. Usually, the largest appear on section fronts. A smaller version appears on inside pages. The *Sun News* in Myrtle Beach, S.C., uses this system (Fig. 19.10).

Consistency in section titles has been a tradition, but it's one that's crumbling, and probably properly so. Some newspapers have introduced section labels that reflect the content of that section. The *San Antonio Express-News* is one of many newspapers that varies one or more section headers to reflect the content. One way to assure readers where they are is to build a miniature version of the newspaper's flag into the section header (Figs. 19.9 and 19.10).

BYLINES

Bylines help readers make the transition from the headline type to the text. There are several possibilities, but the byline style selected should be harmonious with the overall style of the paper. For instance, you wouldn't want to use a thick and thin line over and under a byline unless the overall design involved thicks and thins. Unity is the controlling principle. There are two general guidelines for all bylines. First, flush left is the most natural because people read from left to right; however, if headlines are centered, it would make sense to center bylines. Second, bylines should be distinctive from the text. If you use the same type as the text, then the weight, size or form can provide contrast. If you choose sans serif to contrast with the text, you can

19.8   Many publications incorporate an icon that identifies them with the geographic region they serve. The *Kingstree News* successfully integrates the pine so familiar to its residents into its flag.

19.9   The *San Antonio Express-News* deviates from its normal header style when it gets to the life section. The Sports header format appears on the top of the rest of the sections. All of them, however, have a small version of the newspaper's flag with the section name.

19.10   The *Sun News* of Myrtle Beach, S.C., uses the same typographic style for its section headers as for its flag. Notice the small version of the flag that also appears on the section fronts. This is a way of branding all sections of the paper.

add weight as additional contrast. Here are some bylines showing variation
in font, weight, size and form:

By Gary Roets   **By Gary Roets**   **BY GARY ROETS**
Tribune writer   *Tribune writer*   Tribune writer
By Gary Roets   **By Gary Roets**   **By Gary Roets**
Tribune writer   *Tribune writer*   **Tribune writer**

LOGOS

If you opened your local paper every day and saw a variety of column
logo designs, you would probably wonder if anybody at the newspaper was
reading it. Designers rely on column logos (also know as sigs and standing
sigs) to achieve unity, create a personality for writers and help readers locate standing features. Because these three functions are critical to the success of a newspaper, designers spend a lot of time working on logos.

Good logos reflect the marketing philosophy of the newspaper. If the
newspaper is trying to develop and sell personalities, the logos might contain a picture of the writer. Good logos used correctly help guide the reader
through the newspaper. They should be used as locators, not headlines.
Headlines attract the casual and infrequent reader to the content of a specific column; logos identify the feature for the faithful reader. The phenomenon is not unlike highway travelers who look for the billboard of a specific
motel chain. For some, the billboard is sufficient; others take a look at the
motel itself before they decide whether to stay.

Good logos also unify the newspaper. A consistent logo style identifies
the paper to subscribers no matter which section they pick up. This consistency is one more indication that the editors are in control of the product.
Inconsistency, whether in writing, editing or graphics style, damages credibility. Some newspapers, particularly large ones, have different logo styles
in different sections. Varying a logo theme may be a better approach than
completely changing the style.

When designing column logos, here are five considerations:

1. *Size.* Logos should be compact. They have more in common with the
   Izod alligator than a neon sign.
2. *Flexibility.* Are they proportioned so they can be set in one, one and a
   half, and two columns? Normally, one-column logos are slightly
   wider than they are deep, and larger ones are horizontal rectangles.
   While you vary the size, maintain the format.
3. *Marketing.* If you are trying to sell the name of the column, emphasize
   it. If you are trying to sell the author, use a photograph. Column logos
   without pictures are not as warm or personal as those with them.
   Even artists' renderings of authors are less personal than pictures. On
   the other hand, caricatures convey humor and informality.
4. *Unity.* Design of the column logos should be consistent with the design of other standing elements (such as the nameplate and sectional
   logos) and the tone of the publication.
5. *Cropping.* Crop tight but pause before amputating parts of the head.
   Some newspapers have tried to use pictures with parts of heads cut off
   in logos only to redo them because of reader complaints.

The column logos in Figure 19.11 illustrate the variety of approaches. Usually, one-column features are placed above the headline to allow the reader

to proceed directly from the headline to the column. Logos on horizontal features usually appear at the top of the second column, or they are inset in the copy.

STORY LOGOS

A package of stories on a single day or a story that runs more than one day should have a graphic identifying element. Logos help editors get around the problem of labeling something as a series, which readers generally avoid unless the content is gripping. It's easy to scare off readers, who don't want to make a long-term commitment or may have missed one or more parts, by labeling related stories as a series. Each story should stand alone; the graphic logo provides the continuity (Fig. 19.12). Space for a teaser line for the next day's story can be built into the logo. When you are dealing with sensitive stories, such as investigative reports, be careful not to express an editorial opinion in the logo design. The *San Jose Mercury News* removed from its web site the logo from its series on the CIA's alleged Nicaraguan drug connections because the image of a crack smoker over the CIA logo appeared to some to suggest that the CIA was guilty.

ICONS

Iconography is the use of drawings, or icons, to represent objects, actions and qualities. Linguists have found that most people interpret certain drawings or symbols the same way. One team of linguists found 620 concepts common to the 26 language-culture communities they studied. By combining icons with words, designers should be able to eliminate much of the ambiguity in messages. Designers don't have to invent these symbols. Several books are available that show international and other useful symbols (see Additional Readings).

ALICE KAHN

ON THE REBOUND

— *Tim Gallimore* —

CITYSIDES

ALICE KAHN

MONEY MATTERS
Tim Gallimore

19.11 Column logos with pictures generally are considered more personal than line drawings. They humanize the writer. The typography should be harmonious with all labeling within the paper.

19.12 Story logos are useful for a series or a frequently recurring subject. Logos should not express an opinion on the subject.

Glossary

Agate Traditionally, $5^1/_2$-point type, although now commonly used for type up to 7 points; agate line is an advertising space measurement $^1/_{14}$ of an inch deep.

Ascender The part of a letter that extends above the body of the type.

Balance Placement of elements to produce a harmoniously integrated page.

Banner A large headline that extends across the top of the front page above the most important story of the day.

Bar In type, a horizontal or slanted line connected at both ends.

Baseline Line on which the center body of type rests.

Bastard type Type set a different width than the standard column setting.

Black letter See Text letter.

Bleed   An illustration filling one or more margins and running to the edge of the page.

Blurb   A quote or a small part of a story displayed in type larger than text, usually 14 to 18 points.

Body type   See Text type.

Boldface   Type that has thicker, darker lines than the medium or lighter weights of the same face.

Border   An ornamental rule.

Bowl   In type, the curved line that creates a hollow space in a letter.

Broadsheet   Large-sized newspaper, usually about six columns wide by 21 inches deep.

Burn   To transfer type and images to a sensitized photographic plate.

Byline   Line crediting the writer, photographer or designer. Most commonly, it refers to the writer's credit at the top of the story.

Characters per pica (CPP)   Measurement of the width of a typeface, computed by counting the average number of letters that will fit in a given horizontal space and dividing by the number of picas.

Cold type   Type produced by a photographic or digitized process rather than by pressing inked metal forms against paper.

Color filter   Filter that absorbs all but one color.

Color separation   The product of a method of separating a color print or transparency into its three primary colors and black.

Concord   Blending of typographic elements to form a uniform impression.

Contrast   Effect achieved by varying shapes, sizes and weights of the elements on a page.

Contrast and balance   Layout technique in which a page is balanced by using contrasting shapes and weights.

Counter   White space within the letter.

Cursive   Race of type that is a stylized reproduction of formal handwriting. Also known as script.

Cutline   Information under a picture or artwork. Also known as a caption.

Cutoff rule   A horizontal line used to separate elements on a page.

Deck   One or more lines of display type that are smaller than the main headline.

Descender   The part of a letter that extends below the body of the type.

Design   A system of planning in which the person who arranges the elements on the page has some influence over the collection and selection of those elements.

Display type   Type larger than that used for text. In newspapers, display type ranges upward from 14 points.

Double truck   Facing pages in which the space between the pages is also used.

Dummy   The page, usually half the size of the page being produced, on which the editor shows where all the elements are to be arranged; the blueprint of the page.

Duotone   One color plus black, achieved by shooting two halftone negatives of the picture and producing two plates for the page.

Dutch wrap   Extending copy beyond the headline; also called a raw wrap.

Ear   The distinctive stroke at the top right of the letters g and r.

Em   A unit of space equal to the space taken by the capital M of the type size being used.

En   Half an em, or half the size of the capital M of the type being used.

Family   In type classification, typefaces that are closely related in design and share a common name. They differ in width, weight and form.

Flag   See Nameplate.

Flush left   Type that begins at the left hand edge or border of the column.

Flush right   Type that ends at the right hand edge or border of the column.

Focus   Starting point on the page, achieved by selecting a dominant element or elements.

Font   A complete set of type in one style and size.

Frame   Those elements of the page that are the same each issue. Teasers or a column are often part of a page frame.

Gutter   The vertical white space between columns of type.

Hairline   The thin stroke of a letter.

Halftone   Reproduction in which tones have been photographed through a screen to break up the areas into dots whose size determines the dark and light areas.

Hammer   One- or two-word headlines in large type, usually over a deck.

Hues   Pure colors such as red, yellow, green and blue.

Inset   Photograph or copy contained within the borders of a photograph.

Inter-letter spacing   Applying principles of kerning to display type.

Italic   Serif type sloped to the right.

Jim dash   Cutoff rule that does not cross the entire column.

Justified type   Type set so that the lines are all of equal length by hyphenating words and placing more or less space between words.

Kerning   Selective reduction of white space between irregularly shaped letters to create even optical spacing.

Key plate   Printing plate that puts the first image on the paper.

Kicker   Three or four words that are set about half the size of the main headline and usually appear flush left above the main headline.

Layout   Arrangement of elements on the page, usually done without any voice in the preparation or selection of those elements.

Leading   Sometimes written "ledding," this is the space between lines of type.

Leg   A column or wrap of type in a story.

Legibility   Measurement of the speed and accuracy with which type can be read and understood.

Letterpress   Method of printing in which raised letters are inked and pressed against paper.

Ligature   Two or more characters designed as a single unit. Common ligatures include the combinations of ff, ffi, fi, ffl and fl. A ligature has to be created by design, not by kerning.

Logo   An insignia of type, art or both that ties together stories in a series or identifies a regular feature such as a columnist.

Loop   The curved part of letters such as o, c, and e, which is often drawn distinctively.

Masthead   A listing of the publication's managers and editors, name of the paper, date, volume and sometimes the publication's creed.

Modern   Sometimes used to differentiate among types in the roman race. The type is geometric and symmetrical.

Module   A rectangular or square shape on a page. To run a story in modules means that each column of type is the same depth.

Mortise   Overlapping of two or more photographs or of a headline and a photograph.

Nameplate   The newspaper's name as it appears at the top of page 1. Also know as the flag.

Novelty   See Ornamental.

Nut graph   A conversational headline deck; it includes subject, verb and articles.

Oblique   Sans serif type slanted to the right.

Offset   A printing method in which the inked image transfers from plate to rubber blanket to paper. It is based on the principle that grease and water do not mix.

Old style   Sometimes used to differentiate among typefaces in the roman race. The type is asymmetrical and less formal looking than other roman faces.

Optimum format   The layout in which columns are set at the most legible line length.

Ornamental   Race of type designed to create such a specific mood or emotion that it is not useful for other purposes. Also known as novelty.

Pagination   System of producing pages from a typesetting machine, thus eliminating the need for a composing room.

Photocomposition   Method of producing type by exposing negatives of the characters on film or paper or reproducing them digitally.

Pica   A unit of measurement; 6 picas equal 1 inch.

Plate   The metal on which the photographic image of a page is developed by exposing it to a negative. The plate is then placed on the press.

Point   A unit of measurement; 12 points equal 1 pica. Headlines are measured vertically in points.

Poster   The space on the page left after framing to be used for display. A poster or billboard page is one devoted to a single subject. A miniposter is a small space, about tabloid size, devoted to a display.

Process color   Full- or four-color reproduction achieved by separating each color on individual pieces of film and burning them on separate printing plates. The process colors are yellow, magenta, cyan and black.

Proportion   Proper size and spacing relationships among the elements on the page.

Pullouts   Any typographic devices pulled out of a story and displayed in a form other than text. Pullouts include blurbs, summary boxes, fact boxes and quotes.

Pyramid format   Arrangement of advertisements in a stack up the right or left side of the page.

Quad   An empty printing unit for spacing. An em quad is the square of the type size.

Race   The broadest category of type classification. Type is divided into six races: roman, square serif, sans serif, text letter, cursive and ornamental.

Ragged right type   Type set with a fixed left starting point but with an irregular ending point at the right of the line.

Read-in   Type subordinate in size to the main head and placed above it. The main head completes the thought started in the read-in.

Read-out   A deck that reads directly out of the main head. Unlike the main head, it is written in a conversational tone.

Roman   A race of type characterized by serifs and thick and thin strokes. Also used to mean straight-up-and-down type as opposed to italic or oblique.

Rule   A plain line that ranges upward in width from 1/2 point. See Border.

Sans serif   A race of type without serifs and with uniform strokes. Also referred to as gothic.

Scanner   Electronic or laser machine that reads one color of a photograph at a time and transfers the image to a separation.

Screen   Glass or film used in cameras to break copy into halftone dots. The number of lines per linear inch of the screen determines the fineness of the reproduction; the higher the number, the better the reproduction.

Script   See Cursive.

Segmenting   Dividing a story into smaller bites.

Separation   A negative containing elements to be printed in one of the process colors. A full-color picture normally requires four separations.

Series   The range of sizes in a typeface. With photocomposition and digital typesetting, the range of sizes includes fractions of points.

Serif   The cross-stroke at the end of the main stroke of a letter.

Shades   Color formed by mixing pure colors with black (see Hues).

Sidebar   A secondary story intended to be run with a major story on the same subject.

Sidesaddle   Placement of type to the left side of the story rather than over it. Also called side head.

Slug   One-word designation for a story as it moves through the production system.

Spot color   Any color printing other than process.

Square serif   A race of type with monotone strokes and squared-off or blocked serifs.

Stereotype   A flat or curved metal plate cast from a papier-mâché mold; the process.

Stress   The thickness of a curved stroke; the shading of the letter.

Stroke   The primary line of the letter.

Tabloid   A publication whose pages are approximately half the size of a broadsheet or full-sized newspaper and usually printed on newsprint.

Teaser   A graphic written and designed to draw readers' attention to something in the publication, usually on an inside page.

Terminal   The distinctive finish to the stroke on sans serif type.

Text letter   Face of type that has a medieval appearance of early European hand lettering. Also known as black letter.

Text type   Also referred to as body type; used in newspaper stories and editorials.

Tints   Color formed by mixing pure colors with white.

Tombstoning   Bumping of two or more headlines or unrelated graphic elements.

Tones   Color formed by mixing pure colors and white and black.

Tracking   Fixing the spacing between letters in a block of type to achieve a certain color or density. Kerning applies to pairs of letters or a character and punctuation; tracking applies to a block of text.

Transitional   Sometimes used to differentiate among types in the roman race. The type has characteristics of both old and modern faces.

Transparency   A color photograph on slide film.

Typography   The arrangement and effect of type.

Unity   Harmony among the elements on a page and among the parts of the publication.

Value   The degree of lightness or darkness of a color.

Well format   Arrangement of advertisements in the shape of a U on a page.

Wrap   A column or leg of type. Type set over six columns would have six wraps.

x-height   Height of the lowercase x, the standard for measuring type.

References Cited

Aaronson, Bernard. 1970. Some affective stereotypes of color. *International Journal of Symbols* 2(2): 15–27.

Anonymous. 1997. A brand new look for America's oldest newspaper. *DESIGN*, Winter, pp. 20–23.

Ashe, Reid. 1992. What readers really want. *Nieman Reports* (Spring): 7–10.

Auman, Ann. 1995. Seeing the big picture: The integrated editor of the 1990s. *Newspaper Research Journal* 16: 35–47.

Bain, Chic, and David H. Weaver. 1979. Newspaper design and newspaper readership. Paper presented to the Graphics Division, Association for Education in Journalism, Houston.

Becker, D., J. Heinrich, R. Von Sichowky, and D. Wendt. 1970. Reader preferences for typeface and leading. *Journal of Typographic Research* 1(Winter): 61–66.

Benton, Camille. 1979. The connotative dimensions of selected display typefaces. Paper presented to the Association for Education in Journalism, Houston.

Birren, Faber. 1961. *Creative color.* New York: Reinhold, p. 48.

Black, Roger, and Michael Jones. 1998. *A newspaper has to look like a newspaper,* 2nd ed. Zurich, Switzerland, p. 45.

Clark, Ruth. 1979. Changing needs of changing readers. *American Society of Newspaper Editors Newspaper Readership Project* (May).

Click, J. W., and Guido H. Stempel III. 1974. Reader response to modern and traditional front page make-up. *ANPA News Research Report* 4 (June).

Collins, Tracy. 1997. Who stole the news? *DESIGN,* Spring, pp. 6–8.

Curley, John. 1979. Pilot research tailored to unique needs of each newspaper. *Gannetteer* (March): 6–8.

Dagson, Jones. 1998. Eight graphics lies (and how to fix them). *DESIGN,* Spring, pp. 10–12.

David, Prabu. 1992. Accuracy of visual perception of quantitative graphics: An exploratory study. *Journalism Quarterly* 69: 272–92.

Dowding, G. 1957. *Factors in the choice of typefaces.* London: Wace.

Fabrizio, R., L. Kaplan, and G. Teal. 1967. Readability as a function of the straightness of right-hand margins. *Journal of Typographic Research* (January): 90–95.

Fiquette, Larry. 1993. Story was a hit and miss. *St. Louis Post-Dispatch,* October 17.

Fitzgerald, Mark. 1993. Controversial photo. *Editor & Publisher,* October 23, pp. 14–15.

Garcia, Mario, and Don Fry, eds. 1986. *Color in American newspapers.* St. Petersburg, Fla.: Poynter Institute for Media Studies.

Garcia, Mario, and Pegie Stark. 1991. *Eyes on the news.* St. Petersburg, Fla.: Poynter Institute for Media Studies.

Gentry, James K., and Barbara Zang. 1989. Characteristics of graphics managers at metropolitan dailies. *Newspaper Research Journal* 10(4): 85–95.

Gyles, Barbara. P-o-p goes the **. *Presstime,* February 1998, pp. 34–39.

Hartley, James, and Peter Barnhill. 1971. Experiments with unjustified text. *Visible Language* 5(3): 265–78.

Haskins, Jack. 1958. Testing suitability of typefaces for editorial subject matter. *Journalism Quarterly* 35: 186–94.

Haskins, Jack P., and Lois P. Flynne. 1974. Effect of headline typeface variation on reading interest. *Journalism Quarterly* 51: 677–82.

Hilliard, Robert D. 1990. What power rests in the "Big Chair?" *The Journal of the Society of Newspaper Design* (October/November): 10–12.

Holmes, Grace. 1931. The relative legibility of black print and white print. *Journal of Applied Psychology* 15(June): 248–51.

Hurley, Gerald D., and Angus McDougall. 1971. *Visual impact in print.* Chicago: American Publishers Press.

Hvistendahl, J.K., and Mary R. Kahl. 1975. Roman v. sans serif body type: Readability and reader preference. *ANPA News Research Report* 2 (January).

Itten, Johannes. 1964. *Design and form.* New York: Reinhold.

Kalfus, Marilyn. 1991. Photos often pose dilemmas. *Orange County Register,* March 24.

Kochersberger, Robert C. Jr. 1988. Survey of suicide photos used by newspapers in three states. *Newspaper Research Journal* 9(4): 1–11.

Lee, H.H. 1994. Photographs increase readership of stories and help recall and comprehension. *News Photographer* 49(4): 14–15.

Lewis, Wayne. 1989. Readership of buried ads versus ads placed beside reading material. *Newspaper Research Journal* 10(2): 67–74.

Lott, Pam. 1993. A study of the use of a small non-lead informational graphic on a newspaper page. Master's thesis, Ohio University, Athens, Ohio.

Lund-Seedon, Kathleen. 1996. Would you run these photos? *The Editor* (March/April): 8–9.

Mansfield, Matt. 1997. Details on the new design. *Wordsmith*: 9–10.

Mauro, John. 1986. *Survey of front page color vs. black and white.* Richmond, Va.: Media General.

McDougall, Angus, and Veita Jo Hampton. 1990. *Picture editing and layout.* Columbia, Mo.: Viscom Press.

Moen, Daryl. 1989. Unpublished study. University of Missouri, Columbia, Mo.

Pepper, Miriam. 1998. Compliments on paper's redesign outpace complaints. *Kansas City Star*, November 15.

Pipps, Val Steven. 1985. Measuring the effects of newspaper graphic elements on reader satisfaction with a redesigned newspaper using two methodologies. Ph.D. diss., Newhouse School of Mass Communications, Syracuse, N.Y.

Poindexter, Paula M. 1978. Non-readers: Why they don't read. *ANPA News Research Report* 5(January): 2.

Poulton, E.C. 1955. Letter differentiation and rate of comprehension of reading. *Journal of Applied Psychology* 49: 358–62.

Reaves, Sheila. 1987. Digital retouching. Is there a place for it in newspaper photography? An examination of ethics. *News Photographer*, January, pp. 23–33.

———. 1992/1993. What's wrong with this picture? *Newspaper Research Journal* 13/14: 131–53.

Robinson, David O., Michael Abbamonte, and Selby Evans. 1971. Why serifs are important: The perception of small print. *Visible Language* 5(Autumn): 353–59.

Roethlein, B.E. 1912. The relative legibility of different faces of printing type. *American Journal of Psychology* 23(January): 1–36.

Rose, Bob. 1998. Third time lucky in St. Louis. *DESIGN*, Spring, pp. 16–20.

Ruel, Laura. 1993. The effect of information graphics on reading comprehension in newspapers. Master's thesis, University of Missouri–Columbia.

Sharpe, Deborah T. 1974. *The psychology of color and design.* Chicago: Nelson-Hall.

Siskind, Theresa G. 1979. The effect of newspaper design on readers' preferences. *Journalism Quarterly* 56: 54–61.

Sissors, Jack Z. 1974. Do youthful college-educated readers prefer contemporary newspaper designs? *Journalism Quarterly* 51: 307–13.

Stark, Pegie. 1992. *Information and graphics.* St. Petersburg, Fla.: Poynter Report, pp.8–10.

Tannenbaum, Percy, Harvey K. Jacobson, and Eleanor L. Norris. 1964. An experimental investigation of typeface connotations. *Journalism Quarterly* 41: 65–73.

Thornburg, Ron. 1986. *The ethics of the controversial photo.* APME Photo and Graphics Committee Report, pp. 2–11.

Tinker, Miles A. 1963. *Legibility of print.* Ames: Iowa State University Press.

Tinker, Miles A., and D.G. Paterson. 1929. Studies of typographical factors influencing speed of reading: III. Length of line. *Journal of Applied Psychology* (June): 205–19.

Tufte, Edward R. 1983. *The visual display of quantitative information.* Cheshire, Conn.: Graphics Press.

Vessey, Iris. 1991. Cognitive fit: a theory-based analysis of the graphs versus tables literature. *Decision Sciences* 22: 219–40.

Ward, Douglas B. 1992. The effectiveness of sidebar graphics. *Journalism Quarterly* 69: 318–28.

Wurman, Richard Saul. 1990. *Information anxiety.* New York: Bantam.

Zachrisson, Bror. 1965. *Studies in the legibility of printed text.* Stockholm, Sweden: Almquist and Wiskel.

Adam, Pegie Stark. 1995. *Color, contrast, and dimension in news design.* St. Petersburg, Fla.: The Poynter Institute for Media Studies.

Bain, Eric K. 1970. *The theory and practice of typographic design.* New York: Hastings House.

Baird, Russell N., Arthur T. Turnbull, and Duncan McDonald. 1987. *The graphics of communication*, 5th ed. New York: Holt, Rinehart and Winston.

Beach, Mark. 1992. *Graphically speaking.* Cincinnati: North Light Books.

Best of newspaper design. Annual. Reston, Va.: Society of News Design Annual.

Bierut, Michael, William Drenttel, Steven Heller and D.K. Holland, eds. 1994. *Looking closer: Critical writings on graphic design.* New York: Allworth Press.

Birren, Faber. 1969. *Principles of color*. New York: Van Nostrand Reinhold.

Black, Roger. 1990. *Roger Black's desktop design power*. New York: Bantam.

Bohle, Robert. 1990. *Publication design for editors*. Englewood Cliffs, N.J.: Prentice-Hall.

Bringhurst, Robert. 1996. *The elements of typographic style*, 2nd ed. Point Roberts, Wash.: Harltey & Marks.

Burt, Sir Cyril. 1959. *A psychological study of typography*. Oxford, U.K.: Cambridge University Press.

Craig, James. 1981. *Designing with type*. New York: Watson-Guptill.

Dair, Carl. 1982. *Design with type*. Toronto: University of Toronto Press.

Evans, Harold. 1973. *Newspaper design, book five*. New York: Rinehart and Winston.

Finberg, Howard I., and Bruce D. Itule. 1990. *Visual editing: A graphic guide for journalists*. Belmont, Calif.: Wadsworth.

Garcia, Mario R. 1993. *Contemporary newspaper design, a structural approach*, 3rd ed. Englewood Cliffs, N.J.: Prentice-Hall.

Gregory, D.L. 1970. *The intelligent eye*. New York: McGraw-Hill.

Harrower, Tim. 1998. *The newspaper designer's handbook*, 4th ed. Dubuque, Iowa: William C. Brown.

Holmes, Nigel. 1984. *Designer's guide to creating charts and diagrams*. New York: Watson-Guptill.

————. 1985. *Designing pictorial symbols*. New York: Watson-Guptill.

Hurlburt, Allen. 1977. *Layout: The design of the printed page*. New York: Watson-Guptill.

————. 1982. *The grid*. New York: Van Nostrand Reinhold.

Johnson, A.F. 1966. *Type designs*. Norwich, England: Jarrold and Sons.

Kobayashi, Shigenobu, ed. 1987. *A book of colors*. New York: Kodansha America.

Lieberman, J. Ben. 1978. *Type and typefaces*, 2nd ed. New Rochelle, N.Y.: Myriade Press.

Machlup, Fritz, and Una Mansfield, eds. 1983. *The study of information*. New York: John Wiley and Sons.

Merrinian, Frank. 1965. *A.T.A. type comparison book*. New York: Advertising Association of America.

Modley, Rudolf. 1976. *Handbook of pictorial symbols*. New York: Dover Publications.

Muller-Brockman, Josef. 1981. *Grid systems in graphic design*. New York: Hastings House.

Nelson, Roy Paul. 1985. *The design of advertising*, 5th ed. Dubuque, Iowa: William C. Brown.

Ovink, G.W. 1938. *Legibility, atmosphere-value and forms of printing types*. Leiden: A.W. Sijfhoff.

Polk, Ralph W., and Harry L. Gage. 1953. *A composition manual*. Washington, D.C.: Printing Industry of America.

Rehe, Rolfe. 1979. *Typography: How to make it most legible*. Carmel, Ind.: Design Research International.

————. 1985. *Typography and design for newspapers*. Carmel, Ind.: Design Research International.

Rodriguez, Lulu. 1998. Errors and inaccuracies in Iowa's local newspaper information graphics. Paper presented to Visual Communication Division of the Association for Education in Journalism and Mass Communication, Baltimore, Md.

Rooklege, Gordon, and Christopher Perfect. 1983. *Rookledge's international typefinder: The essential handbook of typeface recognition and selection.* New York: Beil.

Rosen, Ben. 1967. *Type and typography*, 2nd ed. New York: Van Nostrand Reinhold.

Roszak, Theodore. 1986. *The cult of information.* New York: Pantheon Books.

Smith, Charles. 1965. *Color-study and teaching.* New York: Van Nostrand Reinhold.

Solomon, Martin. 1986. *The art of typography.* New York: Watson-Guptill.

Spencer, Herbert. 1969. *The visible word.* New York: Hastings House.

Zachrisson, Bror. 1965. *Studies in legibility of printed text.* Stockholm, Sweden: Almquist and Wiskel.

Index

Page numbers in *italics* refer to illustrations.